1. SATURE OF LIMITATION ON CREDIT CARD DEPTS.
   IN GEORGIA.

THE
JACOBY & MEYERS

PRACTICAL GUIDE TO
EVERYDAY LAW

GAIL J. KOFF
PARTNER, JACOBY & MEYERS

A FIRESIDE BOOK
PUBLISHED BY SIMON & SCHUSTER, INC.
New York

The purpose of this book is to educate you about legal matters so that you can deal more effectively with your lawyer. Federal and state laws are constantly changing. Consult your attorney as the laws apply to your current case.

Copyright © 1985 by Leonard D. Jacoby, Stephen Z. Meyers, and Gail Koff
All rights reserved
including the right of reproduction
in whole or in part in any form
A Fireside Book
Published by Simon & Schuster, Inc.
Simon & Schuster Building
Rockefeller Center
1230 Avenue of the Americas
New York, New York 10020
FIRESIDE and colophon are registered trademarks of
Simon & Schuster, Inc.
Designed by Irving Perkins Associates
Manufactured in the United States of America
10   9   8   7
Library of Congress Cataloging in Publication Data
Koff, Gail J.
    The Jacoby & Meyers practical guide to everyday law.

    "A Fireside Book."
    Bibliography: p.
    1. Law—United States—Popular works. I. Jacoby & Meyers (Firm) II. title.
KF387.K577   1985   349.73   85-14643
                      347.3
ISBN 0-671-44174-4
ISBN 0-671-60700-6 pbk.

The map of the twelve federal judicial circuits is from *Finding the Law: A Workbook on Legal Research for Laypersons,* U.S. Government Printing Office.
The diagram of the anatomic interrelationships of heart, lungs, and brain is from *Defining Death: Medical, Legal and Ethical Issues on the Determination of Death,* U.S. Government Printing Office.

Acknowledgments

**I wish to thank Harold Prince
for his inestimable help
in the preparation of this book**

I would also like to thank the following attorneys for their invaluable assistance in the preparation of the material for this book.

John Bray
Steven Davis
Virginia Giddens
Anthony Giambalvo
John Herchenroder
Edward Horn
Robert Lashaw
John Corcos Levy
Gregory Messer
Barbara Morse

Francine Moss
Mitchell Muroff
Don B. Panush
Raymond Pilch
Richard Ribakove
Richard Rocco
Bruce Roistacher
Steve Seidner
Hal Stangler

In memory of my father, Murray Koff.

Contents

CHAPTER

8 Your Business: Your Rights as an Entrepreneur   145

CHAPTER

9 Wills: Your Right to Determine the Distribution of Your Property After Your Death   161

CHAPTER

10 Man and Woman: Your Rights in Marriage and When You Live Together   185

CHAPTER

11 Negligence: Your Rights When Somebody Injures You Accidentally   218

CHAPTER

CHAPTER

CHAPTER

Introduction
You and Your Legal Rights

If there is one clear and indisputable distinction between democratic and totalitarian societies, it is this: In a totalitarian society the law exists for the state; in a democratic society, it exists for you. In our society, you're the linchpin, and the law supports you with a mechanism of statutes, court decisions, and constitutional privileges that guarantee your inalienable right to life, liberty, property, and the pursuit of happiness. It is this full complex of legal rights as established in the United States of America that this book is all about.

Included are not only the headline rights, civil rights and women's rights, but your everyday rights as well. They're your rights when you buy a home, start a small business, or agree to a contract. They're your rights to get credit, and to get out of debt even when you misuse the credit you get. They're your rights when you marry, divorce, or live together, when you buy things, and when you seek medical care. They're your rights to live and to die with dignity. They're your rights to dispose of your property after your death in the way you want to, not in the way the state wants to. They're your rights to seek redress from civil wrongs, and to get a fair hearing when you're accused of a crime.

They're your rights to place behind *you*—one individual among 220,000,000 others—all the power of the world's greatest judicial system.

Curiously, most of us don't know exactly what our rights are, how to use them, and what to do when they are abused. We don't know how to make the law, which exists for our welfare, work *for* us. This book is a crash course in showing you how.

It's also a reference book to put on your shelf next to your Dr. Spock, your family medical handbook, your guide to finance, your cookbook for better health, and your Bible.

It is not, however, a do-it-yourself book. "A man who plays his own lawyer," said Abraham Lincoln, "has a fool for a client." The law is too complex, too subtle, and too tricky to practice without training. Rather, this book tells you what your everyday rights are, and how you and your lawyer can work as a team to be sure you get them. The more you know about the basics of law in that respect, the more powerful a team you'll make. An educated client is the best client.

Read this book from cover to cover. You'll find that we have avoided deadly "legalese." When we use a legal term, it is because we have to, and we explain it right then and there. (And a glossary is available to refresh your memory, if necessary, when the term is used again.) You can even read this book for page-turning interest, because it's about you. *You* could be the person asking the hundreds of questions in it for which we supply the answers.

About those questions. They're the backbone of this book. They're the questions clients have been asking us over the years at our Jacoby & Meyers offices from coast to coast. Jacoby & Meyers is the pioneering national leader of law firms designed to help *you*, places where anybody can go for virtually any legal service at a price that's right. That's why we're bombarded with questions about every aspect of the law, and that's why we have to have the answers at our fingertips—answers that work for our clients. They're the answers you'll find in this book. They can work for you, too, when they're executed by your lawyer.

This is, we repeat, a book about the everyday rights of every American. Not the least important of them is the right to know what those rights are all about. Turn the page, and start using *that* right.

1

The Law in Action:
Your Legal System

- Types of law
- Arenas of legal action: jurisdiction, the courts, and other tribunals
- Legal action in the courts: litigation
- Legal action outside the courts: arbitration

The law in action is based on the adversarial principle. It's you against the other guy. Both of you think you're right. It's a contest fought with words, sometimes with the intensity of hand-to-hand combat. It's a real-life game played for one of the highest stakes in the world: justice.

This chapter is a basic rulebook of that game. It spells out the fundamental guidelines for entering the legal arena—for "going to law" to seek redress of a wrong. It introduces you to the varieties of the game—the different kinds of law. It tells you where the game can be played—in the several kinds of courts and elsewhere. It defines the language used to describe the equipment, strategies, and tactics of the game—the legal terms (they're *italicized*). And it explains the rules of the game, so you can understand it better when you observe it or play it.

TYPES OF LAW

Law is the body of rules that regulates a society. The law of our land is derived from two great bodies of law: *common law* and *statutory law.*

Common law is derived from custom, usage, and court decisions. The common law of the United States has as its source the accumulated court decisions of our mother country, England. The one exception is the state of Louisiana, once a French possession, where the legal system is founded on the laws decreed by Napoleon Bonaparte, the Napoleonic Code. In essence, common law is a court-established law. It is constantly being redefined and reshaped by new court decisions.

Statutory law, on the other hand, is a body of law created by legislators, such as those of the several states or the Congress of the United States. Even statutory law, or *statute*, is subject to interpretation by the courts.

Both common law and statutory law are subdivided into *substantive law* and *adjective (administrative) law.*

Substantive law defines the substance of the law—the rights and duties of the individual.

Adjective (administrative) law deals with the forms and procedures for carrying out the substantive law.

Both substantive and adjective law play roles in the major subdivisions of common and statutory law: *criminal law* and *civil law.*

Criminal law provides governmental protection against acts of individuals harmful to the peace and order of society. Any violation of criminal law is an *offense.*

Civil law determines the rights of individuals to protect their persons and properties against the wrongful acts of others.

Civil law has two subdivisions: *business law* and *law and equity.*

Business law regulates business transactions. It is incorporated in the Uniform Commercial Code, adopted by most states.

Law, as it pertains to civil law, involves violations which can be remedied by the payment of money (damages).

Equity, on the other hand, involves violations for which there is no remedy at law (as it pertains to civil law)—that is to say, equity involves violations which cannot be remedied by money but which require the violator to take some specific action instead which would restore the innocent party (non-violator) to his position prior to the breach or violation.

ARENAS OF LEGAL ACTION: JURISDICTION, THE COURTS, AND OTHER TRIBUNALS

The answer to the question "Where can my case be heard?" begins with the concept of *jurisdiction*. Strictly speaking, jurisdiction is a level of government at which authoritative bodies can enact laws and enforce them. In this country, there are three levels of government: the federal, the state, and the local. Hence, there are three jurisdictions, each with its own courts.

Since a locality is part of a state and a state is part of the federal union, each level of government can have jurisdiction in the same locality; and each of three jurisdictional courts—federal, state, and local—can coexist there. Which of the courts will hear your case depends on whether federal, state, or local laws are involved.

Within the three major jurisdictions, courts are said *to have jurisdiction*—here meaning the right to hear cases—only on matters of law on which they are empowered to make decisions. For example, a criminal court has no jurisdiction over a civil matter, and a tax court has no jurisdiction over a traffic dispute.

Let's look at the kind of courts in each of three major jurisdictions.

• **THE FEDERAL COURTS.** The federal court system is divided into eleven *circuits*.* (The term "circuit" is a holdover from pioneer days when a judge would saddle up and ride a roughly circular route from town to town dispensing justice—that is, "ride the circuit.") Within the circuits are ninety *District Courts*. There is at least one District Court in each state, and in some as many as four.

The District Courts hear civil and criminal cases involving

*There are twelve when the District of Columbia is included. See map on following page.

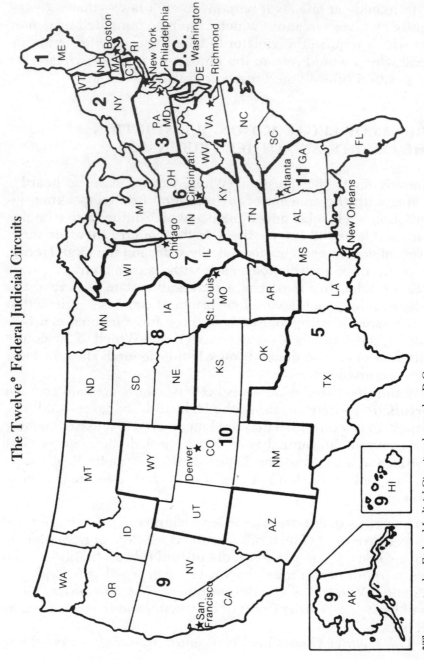

The Twelve* Federal Judicial Circuits

*There are twelve Federal Judicial Circuits, eleven plus D.C.

federal laws, except for cases under the jurisdiction of *special federal courts*, such as the U.S. Tax Court and the U.S. Court of Claims (for cases involving claims against the U.S. government). District Courts also have jurisdiction in cases between citizens of different states in which more than $10,000 is involved. (If less than $10,000 is involved, the case is tried in the state which has jurisdiction by reason of statute or contractual agreement between the parties involved.)

Appeals (see page 27 for definition) of decisions handed down in U.S. District Courts can be made to the *U.S. Court of Appeals*, a branch of which is in each of the eleven circuits. However, appeals from one special federal court, the U.S. Customs Court, can be made only to the U.S. Court of Customs and Patent Appeals; and appeals from another special federal court, the U.S. Court of Claims, can be made directly to the U.S. Supreme Court.

The *U.S. Supreme Court*, the highest court in the land, also hears appeals from the U.S. Court of Appeals, the U.S. Court of Customs and Patent Appeals, and directly from the highest state courts as well (but only in cases involving constitutionality). The nine judges of the U.S. Supreme Court decide on matters involving the *constitutionality* of all laws, federal and state—that is, whether the laws agree with the letter and spirit of the Constitution of the United States. They also hear cases involving the general welfare in which inferior courts have given conflicting opinions or rulings concerning the law, the object being to resolve the conflicts and to establish the rules of law.

• **THE STATE COURTS.** The state court systems, set by state law, are divided into *lower courts*, which are essentially trial courts, and *higher courts*, which are appeals courts (*appellate courts*). There are courts of both types in every county. Among the lower courts, *district courts* hear general civil cases, and criminal courts hear criminal cases. Lower courts, depending on the state, can also include special jurisdictions, such as family courts, juvenile courts, probate courts, and courts of claims (for adjudication of cases involving claims against the state). Appeals from the decisions of lower courts are made to the appellate courts.

• THE LOCAL COURTS. These are county, municipal, town, and village courts. They have limited jurisdiction geographically (they are empowered to act only within their own borders), financially (cases involving sums over statutory dollar ceilings must be tried in state courts), and criminally (only minor offenses can be tried). Local courts usually include a police court, a traffic court, a small claims court, and a justice of the peace. Appeals, although theoretically possible, are almost never made because of the relatively minor nature of the legal matters involved.

Now that you have an overview of the courts in the three major jurisdictions, you have a good idea where your case will be heard within the court system. But your case could be heard legally outside that system in the following two ways.

Through administrative agency hearings. Government administrative agencies—such as the federal Nuclear Regulatory Agency, a state liquor authority, or a municipal taxi and limousine commission—have the statutory right to make their own regulations and enforce them. At a *hearing*, authorities of an administrative agency can rule on infractions of its regulations. The hearing generally follows conventional court procedure (see the following section).

Appeal can be made to a court, but only on the grounds that the agency decision was "unreasonable, arbitrary, or capricious"—usually not an easy thing to prove. Should you be granted an appeal and win, the court can decide in your favor, and that's the end of the case; or it can send the case back to the agency for another hearing.

Through arbitration. This is sometimes an alternative to trying civil cases in court. It is described in the section in this chapter beginning on page 29.

LEGAL ACTION IN THE COURTS: LITIGATION

Litigation means to carry on a legal contest by *judicial process*— the procedures of the court. Here is a look at that process in action in the civil case—an action you and your lawyer might bring to court to obtain satisfaction on a claim.

The contestants are you, the *plaintiff*, and whomever you're bringing action against, the *defendant*. But there can be more than one plaintiff involved in a suit and more than one defendant. Both plaintiffs and defendants can be individuals, corporations, unincorporated businesses, institutions, and those branches and agencies of the government not prohibited by statute from being party to a civil suit.

Your attorney is known as the *attorney for the plaintiff*, your opponent's attorney as the *attorney for the defendant*. For the sake of brevity, and following the example of the courts, your attorney in the description that follows will be known as the plaintiff, and your opponent's attorney as the defendant, unless otherwise noted.

An example of the legal process is presented here in twenty-one start-to-finish steps.

1. The action is started by the plaintiff issuing a *summons* or a *summons and complaint*.

    A *summons* names the plaintiff and defendant, names the court to which the defendant is summoned to answer your complaint, and specifies the time the defendant is given to file an answer (thirty days, for example).

    A *complaint* is an expanded version of the summons, listing your claim in some detail, and stating the *causes of action*—the legal grounds for the claims (there may be several).

2. The summons and complaint are then *served* on the defendant—delivered to him—usually by hand, and sometimes by mail, which can be regular mail or registered. When service is by hand, it is customarily made by a professional *process server*.

3. The defendant files an *answer* to the complaint with the *clerk of the court*, an official responsible for the processing of documents. The answer may be a *general denial* of the claim, known also as a *demurrer*; or an *affirmative defense*, the introduction of new information which destroys your claim; or a *counterclaim*, a claim made by your opponent to offset your claim.

4. *Pretrial* or *discovery examinations* follow. In these sessions, usually held in the office of one of the lawyers, the opposing lawyers question you and your opponent, the object being to discover the basis of your action and of your opponent's defense. In some states pretrial examinations are mandatory, in others voluntary, but regarded as necessary by lawyers on both sides. Lawyers can also obtain information in writing by submitting a series of questions, called *interrogatories*, to both parties; by requesting a *bill of particulars*, a detailed revision of the complaint; or by asking for *oral depositions* or *affidavits*, written statements made under oath.

5. The case is placed on the *court calendar*, a listing of the dates on which the cases ready for trial will be heard. Cases seldom come to trial on the date set, because opposing attorneys almost as a matter of course request, and are usually granted, a reasonable number of postponements.

6. The case comes to court. The courtroom, familiar to Americans from its depiction on movie and TV screens, is divided into two areas separated by a rail. One is an austere arena in which the trial takes place before a judge sitting behind a massive desk (*judge's bench*) on a dais. Physically and metaphorically, the judge remains above the battle. The other area resembles the orchestra of a theater, and is usually open to spectators.

7. The *jury* is chosen. From a *jury panel*—twenty to several hundred men and women—twelve, or in some cases six, are selected to hear the case, unless by reason of statutory requirement or by mutual consent of both sides, the case is heard only by the judge. (All cases in equity are also heard only by a judge.) Common law calls for a jury of your peers. Today's peers—the people on the jury panel—are drawn by lot from voter registration rolls, motor vehicle registrations, and lists of real estate taxpayers. Jurors, by and large, are required to be over legal age but under seventy, to own some property, and to have normal health (hearing and vision impairment are usually grounds for disqualification). Some deaf people recently demanded their right to serve on a jury; some courts acquiesced, some didn't.

The twelve or six jurors who hear the case plus one or two alternates are survivors of the *voir dire*—the period of questioning by the opposing attorneys, who try to eliminate prospective jurors who cannot be fair and impartial. Some prospective jurors are *challenged for cause*—an overt display of bias—by the lawyers, and if the judge concurs they are dismissed. Others are dismissed as a result of challenges without cause—*peremptory challenges*—arising from a lawyer's gut feelings that these prospective jurors would be biased against his client no matter how unbiased they may claim to be. While any number of prospective jurors can be challenged for cause, only a certain number can be peremptorily challenged by each side.

There is one exception to voir dire. Most federal judges select jurors themselves, eliminating lawyers from the jury selection process. But a panel of trial judges and practicing lawyers has recommended voir dire in federal cases, and Congress is considering two bills to give each side the right to examine prospective jurors in federal criminal cases.

The jury, which sits in a raised two-tiered *jury box*, is led by a *foreman* whose only qualification for leadership is that he was the first juror selected. It is *the duty of the jury* members to determine the facts in the case—to decide for themselves which evidence is valid, which is phony, who's telling the truth, who's lying— and to apply the facts as they find them to the law in the case. They're *instructed* on that law by the judge.

8. The trial is conducted according to rules. The basic rule in a civil case is this: The plaintiff has to prove his case by a "fair preponderance of credible evidence." In other words, *the burden of proof* is on the plaintiff. The defendant doesn't have to prove a thing. What he has to do is *disprove* the plaintiff's evidence.

9. The trial begins. Because the plaintiff is handicapped by the burden of proof, the rules permit him an advantage: It allows him to address the jury first. That's like getting possession of the football without the pregame coin toss. (Remember, in our discussion "plaintiff" means the *attorney* for the plaintiff.)

The opening addresses (the defendant will make one after the plaintiff) are called *opening statements*. The plaintiff's opening statement presents his view of the case and a preview of the proof of his claims. The defendant's opening statement presents his view of the case and a preview of the disproof of the plaintiff's claims.

Now it's up to the plaintiff to present the *evidence*— the means of proving his case.

10. Evidence that is *legally admissible* in the trial—that is, the means of proof the jury is permitted to consider— is governed by *the rules of evidence*. These rules are voluminous and extremely complex. The standard text on the subject in the State of New York (*Richardson on Evidence* by Jerome Prince) contains more than a thousand oversized pages of packed fine print, and is revised periodically. In essence, the rules demand that the evidence be *relevant, competent*, and *material*.

Relevant means the evidence must be related to the fact to be proved. (If you're attempting to prove you've been embezzled by the defendant, and you try to introduce evidence that the defendant's grandmother was an embezzler, that's *irrelevant*.)

Competent means that the evidence must be admissible under the rules of evidence. (Otherwise, it's *incompetent*.)

Material means that the evidence must be directly related to the fact in such a way that it helps to prove the fact. (If you're attempting to prove that the defendant embezzled you of $18,000 in July 1984, and you try to introduce evidence that he embezzled you of $1,000 in July 1974, that's *immaterial*.)

During the trial the judge makes decisions, based on the rules of evidence, on the admissibility of the evidence. In the legal contest, he plays the part of umpire. Objections by either side to his decisions are called *exceptions*. ("Inadmissible," a judge will rule. "Exception," one of the lawyers will respond.) Exceptions help lay the basis for an appeal.

11. The plaintiff presents his evidence first. There are two major classes of evidence: *testimony* and physical *evidence*.

Testimony is that form of evidence given orally by a witness.

Physical evidence is all other forms of evidence, such as documents, films, photographs, recordings, videotapes, and natural and artificial objects.

Both major classes of evidence are divided further into *direct evidence* and *indirect evidence*.

Direct evidence immediately establishes the fact to be proved.

Indirect evidence establishes facts from which the fact to be proved can be inferred. (*Circumstantial evidence*, a form of indirect evidence, establishes circumstances from which the fact to be proved can be inferred.)

12. Witnesses are called. A witness in a court case is a person who gives testimony. Witnesses appear voluntarily or by *subpoena*, an order by the court to appear and testify. When the witness is required to bring to the court substantiating evidence, such as commercial and financial records, a special kind of subpoena is issued called a *subpoena duces tecum* (freely translated as "bring the goods with you").

The witness testifies from the witness box, a raised three-sided enclosure to the immediate right of the judge's bench. Before being seated there he *swears an oath* (a sacred pledge) or *makes an affirmation* (a binding promise according to the dictates of conscience) to tell the truth, the whole truth, and nothing but the truth. (Violation of either is *perjury*, and is punishable by law.) The witness is then seated and *examined*—that is to say, questioned—by the plaintiff to establish the facts on which proof of claim is made. The witness is then *cross-examined*—questioned by the opposing lawyer— in an attempt to break down his testimony *directly* ("You testified that this transaction took place on June 12, when as a matter of fact these receipts prove it occurred on June 11. What do you say to that?") or to break it down indirectly by casting doubts on his credibility ("Isn't it true that you were fined by the State Real Estate Board for false entries on your application for a license renewal?").

Documents or other evidence introduced by witnesses, or directly to lawyers for the plaintiff and defendant, when accepted by the judge as admissible are tagged "Exhibit A as evidence," "Exhibit B as evidence," and so forth.

13. The plaintiff *rests his case*—that is to say, finishes his presentation of the evidence—when all his witnesses have been examined and cross-examined, and all the

evidence he has to offer has been ruled admissible or inadmissible.

14. Remember, the burden of proof is on the plaintiff. At this point in the trial, he must have *made a prima facie case*—a presentation that "on first view" (that's the meaning of "prima facie") supports his claims with sufficient evidence. The defendant can now *make a motion*—a spoken request to the judge—to dismiss the case on the basis that a prima facie case has not been made. (When making a motion, the lawyer says, "Your Honor, I move that...")

    It's up to the judge, not the jury, to decide whether a prima facie case has indeed been made. Should he decide that it has *not* been made, he will grant the defendant's motion to dismiss, and that's the end of the case, with a victory for the defendant. If he decides a prima facie case *has* been made, the case continues. The final decision will now come from the jury.

15. A prima facie case has been made here, and the case continues. Now it's the defendant's turn to take testimony from *his* witnesses and introduce other evidence. The object: to show that the facts presented by the plaintiff do not support his claims. The plaintiff has the right to cross-examine the defendant's witnesses. When direct examination and cross-examination of the defendant's witnesses are completed, and the defendant has entered all other evidence, the defendant rests his case.

16. Now the plaintiff has the right to bring in *rebuttal* witnesses. The purpose of their testimony is to destroy the effect of the evidence introduced by the defendant. These witnesses, like all others, are subject to cross-examination.

17. When both sides have completed the presentation of evidence, each side in turn is permitted to address the jury. These *closing speeches* or *summations* are attempts to influence the jury's *verdict* (decision) by reviewing the evidence, using the arts of persuasion, of which logic is only one. The defendant sums up first. That gives the plaintiff another advantage: the last word, a chance to undo the effects of the defendant's summation.

18. Following the summations, the judge *charges* the jury—

that is, he tells the jury about the law in the case, and how to apply the facts in the case to that law to come to a verdict for the plaintiff or defendant. Simply stated, the essence of what the judge says is this: "The law says if the facts are so-and-so, you must bring in a verdict for the plaintiff. If the facts are this-and-that, you must bring in a verdict for the defendant. You decide on the facts, and bring in the verdict accordingly." Unfortunately, charges to the jury are never that simple; and frequently juries interrupt their deliberations to return to the courtroom to ask clarification of the judge's *instructions*.

Both sides can take *exceptions* to (object to elements of) the charge, which the judge denies or accepts by altering those portions of his charge to which exceptions had been made.

19. The jury then *retires*—leaves the jury box for deliberations in a locked jury room. After a discussion of the case, the foreman asks for a vote, which can be secret. A unanimous decision is required for a verdict in some jurisdictions; in others, a five-to-one tally becomes a legal verdict on a six-person jury, and a ten-to-two tally on a twelve-person jury. Often the jury is empowered not only to bring in a verdict—*find for*—plaintiff or defendant, but also to find for the plaintiff in the sum of X dollars—the amount to be paid by the defendant in settlement of the plaintiff's claims.

20. An *appeal* to a higher court to reverse the decision can be made mainly on the basis of an *error* in law by the judge (which means exactly what it says). That's why exceptions are so important in the course of a trial. A denied exception, if the exception indeed revealed an error in law, is the basis of an appeal.

The procedure for an appeal follows this general pattern: The *appellant*—the loser in the lower court—serves a *notice of appeal* to the winner in the lower court, now known as the appellee; and at roughly the same time files with the appeals court a *memorandum of appeal*, which details the alleged errors. The appellee then files his memorandum of appeal to counter the appellant's claims of errors. The appellant can then file a reply, and the appellee has one final opportunity to answer the reply.

The appellate court comes to a decision either from an examination of papers submitted or from arguments presented orally by both sides. The decision can either be an *affirmation* of the lower court's, in which case the verdict stands; or it can be a *reversal* of the lower court's, in which case the verdict is canceled. The case, though, may be sent back for a new trial.

A case can also be brought up from a lower court by a *writ of certiorari*—an order issued by a higher court based on a complaint that a party to the suit did not receive justice or an impartial trial.

21. When a final verdict is for the plaintiff, he is entitled to the sum awarded in the suit. Now he has to collect. This isn't always easy. Here's a worst-possible-case scenario:

After the verdict is handed down, the *judgment*—the court's determination of the amount of the award to be paid by the defendant—is filed in an official place of judgment records, such as the office of the county clerk. The former plaintiff is now called the *judgment creditor*, and the former defendant the *judgment debtor*, or simply *debtor*.

The debtor decides not to pay. Because the judgment has been filed, the judgment creditor now has legal recourse. He summonses the debtor to a *proceeding supplementary to judgment* in which the debtor is examined under oath concerning his assets—what they are, where they are, and how much they're worth. If the debtor has any assets at all, he's now vulnerable. If he still doesn't pay, the judgment creditor can now obtain a court-issued *execution*—an order to an officer of the court to seize the debtor's assets. Then the officer of the court may either hold the assets until the debtor pays up, or sell the assets to raise the cash necessary to *satisfy the judgment*—pay the debt. Bank accounts are assets, and if the court officer seizes them, they're frozen—the debtor can't touch them—until he pays up. If he won't or can't pay, the court officer can satisfy the judgment from the seized cash.

LEGAL ACTION OUTSIDE THE COURTS: ARBITRATION

Arbitration is a method of settling a commercial claim by the decision of a person or persons chosen or approved by both parties to the dispute instead of by the verdict of judge or jury. A person deciding the dispute is an *arbitrator*.

Arbitration is sometimes preferred to litigation because it minimizes the need for the services of a lawyer (you can in some cases do it yourself), reduces red tape (the hearing is not as rigidly structured as a court action), cuts costs appreciably (a trial lawyer can cost upward of $185 an hour plus expenses), and sharply reduces the time of the proceedings (on the average twenty-four hours to three months for arbitration as contrasted with up to three years in litigation).

The arbitration method of settling a dispute is usually agreed upon before a dispute occurs by means of a provision in a contract or purchase agreement. Such a provision reads something like this:

"In the event of any dispute under this agreement arising between or among the parties, any party may request any other party to submit such dispute to arbitration in the City of (name of city) in accordance with the rules of the American Arbitration Association."

The American Arbitration Association (AAA) is an organization, unrelated to the judicial system, that sets up *tribunals* of an arbitrator or several arbitrators having the authority to hear and decide disputes so as to bind the *disputants* (parties to the disputes). The AAA also creates the rules governing these tribunals.

What follows is the blueprint for the arbitration procedure arranged in ten start-to-finish steps. The word "you" means you, not you-and-your-lawyer, unless you choose to be represented by a lawyer.

1. You start the arbitration procedure by requesting an AAA *demand form* from the nearest regional AAA office. For a list of regional AAA offices in the East, contact

American Arbitration Association, 140 West 51st Street, New York, NY 10020 (212-977-2070); in the West, American Arbitration Association, 443 Shatto Place, Los Angeles, CA 90020 (213-383-6516).

The *demand form* is just that—a form which when filled in makes a demand on your opponent to satisfy a claim you have against him. The fill-ins, besides supplying names and addresses, describe the agreement on which you base your claim, why the agreement was violated, and how much money and/or other compensation you demand.

2. You send two copies of the filled-in demand form to your regional AAA office, together with a check for a nominal fee.

3. The AAA regional office then sends one copy of the filled-in demand form to your opponent with a notice advising him that if he wishes to file an answer he must do so in ten days. He is under no obligation to do so, however; and should he fail to respond, the arbitration procedure goes on anyway. Should he file an answer, the AAA regional office forwards one copy to you.

4. After you've received a copy of the answer, or after the seven-day period has expired without an answer having been filed, you receive from the AAA regional office a list of proposed arbitrators. It contains the names of men and women in your field and in related fields (they understand your kind of dispute) as well as some lawyers. You're asked to strike from the list those names that for any reason are objectionable to you, and return the list to the AAA regional office by a certain date. If you fail to meet the deadline, the AAA assumes you have no objection to any name on the list. Your opponent has received the same list, and has the right to exercise the same options.

5. From the names that have not been stricken from the list by one party or another, your regional AAA office designates one arbitrator or several. You and your opponent are notified of the selection.

6. You now have seven days to agree with your opponent on where the arbitration will be held. If you can't come to an agreement, your AAA regional office will determine the place and notify both parties. The notification

also includes the date and time of the arbitration.

7. Arbitration takes place usually in a conference room. The arbitrator or arbitrators sit at the head of a conference table, the opponents on either side. Witnesses wait outside closed doors, or are seated in the room away from the table, until they are called. The atmosphere, in contrast to the adversarial climate of the courtroom, is conciliatory and relaxed.

   The arbitrator opens the arbitration by asking for *opening statements* from both sides—similar to the opening statements in litigation. You present an overview of your claim, a preview of how you intend to prove it, and you identify the witnesses you will call. Your opponent counters with reasons for the invalidity of your claim, how he intends to prove it, and what witnesses he will call. Questions are asked by the arbitrator or arbitrators to clarify the facts.

8. You begin your proof by testifying under oath or affirmation, and introducing other evidence. Although arbitrators have the power of subpoena, witnesses usually appear voluntarily. Witnesses who cannot appear are permitted, contrary to the rules of litigation, to testify by means of an *affidavit*, a sworn statement in writing. ("Affidavit" is a general legal term, and its usage is not limited to arbitration.)

   Another advantage of arbitration over litigation is that the rules of evidence, inflexible in a court of law, are relaxed. But you and your witnesses can be cross-examined by the other side; and if the other side is represented by a lawyer, that can be an experience almost as painful as it is in litigation.

   After you have presented your case, your opponent presents his. The procedure that applied to you is applied with equal fairness to him.

9. After each side has presented its case, the arbitrator or arbitrators have six months to come up with a decision, called an *award*. It becomes a true judgment when it is filed as such in a state court. It has the same binding effect as a judgment when the arbitration provision of a contract states that "the award shall be binding on both parties," or words to that effect.

10. There is no appeal from an arbitration award unless it

can be shown that the arbitration procedure was conducted, or the award was arrived at, improperly—that
is to say, in violation of the rules of arbitration. Then
the appellate court can affirm the award or throw the
case back into arbitration.

"A COURT WHERE YOU DON'T NEED A LAWYER": SMALL CLAIMS COURT

Small claims courts are local courts designed to permit you to
bring some civil actions involving small sums, at nominal expense and sometimes without the need of a lawyer. Although
the kinds of cases that fall within the jurisdiction of these courts
vary from state to state, in general they involve personal injury,
property damage, and losses due to bad checks, bad debts, and
nonpayment of goods or services sold. Ceilings on claims range
from $300 in most states to $3,500 in Missouri.

Action in small claims court is characterized by speed and a
brand of informality found in no other legal tribunal. "Because
you are a layperson and unfamiliar with the mysteries of the
law," explains small claims court expert Douglas Matthews, "you
gain the benefit of a certain indulgence by the judge or arbitrator." Yet, while small claims courts are relatively hassle-free,
they can present difficulties when you don't have the advice of
a lawyer. Here is the procedure to follow in bringing an action
in small claims court, and the difficulties to beware of.

1. Find the small claims court. *Beware*: Small claims courts
   are not always listed under S in the White Pages of your
   telephone directory. The reason is that in many states
   small claims fall under the jurisdiction of other courts.
   Small claims are handled by "Justice of the Peace
   Courts" in Arizona, Arkansas, Delaware, Indiana, Iowa,
   Kentucky, Louisiana (except in New Orleans, where the
   "City Court" rules on small claims), Mississippi, Nebraska, Tennessee, West Virginia, and Wyoming. In Alabama and Montana, small claims are heard before
   "Justice Courts"; in Alaska, before a "Small Claims Di-
   vision of the District Court"; in Florida, before "County
   Courts"; in Missouri and South Carolina, before "Mag-

istrate's Courts"; and in Virginia, before courts called "Courts Not of Record." In Georgia, small claims are settled in either "Small Claims Courts" or "Justice of the Peace Courts." To find a small claims court in New York White Pages, you'd have to look under "Civil Courts, Small Claims" in New York City, and under "District Courts, Small Claims" outside New York City.

2. Appear at the small claims court in person, and fill out a simple form. The fee in New York is $4.53, and about the same nominal amount throughout the nation. *Beware*: Your claim may be rejected forthwith because the court has no jurisdiction. Jurisdiction may not extend beyond the county you're in, so you can't sue anybody who resides elsewhere; or jurisdiction may not cover government agencies or certain kinds of suits. Here's an example of the latter cause for rejection: Your company's mail-order piece is copied by a rival. You bring suit for $3,500 (you're in Missouri), claiming infringement of copyright. The small claims court will not entertain the suit because only a federal court has jurisdiction over copyright matters.

3. Rely on the small claims court to serve a summons on the defendant. *Beware*: The summons is sent by registered mail, return receipt requested, in an envelope bearing the name and address of the court. Since it's not hard to guess the contents of the envelope, delivery is often refused. The unopened envelope is returned to the clerk of the court, who notifies you that unless service is made on the defendant, the case cannot be placed on the court calendar—and that responsibility for the service is now yours. If you can't get a friend or relative to make the service (it's not legal if you do it yourself), or if you don't know how to go about hiring a professional process server or don't want to pay the fee, your case is over before it begins.

4. When service has been made, prepare your case. *Beware*: You'll have to prepare your case in much the way a lawyer would prepare it for you, but you're not a lawyer. Remember, this is a civil case and the burden of proof is on you. You'll have to prove, for example, that you had a transaction with the defendant (got the receipt for those dresses you sent out to be cleaned?); that the defendant caused damage to your property (can

you produce witnesses to swear that the pink dresses you offer in evidence were red before they went to the cleaners?); that the dresses cost you X dollars and you had worn them only twice (can you produce a dated sales slip?); and that the defendant did actually clean your garments (what's your response should he say, "The dresses were uncleanable, so I returned them to her uncleaned"?). You also may have to show that you are acting in good faith, and that you made reasonable attempts to arrange a settlement, but were rebuffed (if all that happened on the telephone, how are you going to prove it?).

5. Appear on the date of the trial. *Beware*: If you don't show up for any reason, you lose automatically. But if the defendant doesn't show up, you still have to make out a prima facie case before you are declared the winner. If you're late, and the court has already decided in favor of the defendant, you may be able to reopen the case by explaining the reason for your default.

6. When you appear in court, choose between having your case heard by a judge or by an arbitrator (usually a volunteer lawyer). One advantage of choosing an arbitrator is that there are usually five arbitrators in the courthouse to one judge, so your case will come up faster. Another advantage is that your case is heard privately across a table in a small room, rather than in a crowded, noisy public courtroom. *Beware*: You can't appeal an arbitrator's decision. You can appeal a judge's, but it is so costly to do so (you need a lawyer) that you're almost certain to end up in the red.

7. Don't be surprised if, when you come to trial in this "court where you don't need lawyers," you find yourself opposed by a lawyer. Actually, only six states bar lawyers in small claims courts. In thirty-seven states, the appearance of lawyers is optional. In nine states, it's mandatory for lawyers to represent defendant corporations, on the theory that it's so expensive to bring lawyers into court that corporations will tend to settle out of court—and that's an advantage to you, the plaintiff. But when no out-of-court settlement can be arranged, then it's lawyer vs. layperson—and that's an advantage to the corporation. *Beware*: You're no match for a lawyer. You could get a lawyer of your own. But

then you lose most of the advantages of small claims court: It's no longer fast (delay is a legitimate legal tactic), it's no longer informal, and it's costly.

The states that require lawyers to represent corporations are Alaska, Arizona, Colorado, Florida, Illinois, Indiana, New York, Pennsylvania (Philadelphia only), and Rhode Island (but only when the corporation is the plaintiff, and then the defendant must have a lawyer too). The six states that bar lawyers are California, Idaho, Iowa, Kansas, Minnesota, and Nebraska. In all other states, lawyers are not required but may appear (but in Oregon and Washington, appearance is subject to the court's approval).

8. Go through a cameo version of a court trial or an arbitration procedure. *Beware*: A trial of any sort, even one in small claims court, can be nerve-racking. Without a lawyer to do your fighting for you, it can be even more so.

9. Be prepared to lose, especially when you are opposed by a lawyer. Assessing the value of small claims courts, the City of New York Commission on Human Rights said: "You can sue...but winning your case is a more difficult task." *Beware*: When you lose, you get nothing, and you have to pay the defendant's court costs and sometimes legal fees.

10. When you win, be prepared to struggle for your money. A decision in your favor gets you a judgment in the amount of X dollars (that includes costs and legal fees). *Beware*: Now you have to collect, and that's probably the biggest difficulty you face in a small claims court case. The defendant—now known as the judgment debtor—has ten days to pay. If he doesn't, your only recourse is to hire the sheriff or marshall of the county (name and address supplied by the court) to act as your collection agent (for expenses and a fee, usually 5 percent of the amount collected). The sheriff has the power to attach the judgment creditor's assets, wages, bank accounts, and other properties), but if the sheriff doesn't know where and what they are, he's powerless—which is not infrequently the case. In small claims court, even when you win you sometimes lose.

Before you begin any legal action, no matter how small, consult your lawyer.

2

Medical Malpractice: Your Right to Standard Medical Care

- A definition of medical malpractice
- Some questionable medical practices that are *not* malpractice
- Some questionable medical practices that *are* malpractice
- "Informed consent" and the role it plays in malpractice
- Conducting a malpractice suit and what it costs to win or lose

In one of Fletcher Knebel's novels, a computer company markets a video game in which, instead of zapping monsters from outer space, the players zap doctors. The game is called DoctorBlast. It expresses a perception among some Americans that the doctor has become the enemy.

Behind the perception, critics of the medical profession point out, is a hard-core compendium of shocking statistics. Doctor-prescribed drugs hospitalize 1,500,000 patients yearly. In hospitals one out of five patients are afflicted with a disease *after* admission, three out of four are malnourished on hospital food, and up to twelve in a hundred of those undergoing coronary bypass surgery die. This year 35 million Americans will suffer from high blood pressure, 12 million will have diabetes, 1.25 million will be victims of heart attacks and 500,000 of strokes, and one out of three Americans will contract cancer before the age of seventy-four. Lack of emphasis on preventive medicine may contribute to this widespread ill health.

Critics of the medical profession also point out the unfortunate breakdown in patient-doctor relations. They cite the doctors' cold, detached manner and lack of compassion; the humiliation, particularly to women, of routine examinations; the disrespect doctors show to patients when they call them by their first names or demeaning nicknames (Doll, Sweetie, Granny). They lament the virtual disappearance of house calls, and the absence of the bedside manner which in the past has helped speed healing. They also remind us that doctors are prone to alcoholism, addiction, and depression—more so than those in any other profession.

Additional counts of the indictment of medicine include the soaring profits from human suffering (seven hundred of the nation's cardiovascular surgeons earn around $350,000 a year, yet they average only three operations a week); the frequency of overcharges on hospital bills; the high cost of specialist services and hospitalization for the treatment of conditions formerly handled with competence by the family doctor; and the prisonlike environment of many hospitals in which patients are stripped of their clothes and belongings, dressed in institutional garments, and given numbers in place of names.

The defenders of our medical establishment, however, argue that it is the best-equipped, the most technologically advanced, and the best-staffed in history. They point with pride to the unparalleled achievements of modern medicine, to the extension of the life span to an unprecedented high, to the triumph over pain, to the conquest of infectious diseases that in the not too distant past decimated populations, and to the miracles of surgery. Doctors on the whole, they contend, are humane people devoted to serving the community and providing the best possible care for their patients. They act with moderation and integrity in their financial transactions.

But even these supporters of the medical establishment admit that doctors, in the words of Dr. David E. Reiser, director of

Psychosocial Medicine at the University of Rochester Medical School, "face a hostile and distrustful public." This public is striking back with malpractice suits.

Malpractice litigation, soaring at increasingly accelerated rates, is today compensating patients for medical negligence and incompetence with awards averaging about $300,000 each and totaling about $15 billion annually, with individual awards not infrequently in the millions. The severity of these awards is rooted in the common law, which has established suitable dollar payments as the means of redress for wrongful acts resulting in bodily harm, particularly in cases of irrecoverable loss, say of a limb, a part of the brain, or life itself.

But not every flagrant act of a doctor or hospital is malpractice. The patient can be insulted, humiliated, sickened, or maimed or even die under medical care and have no basis for a malpractice claim. Medical malpractice is a specific legally defined wrong, and unless a doctor's act satisfies that definition it is not considered malpractice.

A DEFINITION OF MEDICAL MALPRACTICE

Malpractice is a form of negligence committed by a professional whose departure from standard practice in the performance of his duties results in harm to others. Professionals of all kinds can be liable for malpractice—lawyers, accountants, architects, engineers, clergymen, and so on. Today, some even regard parenting as a profession; recently a young man brought suit against his mother for parental malpractice.

When malpractice is committed by a doctor, it is medical malpractice. Legally, a doctor commits medical malpractice when he departs from standard practice in two specific ways: when he fails to live up to the standards set by his education and training, and when he fails to treat a condition in accordance with the standards in his community. (The current tendency of the courts is to expand the concept of "community" to include the nation; so a rural doctor is likely to be held to the same standards as a doctor in a metropolis.) Hospital malpractice, another form of medical malpractice, is defined the same way as doctor malpractice.

SOME QUESTIONABLE MEDICAL PRACTICES THAT ARE *NOT* MALPRACTICE

· *I spent thousands of dollars for the treatment of my sciatic condition, but the pain is now worse than ever. Malpractice?*

Some medical treatments don't work for some people, and a doctor is not required to produce the results you desire. Provided your doctor treated your sciatic condition with standard therapy, his failure to help you is not malpractice.

· *I have deep laugh lines. My cosmetic surgeon promised that a face lift could almost make them vanish. It didn't. Malpractice?*

Not if his surgery conformed to standard practice. However, you still have recourse under the law. The arrangement you make with a plastic surgeon (but not with any other type of doctor) is regarded as a contract. If you don't get what's been promised (contracted for), you can sue for breach of contract.

· *My husband went for his yearly checkup and was given a clean bill of health. The next day while jogging, he had a heart attack. Malpractice?*

The standard annual medical checkup has built-in limitations, one of which is the incapacity to detect an impending heart attack. If the checkup your husband received was standard, the doctor did not commit malpractice.

· *I have a form of cancer that all the textbooks say is incurable, yet my doctor insists on treating me, and the bills are staggering. Malpractice?*

Doctors treat incurable diseases like yours with palliatives—medicines and procedures that ameliorate symptoms but do not curb the course of the disease. Since this is standard practice, it is not malpractice.

• My doctor pooh-poohs nutritional therapy. For a year he treated my high blood pressure with pills that made me sick. I switched to a salt-free diet with supplements, my blood pressure dropped, and I feel great. Malpractice?

Most doctors are uneducated and untrained in the application of nutritional therapy. In prescribing pills, your doctor acted in conformity with standards set by his education and training, and the standards practiced by other doctors in his community. That's standard practice, not malpractice.

• I had the flu, and I didn't want to go out in a snowstorm. But my doctor said he doesn't make house calls. Malpractice?

No. It's now standard practice not to make house calls.

• I had an ingrown toenail. My family practitioner said, "That could be dangerous if you have diabetes. Let's find out." The tests cost me a bundle, and then he said, "You don't have diabetes. Now I'll refer you to a podiatrist to take care of your toenail." Malpractice?

It's now standard medical practice in many cases not to proceed without exploratory tests and to refer patients to specialists. Frustrating and costly as this is, it is not malpractice.

• My doctor prescribed an oral birth-control pill and gave me correct instructions on how to use it, but I became pregnant anyway. Malpractice?

The oral contraceptive is the most effective birth-control method in history, but it is not perfect. As long as your doctor didn't promise you absolute protection, he behaved in conformance with standard practice, and your pregnancy is not the result of his malpractice.

• I've read that there's no drug without a side effect, and that every surgery, no matter how minor, does some injury to the body. Since a guiding principle of medical practice is "Do no harm," isn't every prescription for a drug or recommendation for surgery malpractice?

Actually, "Do no harm" is no longer a directive of standard medical practice. The new directive is: A treatment or procedure is acceptable when the benefits outweigh the harm done. Prescribing pills and performing operations that are considered to help more than they harm are standard practice, not malpractice.

· *I've heard about "iatrogenic diseases"—diseases actually induced by doctors. Malpractice?*

Not necessarily. These diseases—a spectrum of ills including infections, hypertension, heart disease, acute allergic reactions (anaphylactic shock), liver tumors, deafness, cancer, and cardiac arrest—result from the use of diagnostic X rays (mammography is an example), therapeutic drugs, radiation therapy, exploratory surgery, and other treatments and procedures in accordance with standard practice. However, should a doctor-induced disease result from nonstandard practice—say, the excessive use of X rays—a malpractice claim could be made. The same rules apply to "noscomial diseases"—diseases induced by hospitals.

SOME QUESTIONABLE MEDICAL PRACTICES THAT *ARE* MALPRACTICE

· *My doctor prescribed a drug that is not approved by the FDA for my illness, and I was hospitalized as a result. Malpractice?*

Yes. His act was contrary to standard practice. To find out whether a drug your doctor prescribes is approved by the FDA (Federal Drug Administration) for your illness, ask your pharmacist for the "package insert." It's a complete description of the drug and how it should be used.

· *My doctor prescribed the right drug in the wrong amounts, and I became ill. Malpractice?*

Yes. His prescription was not in accordance with standard practice. In a recent case a prescribed overdose of barbiturates resulted in a young woman's death. The doctor faced not only a malpractice suit but also a criminal indictment. (He was in fact sentenced to three years in a state penitentiary.) You can check for the FDA-approved dosage by referring to the package insert.

· *I was put on painkilling drugs and became addicted. Malpractice?*

Yes, if your doctor prescribed the addictive drugs carelessly, that's obviously not standard practice. In a recent case in New York, a patient whose addiction was doctor-caused was awarded $800,000.

· *Is misdiagnosis malpractice?*

Yes, if the misdiagnosis is the result of departure from standard practice or the failure to exercise the skill and ability of a doctor of reasonable competence, and results in injury to the patient. In one recent case, a young man was placed in a hospital for the mentally retarded. It turned out he wasn't retarded, just deaf. His doctor had misdiagnosed the condition because he hadn't tested the young man's hearing. That was a departure from standard practice. The malpractice award was $2,500,000. In another case, without making standard tests, a doctor misdiagnosed a brain hemorrhage as an ordinary headache. The award was $10,000,000. (These large awards are the exceptions, not the rule.) However, medicine is not an exact science, and if the misdiagnosis is arrived at through standard tests and procedures, it is not malpractice. At one hospital, autopsies proved that the illness of one out of four patients had been misdiagnosed, yet there was no malpractice.

· *My doctor diagnosed my condition over the phone as indigestion. Actually, I was having a heart attack. Malpractice?*

In a case of this type, standard practice requires the doctor to insist on a physical examination before making the diagnosis. The misdiagnosis is malpractice.

· *My wife suffered severe burns when her pressure cooker exploded. I called my doctor to get emergency advice, but his secretary said, "Sorry, you can't speak to the doctor. This is not his telephone hour." Malpractice?*

If the secretary was ignoring an emergency request on your doctor's orders, that's a departure from standard practice, and it's malpractice. If the secretary took it on herself to prevent your talking to the doctor, it's still malpractice. In accordance with standard practice, a doctor is responsible for the actions of his staff.

• *My baby was born with brain damage because the anesthesiologist cut off the supply of oxygen during birth. Malpractice?*

Obviously, cutting off the supply of oxygen is not standard practice. You have a malpractice claim not only against the anesthesiologist but also against the obstetrician, since the doctor in charge is responsible for the acts of every member of his team. The hospital is also liable. Other acts of malpractice during childbirth include the administration of improper drugs during labor, the improper monitoring of fetal well-being, and the failure to recognize an obstetrical emergency and perform a cesarean section.

• *I was operated on at the insistence of my surgeon. Later I was told by another doctor that drug therapy would have been as effective as surgery, and that the expensive operation was unnecessary. Malpractice?*

Only if surgery for the treatment of your condition is not standard practice. If it's standard practice to prescribe surgery or an alternative therapy—say, drugs—for your condition, your doctor has the legal right to choose, subject to your informed consent. A doctor's choice, for example, of coronary bypass surgery—an expensive, risky operation which does not, except in rare cases, prolong the life of heart attack candidates—instead of inexpensive, minimal-risk, and possibly more effective therapy based on therapeutic drugs, diet, and exercise, is standard practice, not malpractice.

• *My daughter's baby was delivered by cesarean section although the child could have been delivered naturally. My daughter died. Malpractice?*

A cesarean, or C-section, which extracts the fetus surgically by cutting through the abdominal wall and uterus, was once performed only when the life of the mother or the child was in danger. More costly than natural birth, the C-section is now not only standard practice when no such danger exists, but according to Dr. Thomas H. Ainsworth, a former director of the American Hospital Association, "is being touted…in some quarters of the medical establishment…as the new wave, the 'normal' birthing method of the future," even though it has produced an increase in maternal mortality. The death of your daughter because of her doctor's choice of a C-section was not malpractice in and of itself. On the other hand, if there was incompetence in the performance of the operation, it would be malpractice.

"INFORMED CONSENT" AND THE ROLE IT PLAYS IN MALPRACTICE

• *What is informed consent?*

A doctor is required to inform you about everything concerning your illness and his proposed treatment, and, on the basis of that information, to obtain your consent to the treatment before proceeding.

• *What is the relation between informed consent and malpractice?*

If a doctor proceeds with a treatment without your informed consent, that's malpractice. Informed consent is now a principle of standard medical practice.

• *Isn't it reasonable to assume that a doctor knows more about my medical condition than I do, and that I should give my consent to whatever he decides is best for me?*

Your doctor's assumed superior knowledge of medicine has no bearing on your right to determine what will be done to your own body. The court decision that in 1960 established that right states:

"A man is the master of his own body and may expressly prohibit the performance of life-saving surgery or other medical treatment. A doctor may well believe that an operation or other form of treatment is desirable or necessary, but the law does not permit him to substitute his own judgment for that of the patient."

In the court's decision, the word "man" stands for the human race, and includes women as well as men.

· *Exactly what must my doctor tell me before I can give informed consent?*

"Medical jurisprudence contains few concepts as controversial as 'informed consent,'" comments Dr. Martin S. Pernick, a leading authority on the social history of medicine. "Since the phrase was first applied to the doctor-patient relationship in the 1957 case of *Salgo* v. *Leland Stanford Jr. University Board of Trustees* ...judges, lawyers, physicians and medical humanists have debated the definition, application, and purpose of informed consent, yet most of these basic issues remain unresolved."

Exactly what a doctor must tell you is among those unresolved issues. Nevertheless, according to the consensus of court decisions, you're likely to be adequately prepared to grant or withhold informed consent if a doctor tells you all of the following:

- What's wrong with you
- What the proposed treatment is and what it's supposed to do
- The chances of success. If the treatment is surgical, you should be told of the success-failure record of the surgeon and hospital in performing the prescribed operation
- The risks involved, including the possibilities of disfigurement, permanent impairment, or death, particularly if surgery is involved
- Probable side effects, particularly from drugs
- Disagreeable aspects of the therapy other than side effects, including hospitalization, extensive and/or painful tests, and periodic injections
- Available alternative treatments

- Why the treatment selected is better for you than the available alternatives
- The risk to your health should you reject the treatment

Since lack of informed consent is a cause for a malpractice claim, ideally the information supplied by the doctor which forms the basis of consent should be taped, and copies retained by both doctor and patient. While some doctors do tape information sessions for their own protection, others bristle when taping is suggested by the patient. If the information session with your doctor is not recorded, it's a good idea to make complete notes at the session itself, or as soon after it as possible while the information is still fresh in your mind. Then obtain written corroborative material from your doctor (otherwise, should you bring an action against him, it will be your word against his).

· What happens if a doctor intimidates me into giving informed consent?

Informed consent must be given freely. If it's not obtained freely, it's not consent, and should you be injured as a result of the treatment, you can make a claim of malpractice against the doctor. Here's a case in point:

Malignant (cancerous) breast growths are now treated surgically in three ways: by radical mastectomy, the complete removal of a breast, nearby lymph tissue, and some muscle; by simple mastectomy, the complete removal of a breast, but less of the lymph and muscle tissue; and by lumpectomy, just the removal of the lump.

A doctor recommended that a lump in a woman's breast, diagnosed as probably benign, be removed surgically. He asked for permission in writing to perform a radical mastectomy should a biopsy (a medical test for the presence of cancer) taken during the surgery reveal malignancy. The patient said she would not sign because if malignancy was found, she would prefer lumpectomy. The angry doctor growled, "What difference does it make? I told you it's probably benign. Sign it." She signed. The biopsy revealed malignancy, and the doctor performed a radical mastectomy.

The malpractice claim was based on physical injury—the unnecessary loss of a breast—and on consequent emotional suffering, both brought on by lack of informed consent because of the doctor's intimidating behavior. The award was in the high six figures.

• *My father is senile. Since he doesn't understand what the doctor tells him, how can he give informed consent?*

He can't. You can give it for him, though, provided you're appointed legal guardian by the court. If you prefer not to assume that responsibility, you may request the court to appoint another relative, your father's doctor, or the court itself to become your father's legal guardian. A legal guardian is required to grant informed consent not only for senile people but for those who are mentally incompetent in any way.

• *I'm a teenager. I've contracted genital herpes, and I don't want my folks to know about it. Can I give informed consent for treatment?*

Yes, in many states, and in most of those states the doctor is not required by law to inform your parents. This right of teenagers to give informed consent applies not only to treatment of venereal diseases, but also to treatment of drug abuse, alcoholism, pregnancy, emotional abnormalities, and the medical application of contraceptive devices and procedures. In all states, teenagers can give informed consent on all medical concerns provided they meet one of the following conditions: They live in their own dwellings; provide for their own living; serve in the Armed Forces; are married; or are parents, wedded or unwedded.

• *As a parent, is it my responsibility to give informed consent for the medical treatment of my minor children?*

Yes, with these exceptions: Teenagers have the right to give consent under certain conditions (see preceding question); and in Delaware and Illinois children as young as twelve can give informed consent to some medical treatments. Also, your responsibility is waived if you can't be reached by your doctor, particularly in an emergency. The doctor, provided he has tried to get in touch with you, is then legally permitted to act as the child's guardian in your place.

· *When I was admitted to a hospital for minor surgery recently, I was asked to sign a "blanket consent," which gave the hospital the right to do anything it wanted to me. Whatever happened to the principle of informed consent?*

Nothing. The principle stands firm. Blanket consents are invalid. Even if you signed one, you can still sue for malpractice if you didn't give informed consent to the specific surgery for which you entered the hospital or any other surgery or treatment decided upon by the hospital.

CONDUCTING A MALPRACTICE SUIT AND WHAT IT COSTS TO WIN OR LOSE

· *I suspect that my doctor committed malpractice, but I'm not sure. How can I find out?*

One way is to consult a malpractice lawyer. His knowledge of the law, his experience in the field, and his ready access to medical experts can help determine whether you have grounds for a malpractice claim.

Another way is to call your local county medical society (try your White Pages or ask your public librarian for the number) and say, "I want to file a complaint against my doctor, and I want you to review it. How do I go about it?" Follow instructions. The county medical society's malpractice review committee will study your complaint and render an opinion solely on its medical merits—that is to say, whether in treating you your doctor departed from the standards of medical practice. Should the opinion confirm your suspicion of malpractice, your next step is to see a malpractice lawyer. If the opinion does not confirm your suspicion, you may opt to drop the case or seek a second opinion—a legal one.

Critics of malpractice review by the county medical society compare a patient going before a panel of doctors to a hen pleading before a skulk of foxes. Proponents, though, point out that this cost-free and relatively red-tape-free way of evaluating a malpractice claim is impartial and has even been praised by some members of the legal profession.

• How much time do I have by law until I can bring a malpractice suit?

Each state has its own statute of limitations which sets the allowable time before a malpractice suit can be instituted. Some states count that time from the occurrence of the alleged malpractice (one year in Louisiana to seven years in Vermont); other states from the time of the discovery of the malpractice (six months in Michigan to as much as five years in Montana). If you suspect malpractice, it is prudent to pursue the matter without delay.

• What do I do when I decide to make a malpractice claim?

Provide your lawyer with all the facts in the case and all the relevant documents in your possession, including the notes you made after each visit or telephone conversation with your doctor. Answer all your lawyer's questions honestly and to the best of your ability. Don't embroider the facts and don't editorialize.

• What does my lawyer do after I've given him the facts?

He attempts to confirm your version of what happened with whatever records of your case he can obtain from your doctor, your hospital, your pharmacist, the medical laboratories that conducted your tests, and from any other relevant sources. He obtains the services of medical consultants. He searches the legal literature to determine how cases like yours have been decided in the past.

Your lawyer then normally conducts a "discovery." It's a procedure that allows each side to discover as much as possible about the other's position—with the hope that the open review of the facts will lead to a settlement before litigation. This is a time-consuming and expensive process, involving the examination of as many relevant witnesses as possible.

If the claim cannot be settled as a result of discovery, your lawyer may ask for a review by the local county medical society (if you have not already done so). Decisions are not binding, but they provide guidance for rapid out-of-court settlements. Should you and your lawyer decide to bypass a nonbinding review, or to ignore the decision of such a review, your lawyer places the case on the court calendar—that is, sets a date for trial.

Before the case can go to trial, some states require a pretrial hearing—a sort of rehearsal of your case and your doctor's defense. The object, like that of medical-society and bar-association review, is to obtain an out-of-court settlement without prolonged litigation. In those states in which pretrial hearings are not mandatory, opposing attorneys often recommend voluntary pretrial review to their clients.

Cases that seldom reach court are mainly of the open-and-shut variety—in which malpractice is so blatant that it's clear even to a layman. In a recent case of this type, a $75 million lawsuit was filed against a surgeon who left a needle and thread in the chest of a two-year-old girl after open-heart surgery. In this case, and others in which negligence is apparent, the courts hold that the fact speaks for itself (*res ipsa loquitur*), and all the lawyer would have to prove in court would be the facts. In the $75 million needle-and-thread case, the facts to be proved are that the needle and thread were indeed left in the body of the two-year-old, that the child didn't put them there, and that the surgeon or some member of his team did put them there—facts so easy to establish that a trial would be a mere formality. As this book goes to press, an out-of-court settlement is pending.

Should your lawyer fail to reach a pretrial settlement, the case goes to trial. Unless the doctrine of *res ipsa loquitur* is invoked, the lawyer must prove that you suffered an injury as a result of your doctor's departure from standard practice. In presenting your case, your lawyer relies on your own appearance if the injury is obvious (blindness or paralysis, for example), on documents, and on witnesses, particularly medical experts who testify to the extent of your injuries and your doctor's departure from standard practice. Your lawyer also has to counter the opposing lawyer's attempts to discredit your evidence and your experts (usually with experts of his own).

Between the time a malpractice action is initiated and a judgment is rendered, years may pass. You may lose; but should you win, the award may justify the long legal process.

· How much should I sue for?

Your lawyer will help you arrive at a figure that represents just compensation for the wrong suffered. He'll take into consideration such tangibles as dollar losses on earnings and extra medical expenses incurred as a result of the doctor-induced injury. He'll also put a dollar value on such intangibles as physical and emotional distress. Your lawyer also may in some cases recommend that you request punitive damages as well—punishment for your doctor's willful neglect, incompetence, or cover-up.

In some states, though, you're not permitted to specify the amount of the award in your claim; the award is set by either the judge or the jury. In other states you can specify the amount of the award but the jurors are not permitted to know about it during the trial, so it doesn't enter into their deliberations. In still other states, legislation puts a cap on the amount you can be awarded. And in all states, no matter what the jury decides to award you, the judge more often than not cuts it down.

· What are the legal fees for a malpractice suit?

A medical malpractice lawyer operates on a contingency basis— that is to say, the fee is contingent (depends) on his winning the case and on the size of the award. Contingent fees range from one-third to one-half of the award.

The advantages of the contingency system for malpractice cases are: You don't pay your lawyer unless you win. You're free of monthly legal bills during the duration of the case, which can be years. Your lawyer as a matter of self-interest will aim for the highest possible award. In short, even after deducting your lawyer's high percentage of the award, you're almost certain to be better off than had you paid a fixed fee. The disadvantage is: If in the opinion of your lawyer, the award potential is small, he may refuse your case no matter how meritorious it is. You may not find any malpractice lawyer to take it on.

· *When I win, doesn't the court rule that the doctor pay my costs?*

Yes, but that means court costs, not your lawyer's expenses. Those expenses come out of the award, as does your lawyer's fee. If you lose, you pay both your lawyer's expenses and the court costs.

· *Suppose I lose the suit—can the doctor strike back and sue me?*

Yes, he can sue in some states on the ground that your claim was without merit and your suit was frivolous—an abuse of the legal process. This kind of countersuit has resulted in a number of victories for doctors so far, but it's too early to tell how the verdicts will stand up on appeal. But even if the doctor loses the countersuit, the cost to you can be high in legal fees (no contingency here), time, and peace of mind.

3

Medical Life-Support Systems: Your Right to Have Them, and to Reject Them

- New legal definitions of death, and their relation to life-support problems
- Medical standards for compliance with the new legal definitions of death
- The "right to die": when it is legal to reject life support
- The "right to live": receiving life support

A little more than a month ago, Geraldine Goodman, forty-four, was admitted to the Fairchild General Hospital suffering from an incurable disease.

Five days later, she lapsed into a coma and was connected to a respirator. The machine artificially maintained her breathing and her heartbeat.

Three tests taken since indicated no brain activity, according to the Goodman's family lawyer.

Today Geraldine Goodman's husband requested the hospital to disconnect the respirator.

Will the hospital comply?

The names are fictitious but the situation is not. The problem of when to terminate life-maintaining medical support, and who has the right to make the decision, is disturbing people all over the country. It's a problem affecting the seriously ill of all ages—the Baby Does, the Karen Ann Quinlans, and the multitudes of nursing-home aged. It is a problem that has arisen mainly because modern high-tech life-maintaining systems have made it difficult in some cases to distinguish between life and death.

Only ten or fifteen years ago, a doctor could easily diagnose death. He would listen for a heartbeat with a stethoscope and look for signs of breathing, sometimes holding a mirror to the nostrils to detect the faint condensation that signified breath. If there was no heartbeat and no sign of breath, he would pronounce the patient dead. Except in those rare, dramatic instances when a cadaver rose in the coffin during the burial services, his diagnoses were correct.

The law, following the lead of the medical profession, defined death, according to the authoritative *Black's Law Dictionary*, as "a total stoppage of the circulation of the blood [heartbeat] and a cessation...of respiration [breathing]."

By this definition, a person whose heartbeat and breathing are generated by high technology is alive. But is that person alive when consciousness and the other higher faculties of the brain have passed away forever? Does the life-support system then merely mimic life and mask death? Does it just falsely animate a corpse? Clearly, today's high-tech life-support systems have made a new definition of death mandatory.

NEW LEGAL DEFINITIONS OF DEATH, AND THEIR RELATION TO LIFE-SUPPORT PROBLEMS

The new medical definition of death is based on the following current understanding of the *natural* life-and-death interrelations of three vital organs of the body, the heart, the lungs, and the brain; and on the separate functions of the two major parts of the brain, the cerebrum and the brain stem (see the diagram on the next page).

  • When the cerebrum stops functioning, consciousness and the other higher faculties of the brain cease. But should the brain stem continue to function, impulses from it still flow down the phrenic nerves to activate the heart and lungs. The body, deprived of cerebral function but with

brain-stem function intact, becomes a "vegetable," but it is alive. The body is not dead until the cerebrum *and* the brain stem—the whole brain—cease to function ("whole brain death").
- When the heart and lungs cease to function, whole brain death occurs, and the body is dead.

Medically redefined, then, death is either the cessation of the functions of the heart and lungs *or* the cessation of the functions of the whole brain.

The latest edition of *Black's Law Dictionary* now includes an entry under the heading "brain death," citing recent statutes and court decisions indicating a growing legal acceptance in principle of the new medical definition of death. But not all states have altered the traditional legal definition of death; and among the twenty-seven states that have, there are several variations of the basic new medical definition. In states without statutory definitions of death, the legal definition is set by court decisions, many of which adhere to the medical definition of death prior to the recognition of whole brain death.

There is no federal law on the determination of death as yet. But the President's Commission for the Study of Ethical Problems in Medicine and Biochemical and Behavioral Research recommends such a law. "We have concluded," reports Morris B. Abram, commission chairman, "that in light of the ever increasing powers of biomedical science and practice, a statute is needed to provide a clear and socially accepted basis for making determinations of death. We recommend the adoption of such a statute by the Congress for areas coming under federal jurisdiction and by all states as a means of achieving uniform law on this subject throughout the nation."

The commission proposes that a Uniform Determination of Death Act embody the new medical definition of death as follows:

"An individual who has sustained either (1) irreversible cessation of circulatory and respiratory functions or (2) irreversible cessation of all functions of the entire brain, including the brain stem, is dead. A determination of death must be made in accordance with accepted medical standards."

The proposed statute has been endorsed by three influential

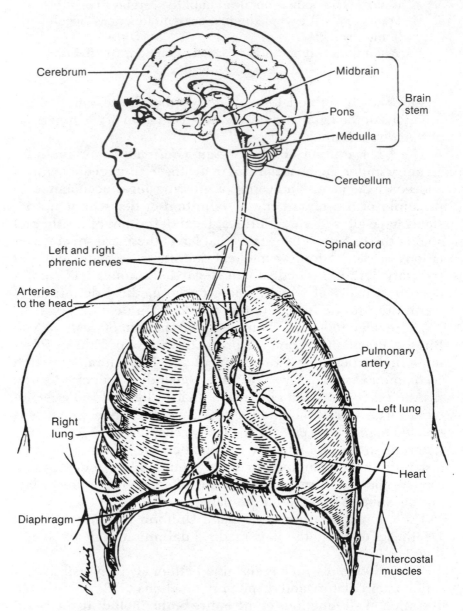

Cerebrum

Midbrain

Brain stem

Pons

Medulla

Cerebellum

Spinal cord

Left and right phrenic nerves

Arteries to the head

Pulmonary artery

Left lung

Right lung

Heart

Diaphragm

Intercostal muscles

Anatomic Interrelationships of Heart, Lungs, and Brain

organizations that previously had proposed their own model legislation on the determination of death: the American Bar Association, the American Medical Association, and the National Conference of Commissioners on Uniform State Laws. Two states, Idaho and Colorado, have adopted it.

The new legal definitions of death can help solve the problem of who is alive on a life-support system and who is not, and consequently whether the system should be disconnected. But it does not solve the legal problem of who has the right to disconnect. Nor, unless the definition of death is to be modified even further, does it solve the related legal problems of the terminally ill: whether they have the "right to die" by rejecting life support, and whether they have the "right to live" when others decide to withdraw life support from them.

• *In the case of "Geraldine Goodman," whose husband requested discontinuance of a life-support system on the basis of whole brain death, how will the hospital respond?*

In those states which have enacted whole-brain-death statutes, the hospital will grant Mr. Goodman's request, although sometimes a court order is necessary. In states which have no such statutes, it's a matter for the courts to decide. In one important case, the court refused to accept whole brain death as a basis for the diagnosis of death, but informally assured the doctors involved that no liability would follow termination of the life-support system.

• *Since the determination of death in one state can differ from that in another, can a legally live body become legally dead when transported across state lines?*

It hasn't happened yet, but it could. In a hypothetical case, an impatient heir might transfer a legally live relative to a hospital in another state which would pronounce the relative legally dead. Such a possibility points to the need for a federal Uniform Determination of Death Act.

• *During surgery, doctors decide that an auto-accident victim is whole-brain-dead. They disconnect the life-support system, then remove the heart and kidneys for transplant. Legal?*

Organs cannot be removed for transplant until after death. Whether in this case it is legal to remove the heart and kidneys depends on the legal definition of death acceptable in that state. If the statutory definition includes whole brain death as a criterion for the diagnosis of death, the removal is legal; if it doesn't, the removal is not. If the definition of death is not governed by statute, the legality of the removal is subject to the court's decision. In one case in New York, a state with no statutory definition of death, the court accepted a definition of death "consistent with the generally accepted medical practice concerned with organ transplants." That practice permits the removal of organs for transplant following a diagnosis of whole brain death.

· *Doctors disconnect a victim of a shooting from a life-support system by mistake. He dies. The woman who confessed to the shooting is accused of homicide. Her defense is: "I didn't kill him. The doctors did." Who's guilty?*

Basing their decisions on the "proximate cause" (initial cause) theory of criminal responsibility, the courts have held that when the accused inflicts the wounds that are the proximate cause of death, subsequent medical action, even if it is in error, does not constitute a valid defense. The woman is guilty.

MEDICAL STANDARDS FOR COMPLIANCE WITH THE NEW LEGAL DEFINITIONS OF DEATH

· *What medical methods for the determination of whole brain death are acceptable to the courts?*

The courts accept the medical profession's up-to-date diagnostic tests and medical procedures. The Washington Supreme Court in 1980 described such methods in the case of five-year-old Matthew Bowman, whose heart and lungs were functioning by means of a life-support system:

"The testifying physician indicated that he believed Matthew's brain was dead under the most rigid criteria available, called the 'Harvard criteria.'...An electroencephalogram (EEG) gave no reading, and a radionucleide scan, which shows whether blood is getting to and through the brain, found a total absence of blood flow. No cornea reflex was present, and Matthew's pupils were dilated and nonreactive to any stimuli. There were also no deep tendon reflexes or other signs of brain stem action, nor responses to deep pain or signs of spontaneous breathing. ...[The medical conclusion drawn from the test results predicted] that Matthew's cardiovascular system, despite the life support systems, would fail in 14 to 60 days."

· *On a life-support system, how can doctors tell that the brain stem is alive?*

The patient yawns, blinks, swallows, makes reflex responses, and carries on all the other vegetative functions of the human body.

· *Are there conditions that can be mistaken for whole brain death?*

Yes. They include deep coma induced by some diseases; severe shock (sudden sharp reduction of blood circulation); hypothermia (extremely low body temperature); and reactions to some therapeutic and recreational drugs. A state of apparent lifelessness is also induced in children, particularly under five, by some forms of brain damage. Doctors are trained to recognize these deathlike states, which do not usually persist long even without medical aid.

"THE RIGHT TO DIE": WHEN IT IS LEGAL TO REJECT LIFE SUPPORT

· *Before I can make up my mind about whether to reject—or accept—life support, I want to know what it is. Is there a legal definition?*

Not a statutory one. But court decisions make it clear that life support consists of medical care to prolong life. That care can take the form of a high-tech apparatus that generates heartbeat and breathing artificially, or it can be conventional medical prescriptions and procedures, including drugs, surgery, and hospitalization.

• *The doctors say my father is dying, but he won't undergo chemotherapy and radiation therapy which they tell him can prolong his life. He's in a hospital. Can the doctors force the treatment on him?*

When a person who knows that he is dying rejects life support, the courts usually follow this procedure: On the assumption that such a person is mentally incompetent, since no one in his right mind would deny the gift of life, the court appoints a guardian to make the life-support decision for him. The guardian could be yourself, a relative, the hospital doctor in charge of his case, or the court itself.

There are, however, exceptions to this procedure. The best-known involves the Quackenbush case in New Jersey. A seventy-two-year-old drifter with no living relatives, Quackenbush (first name unknown) was hospitalized with gangrene in both legs. Told that he would die in two weeks unless both his legs were amputated, he growled, "No way." The hospital petitioned the court to appoint a guardian on the basis of the patient's mental incompetence.

But the judge, after a personal examination of the old man, found him in full command of his senses, and ruled that "as a mentally competent individual...Quackenbush...has the right to make his informed choice about the operation and I will not interfere with that choice."

• *The idea of ending my life as a vegetable on some life-support system is abhorrent to me. I want to give binding instructions to doctors to pull the plug if that ever happens to me. Can I do it legally?*

Bills have been introduced in a number of states which would permit a person to prepare a written directive to his doctors to cease treatment in case of an irrevocable vegetative or terminal illness. Known as a "living will," such a directive has become legally binding only in North Carolina. Whether a living will is legal in the other forty-nine states is now a matter for the courts to decide.

THE "RIGHT TO LIVE": RECEIVING LIFE SUPPORT

· *Shouldn't a vegetative person on a life-support system have the right to stay on that system—stay alive?*

Yes, in those states in which whole brain death is a criterion for the diagnosis of death, and there is evidence of the continuance of brain-stem activity. In other states it's a matter for the courts to decide, as it was in the much-publicized case of Karen Ann Quinlan.

Quinlan, who suffered from brain damage, was apparently kept alive by a high-tech cardiac-respiratory life-support system. She was sometimes in a state of coma, sometimes in a state of awakened awareness, but never conscious. Her parents, believing that she would never again regain consciousness, requested on religious grounds that the doctors terminate the life-support system. The doctors refused, arguing that their disconnection of the apparatus would result in the death of their patient, an act contrary to standard medical practice. The New Jersey court ruled in favor of the parents, holding that the irrevocable absence of a "cognitive state" (consciousness and the higher brain faculties) justified the removal of life support. In essence, this court had defined death as the permanent cessation of the functions of *one* part of the brain, the cerebrum; and had concluded that the girl was dead, and that the removal of the life-support system would have no effect.

The parents had gained their daughter's "right to die"—that is, to end artificially induced heartbeat and breathing. But if the other part of the brain, the brain stem, was still alive—it *was* possible—then by the definition of *whole* brain death, the girl would be alive, and the parents would have denied their daughter's "right to live." As it turned out, the brain stem *was* alive, and after the disconnection of the apparatus Quinlan continued to live in a vegetative state on conventional life support, until her death in June 1985. In a similar case in New York, also decided on the basis of irreversible loss of cognitive function, the brain stem proved to be dead as well, and the patient died when the life-support system was disconnected.

In 1984, nine years after its decision in the Quinlan case, the New Jersey Supreme Court ruled that "all life support can be withheld from incompetent as well as terminally ill competent patients, provided that is what the patient wants or would want."

• *Doesn't a child, even though born hopelessly unable to function as a normal human being, have the right to life support—to live?*

In recent years, possibly because of therapeutic drugs and polluted environment and food, there has been a sharp increase in the birth of defective infants. Some newborns arrive irreversibly deformed, retarded, comatose, in permanent pain, and in many instances terminally ill. In these cases in which life is likely to be a tragic travesty of human existence and a nightmare of pain, are heroic medical efforts to prolong life justified in opposition to the parents' wishes?

In 1983, the media spotlighted this dilemma for the American public in a case that would involve vicious controversy and litigation, incite the Reagan administration to acts that would be widely and hotly debated, and result in pending federal legislation to deny such unfortunate children the right to die— which is to say, to enforce their right to live.

Baby Jane Doe, a fictitious name employed by the courts and media to protect the privacy of the parents, was born likely to die, with an open spinal column, an abnormally small head, and excess fluid on the brain. Surgery was prescribed that could prolong the child's life but could not improve the severe mental retardation or ameliorate the pain. After consultation with lawyers, social workers, and doctors, the parents decided on nonsurgical care.

To Lawrence Washburn, a lawyer associated with the Right to Life Group, the parents' action was tantamount to a decision to let the baby die. He petitioned a New York court to appoint a legal guardian who would consent to the operation. The court ruled against Washburn, calling the parents' decision "a reasonable determination based upon...reasonable medical authority," and denouncing Washburn's suit as offensive.

Prodded by massive media coverage of the event, the Reagan administration then filed suit in federal court to force a disclosure of hospital records on the unusual grounds that Baby Doe's civil rights had been violated in that she had been discriminated against as a handicapped person. The federal court rejected the suit, indirectly rebuking the administration by upholding the parents' decision as "compassionate." Undeterred, the federal Justice Department appealed (the appeal has since been dropped), and Washburn threatened to take the case to the Supreme Court of the United States, and if defeated there, to Congress.

Thwarted by the courts, the Reagan administration through its Health and Human Services Administration in January 1984 promulgated regulations which permitted the government to intervene to preserve the lives of newborn handicapped children. The regulations, among other things, required the hospitals to post in all nursing stations antidiscrimination notices involving handicapped newborns, and hot-line telephone numbers to appropriate state child service agencies for anybody to use to report life-involving parental decisions contrary to doctors' decisions. It was inevitable that the courts would strike down these regulations; and later in 1984, a Manhattan federal court judge ruled that the so-called "Baby Jane Doe Regulations are invalid, unlawful and must be set aside...because [they were] promulgated without statutory authority."

In the meantime, as a result of nonsurgical medical treatment, the skin over Baby Doe's open spine has healed, reducing the risk of infection. Overall, the improvement in the infant's condition has been so marked that she's been released from the hospital. "She's been making a joke of all who've been screaming for surgery," her mother said. "We looked at all the options ...got the best advice...and made our decision out of love of her." Apparently, the courts have agreed.

If there's any guideline to be found in the Baby Jane Doe case so far, it's this: The courts look favorably on giving parents the right to life-and-death decisions over newborn infants whose early death seems likely. However, when infants, although seriously impaired, have a prospect for long life, however abnormal, the courts usually decide against the parents' petition to terminate life-support systems. A court recently denied such a petition in a case involving an infant born with Down's syndrome (mongoloidism).

· *When parents and doctors disagree concerning the use of life-support systems for infants, who decides?*

A federal law passed in 1984 requires treatment and feeding of all handicapped newborns, unless they are irreversibly comatose, or when treatment would just prolong dying, or when treatment would not prolong the infant's life.

· *Shouldn't the hopelessly ill aged have the right not to be deprived of life support by doctors—the right to live?*

In October 1982, a group of medical doctors meeting at Harvard Medical School issued a little-known, but potentially influential, report that made the following major conclusions concerning the care of the hopelessly ill aged:

Doctors are always to obey the patient's own wishes, but if hopelessly ill patients are too sick or deranged to say how much care they want, it is ethical for the doctor to withhold drugs, and even food and water, provided the patients are kept comfortable while they die.

This controversial recommendation was echoed some two years later in a much-publicized statement by Colorado's governor, Richard D. Lamm. He said that the terminally ill aged have "a duty to die and get out of the way instead of trying to prolong their lives by artificial means."

He explained, "We are really approaching a time of almost technological immortality when the machines and the drugs and the heart pacemakers ... literally force life on us. I believe that we should really be careful in terms of our technological miracles that we don't impose life on people who are suffering beyond the ability for us to help."

The governor added that the costs of life-prolonging treatment for terminally ill people were ruining the nation's economy. Conventional life support for the hopelessly ill aged, such as is provided by nursing homes, is expensive: and high-tech life-support systems are estimated to cost upward of $1,000 a day—virtually all of which for indigent patients comes from state and federal funds.

Statutes and court decisions grant the rights to live and to die to all patients, including the hopelessly ill aged, on high-tech life-support systems. But there is now no body of law, or pending legislation, that deals specifically with conventional life support for the hopelessly ill aged. Disputes between those patients and their doctors concerning the right to live will have to be contested individually in the courts.

4

Credit: Your Right to It, and to Its Fair Use

- How you're protected when you apply for credit
- How you're protected when your credit record is checked
- How you're protected when you pay for credit
- How you're protected when you use your credit cards

"In the world we live in," advises consumerism pundit Bernard Meltzer, "using credit is morally right and financially sound when...you're borrowing for the right purpose." There are actually six right purposes, according to another leading consumer expert, Sylvia Porter:

- To establish a household or begin a family
- To buy big-price-tag items—a house, a car, appliances, furniture, or that energy-restoring trip to faraway places with strange sounding names
- To pay for otherwise unpayable major emergency expenses—catastrophic medical bills, for example
- To meet the high costs of college or other educational expenses
- To take advantage of sales when you don't have the ready cash
- To buy something you need today because not only will it cost more tomorrow, you'll also be paying for it with cheaper (inflated) dollars

The items Sylvia Porter is talking about—a family, a home, a car, vacations, education, the best medical care money can buy, a shelter against chronic inflation—are, these days, the normal expectations of the average American. But the average American could never achieve these goals without credit. Bernard Meltzer gives some homespun examples:

"Your single days are over, the wedding bells have chimed, and now there are two of you with a single thought: Let's buy a house.... If you waited to save $50,000, by the time you saved it, the house would cost $100,000; and if you waited until you saved $100,000, it would cost $200,000, and so on. You could never catch up, and you would never live in your own house. The only thing to do—and millions and millions of American families do it—is to borrow. Mortgages were invented for people like you....

"Kids.... A baby is one of the big, big expenses of a lifetime. What are you going to do about it? Dig into your savings and leave yourself with little or nothing for a rainy day? The wise and sensible thing to do is borrow, and pay it back in small installments. For a few dollars a week, you can have the joy of children when *you* want them, and not when your *bank balance* says you can have them.... More than ever your kids' futures depend on education.... And how do you finance higher education with the costs going through the roof and heading for the stratosphere?... Borrowing for the kids' higher education is the American way of life, and has been for a long time.

"Unless you were born with a silver spoon in your mouth," Meltzer concludes, "you're going to borrow for many, many things most Americans find to be necessities, not luxuries."

To procure these necessities, credit itself has become a necessity. When you're denied it without legitimate cause, or overcharged for it, or misled about it to your detriment, you're deprived of a right that has become an American basis: the right to get credit and to use it fairly.

In the years since the inception of mass consumer credit in 1964 (more about that in the following chapter), a significant body of legislation to protect your credit rights has been established. The Consumer Credit Code, sponsored by the National Conference of Commissioners on Uniform State Laws, was adopted by a number of states. Other states enacted similar codes. From the Congress of the United States came the Fair Credit Building Act, the Equal Credit Opportunity Act, the Fair Credit Reporting Act, the Fair Credit Billing Act, and the landmark Consumer Credit Protection Act, better known as the Truth in Lending Act. The enforcement of these laws falls to federal and state agencies, which are also empowered by statute to provide the regulations for implementation.

This strong network of legislation, regulation, and enforcement has grown out of our lawmakers' realization of the vital role consumer credit plays in our national economy. "The growth of consumer credit in the United States has been largely responsible for...the level of economic growth that the nation has achieved," states consumer-credit authority Melvin J. Kaplan. "Our industrial machine, and the jobs and income it provides, are dependent on credit buying to absorb the goods that are produced.... Destroy the credit system and our economy would suffer a severe—if not a devastating—jolt."

But the credit system is indestructible as long as the average American continues to be willing to buy today with the money he hopes to earn tomorrow. That's "consumer confidence"—and to help keep the "index of consumer confidence" high and rising, our legislators have provided the safeguards that have made fair credit available to the widest number of Americans. What's good for the economy turns out, as it should; to be good for you.

HOW YOU'RE PROTECTED WHEN YOU APPLY FOR CREDIT

• *Am I protected against discrimination when I apply for credit?*

The purpose of the federal Equal Opportunity Credit Act (EOCA) is to protect you from being denied credit, from being given unfair terms for credit, and even from being discouraged from applying for credit for fear of discrimination. Specifically prohibited is discrimination based on race, color, sex, religion, and national origin; as well as discrimination based on marital status, being on welfare or other public-assistance rolls, or being a complainant in an action based on consumer-protection credit laws. All states have enacted versions of equal opportunity credit laws as well.

• *I'm a handicapped person. Does the Equal Opportunity Credit Act protect me against credit discrimination?*

No. But your state credit laws may.

• *I'm a woman and I'm Hispanic. I believe my credit application was turned down for those two reasons. What do I do?*

A credit source (in legal language, a creditor) that turns down your credit application, or offers you terms that are unfavorable compared to those offered most customers, is required to give you the name and address of the appropriate equal credit opportunity enforcing agency. If the bank or company you're dealing with doesn't offer it to you, ask for it. If you still don't get it, use the following list to find the type of creditor that discriminated against you, and address your complaint to the designated enforcing agency, attention: Consumer Complaint Department.

Remember credit legally means straight loans or loans made to finance purchases (as with credit or installment contracts).

Creditor	Enforcing Agency
Nationally chartered bank (a bank with "National" or "N.A." in its name)	Consumer Affairs Division Office of the Comptroller of Currency Washington, DC 20219
State chartered bank and a member of the Federal Reserve System	Division of Consumer Affairs Federal Reserve Board Washington, DC 20551
State chartered bank insured by the Federal Deposit Insurance System (it will display the FDIC symbol)	Office of Consumer Affairs and Civil Rights Federal Deposit Insurance Corporation Washington, DC 20429

Creditor	Enforcing Agency
A federally chartered credit union ("Federal" will appear in its name)	Consumer Affairs Office National Credit Union Administration Washington, DC 20456
A stocks and bonds broker or dealer	Office of Consumer Affairs Securities and Exchange Commission Washington, DC 20549
A federal land bank, federal land bank association, federal intermediate credit bank, or production credit association	Office of Supervision Farm Credit Administration Washington, DC 20578
A retail store, department store, small loan and finance company, gasoline or other nonbank credit card issuer, state chartered credit union, or other creditor	Equal Credit Opportunity Federal Trade Commission Washington, DC 20580

· *What happens to my complaint at an equal credit opportunity enforcing agency?*

It's investigated either on an individual basis or as one of a group of complaints made against a creditor.

· *Can I get fast results from my complaint?*

It could take months.

· *Can a lawyer help speed up my complaint?*

Although equal credit opportunity enforcing agencies were set up for direct consumer-agency relations, lawyers can be helpful. Even formulating the initial letter of complaint in proper legal terms can speed up processing appreciably.

· *Do I have to sue to get my rights under the Equal Opportunity Credit Act?*

Normally, the enforcing agency brings your complaint to a fair conclusion, without resort to the courts. However, when litigation becomes necessary, the U.S. Justice Department may bring suit on your behalf. The action starts when the agency to which you (or your lawyer) made the complaint refers your case to the Justice Department. The Justice Department, though, is more likely to sue your creditor because of a pattern of violations of which yours is just one. You have the option of bringing suit yourself.

If you're dissatisfied with the way an agency or the Justice Department is handling your case, you can write or ask your lawyer to contact: Chief, Housing and Credit Section, Civil Rights Division, U.S. Department of Justice, Washington, DC 20530.

• I know I can be turned down for credit for legitimate reasons. What are they?

Each creditor has the right to set its own standards to determine whether you qualify to receive credit. These standards are usually based on what credit executives call the three C's: character, capacity, and capital. In the world of credit, "character" means a record of paying your debts on time; "capacity" means a steady income sufficient to pay your debts on time; and "capital" means cash reserves, or property that can be converted into cash, to pay your debts on time in case you lose your steady income. The fill-in lines on credit applications are mainly designed to provide basic information on your three C's. When, by the creditor's standards, your three C's rate A-OK you'll get the credit; but if they don't, you won't.

HOW YOU'RE PROTECTED WHEN YOUR CREDIT RECORD IS CHECKED

• Has the creditor the right to check on my credit record?

Yes. Creditors have found that a sound basic way to do this is to draw a report on you from a credit-reporting agency. The federal Fair Credit Reporting Act is the basic law protecting you against credit-reporting abuses. Almost all states have enacted similar legislation.

• Exactly what is a credit-reporting agency?

It's simply a storehouse of consumer credit account payment histories—information reported to the agency by your creditors. Most of your creditors are likely to report, but some won't. Of the numerous credit-reporting agencies, many are interlinked by a computer network for information sharing. You can't be sure anymore of skipping town to leave your bad-debt record behind; it's probably waiting for you on the next town's computer.

• Does a credit-reporting agency question my friends and neighbors about me?

No. That's the function of a credit investigation agency, which will also question your business associates, your former employers, and you. It will also search court records and other public records. Investigation agencies are usually employed only when there's a great deal of money at stake.

• Does a credit-reporting agency make yes-no decisions concerning my credit application?

No. It simply supplies your credit record to the creditor considering your application.

• What appears on my credit record?

Credit-reporting agencies prefer to call a credit record or a credit report a "credit profile." It contains payment-performance information on your open and closed loans, your charge accounts, and your credit card accounts and on the following two legal items, either of which could give your three-C's rating an F: tax liens and bankruptcy.

Your credit profile does *not* contain information on your income, length of time on the job, length of residency, checking and savings account records, and aspects of your personal life— all of which can be of importance in determining your creditworthiness.

In short, your credit profile is your credit-payment track record. That's all.

• Does a creditor need my consent to draw a credit profile on me?

No. But the creditor must advise you that it's doing so or otherwise investigating you. The creditor must also inform you that you have the right to a copy of the information disclosed. Some creditors, even though they don't have to, do request your consent before beginning a credit checkup.

• Isn't drawing a credit report on me without my consent an invasion of my right to privacy?

No, provided the information is used for lawful purposes. However, drawing a credit profile on you without your *knowledge*— not necessarily without your *consent*—is a violation of federal law. That works out to: You can't call up a credit-reporting agency and ask for your boss's credit profile unless you tell him you're doing it.

• I have reason to suspect that a creditor has drawn a credit report on me without advising me. How can I be sure?

Easily, if you know the name of the credit agency. Just call it and ask for the names of all the creditors who have drawn credit profiles on you in the previous six months. The agency is required to give them to you (there's a small charge).

• I was turned down for credit on the basis of a credit profile. But my credit rating has always been A-1. What can I do?

You can set the record straight by taking the following steps:

1. Write to the credit-reporting agency for a copy of your credit profile. The agency is required to comply with your request without charge in a reasonable amount of time. The name and address of the agency is usually supplied in the creditor's letter of rejection. If it's not, request this information from the creditor. He has to give it to you.

2. Examine the credit profile for negative information that doesn't belong on it. Remember this: A credit-reporting agency is not permitted to report any negative information that's more than seven years old, except bankruptcy, which can be retained on your credit profile for ten years. On the other hand, all information on revolving accounts, good or bad, can be retained indefinitely. A revolving account is one in which your credit is automatically restored as you make payments.

3. Report the illegal negative information to the credit-reporting agency in writing. The agency then has a reasonable time, usually about ten days, to verify your claims with the creditor who supplied the information or with court records. Should revision of your credit profile be necessary, it will be made automatically, and you will be provided with a copy of the revised profile. At your request, the agency will also send a copy of the revised profile to any creditor that had previously requested a credit profile on you.

4. Should the credit-reporting agency inform you that your claims cannot be verified, put your corrections in the form of a one-hundred-word-or-less statement. The agency must include that statement in all your future credit profiles. At your request, the agency must send a revised copy of your credit profile to all creditors who had received a credit profile on you in the preceding six months.

• Can I get a copy of my credit profile even though I'm not applying for credit?

Yes. Try any of the agencies listed in your Yellow Pages. Chances are, if you've had a credit account in the last seven years, the agency's computer will output your credit profile. You can telephone your request, but it's better to put it in writing. The credit-reporting agency is required to comply with your request (there's a small fee). It's a good idea to review your credit profile from time to time; false negative information has been known to slip into the best of credit profiles.

• I'm angry. My credit profile contains a mess of false information, but the credit-reporting agency won't tell me where it got it. What can I do?

Nothing. The credit-reporting agency is not required to reveal its sources, even though the information supplied is injurious to your credit standing and reputation.

HOW YOU'RE PROTECTED WHEN YOU PAY FOR CREDIT

· *What is the Consumer Credit Protection Act?*

It's a law passed by Congress in 1968 essentially to protect you against hidden credit charges by requiring the creditor to reveal the true annual interest rate and the finance charges. The law is known appropriately as the Truth in Lending Act. It applies whether you're borrowing money, or charging goods or services.

· *Before the passage of the Truth in Lending Act, how could a creditor get away with misleading annual interest rates?*

Easily and legally. What happened is best explained by an example. Let's say the stated annual interest rate was 12 percent. You borrowed $1,000. Now here's the sting—but, repeat, legal. The creditor deducted the full interest of $120 ($1,000 × 12 percent) at the time you received your loan. That left you with $880 for which you were paying $120. Divide $120 by $880 to find the true interest rate, which is not 12 percent but a significantly higher 13.64 percent.

Creditors can still deduct full interest charges at the time a loan is received, but now they must reveal the true interest rate. The true interest rate is called the APR (annual percentage rate). Calculating it is almost never as simple as in this example.

· *How is the APR calculated?*

By adding the annual dollar amount paid for interest to other charges, then dividing by the amount of the loan used during the year. Example: You have the use of $1,000 this year. The interest on it is 18.5 percent. That works out to $185. Other charges add another $50. The total yearly cost is $235. Your APR—$235 divided by $1,000—is 23.5 percent, 5 percent higher than your annual interest rate. For your protection, the creditor is required to display the APR prominently (in larger type face or in boldface type, for example) in the credit agreement.

· *What are finance charges?*

That's what you pay in dollars and cents for the money you borrow. It includes interest plus all other charges. The most common other charges are:

Service charge. This can be whatever the creditor decides to levy.

Annual fee. Many credit card issuers now add an annual fee to the cost of credit.

Points. A point is 1 percent of the value of the loan. Points generally apply to mortgage loans.

Minimum charge. You pay this charge when your interest payment during any billing period falls below a certain figure.

Origination fee. This is a percentage of a loan deducted at the time the loan is made.

Insurance. You may choose to have the creditor take out insurance on your life to cover the amount of the loan, in which case the premium and the interest on the premium are added to your payments.

When you know both the APR and the finance charges you have a quick and sound way to appraise the value of the credit deal.

· *Does the Truth in Lending Act require any other disclosures?*

Yes. The law calls for "full disclosure" to be provided in a written document to be shown to the consumer before the credit agreement is executed. Full disclosure is required for both closed-end and open-end credit agreements. A close-end agreement is for a fixed dollar credit (as for the purchase of a TV set); an open-end agreement is for revolving credit (as with credit card use).

For a closed-end credit agreement, the creditor must disclose the following in addition to the APR and the finance charges:

- The number of payments
- The amount of each payment
- The date of each payment
- The total sum of all payments
- How late penalties are figured
- How prepayment penalties, if any, are figured (prepayment means paying off before final due date)
- Whether rebates are made in case of prepayments, and how such rebates are figured
- Identification of collateral, if required

For an open-end credit agreement, the creditor must disclose the following in addition to the APR and the finance charge:

- How much time the lender is allowed after billing to make a periodic payment without any credit costs
- Whether the cost is determined on the whole balance or differs for specified sections of the balance
- The periodic rates used to figure finance charges, and to what fraction of the balance each rate applies
- The minimum periodic payment due
- A notice of your rights under the Fair Credit Billing Act

· *I'd like to know what my credit account looks like from month to month. Does the Truth in Lending Act provide for that, too?*

Yes. On a closed-end credit account, your coupon book (payment book) gives you a month-by-month accounting. On open-end credit accounts, the creditor is required to supply you with periodic statements (usually monthly) which include the following information for the billing period:

- The dates of the billing period
- A list of the purchases made during that period, with identification of each purchase and the date of transaction
- Payments received

- Other credits (returns, for example)
- Interest and other charges
- Debt balance
- Available credit
- An address and telephone number to which inquiries can be made

· *Does the Truth in Lending Act protect me from misleading credit advertising?*

A creditor does not have to reveal *any* terms in its advertising. But if the advertising features one or more terms, then all important terms must be described. This is to prevent the consumer from being being lured by one or more attractive terms that are offset by other less attractive ones.

· *Does the Truth in Lending Act fix the ceiling on interest rates?*

No. Ceilings on interest rates, or lack of them, are set by federal and state statutes.

· *What recourse do I have if the creditor does not comply with the Truth in Lending Act?*

You can sue for damages plus twice the finance charges, provided the finance charges are not less than $100 and not more than $1,000 for each violation. In some cases, you have the right to bring criminal action against the offender, who could be punished by a fine of up to $5,000 and/or one year in prison. Should you win in a civil action, you can also collect attorney's fees and court costs from the offender.

HOW YOU'RE PROTECTED WHEN YOU USE YOUR CREDIT CARDS

· *Does the Truth in Lending Act apply to credit cards?*

Yes. It applies to bank cards (Visa and MasterCard), travel and expense cards (American Express, Diner's Club, Carte Blanche), retail store cards, airline cards, oil company cards, and all other types of credit cards.

• Are there special requirements for obtaining a credit card?

When bank cards first made their appearance in 1964, there were no requirements. Unsolicited cards were sent in the mail to millions of people. This generated a wave of bad debts, and the practice is now illegal. However, it *is* legal for a bank or other credit card issuer to inform you by mail that your credit card has been preapproved, and all you need do to obtain it is to sign a simple form. (Other types of credit, such as bank loans, are now also offered preapproved.) Most credit cards are obtained the way any other types of credit are obtained—through an application and a credit appraisal.

• Is there a standard form for a credit card agreement?

No, but the agreement must conform to the provisions of the Truth in Lending Act. A noteworthy protective feature of the agreement used by major credit card issuers is the following prominently displayed:

> *Notice to the Buyer:*
>
> (1) Do not accept or sign this credit agreement before you read it or if it contains any blank spaces for agreed terms.
>
> (2) You are entitled to a completely filled-in copy of this credit agreement.
>
> (3) You may at any time pay the total indebtedness under this agreement without incurring any additional charge for repayment.

• I received a credit card agreement but there's no place for my signature. Why?

Your signature is not necessary. The agreement goes into effect the first time you use your card.

• Can I sell my credit card?

No. Credit cards remain the property of the credit card issuer and must be surrendered on request.

· *Is it legal for me to have two or more MasterCards or Visas?*

Yes. You can have as many MasterCards or Visas as there are banks issuing them. You can, for example, get one of these cards from Bank A, then another from Bank B, another from Bank C, and so on. You can also obtain a MasterCard *and* a Visa from the same bank if the bank issues both cards. But be careful: The amount of credit available to you is multiplied by the number of cards in your name. Ten bank cards, each with a credit ceiling of $2,000, for example, give you access to $20,000, and you may be tempted to spend beyond your means.

· *When do I start paying interest on my credit card charges?*

No law provides the answer. But in practice, most bank credit card agreements state that interest on purchases of goods and services begins twenty-five days after the billing date, and interest on cash advances immediately on receipt of funds. This type of interest-payment arrangement provides you with a money-saving advantage when you charge goods or services on, or within a few days after your monthly billing date. Then you have as many as thirty days until billing date, and twenty-five days after that until your due date, for a total of as many as fifty-five days during which you have the use of the bank's money without any interest charges. Some banks, though, have recently adopted the practice of charging interest on purchases of goods and services from the date the purchases are made.

On most bank credit cards, you can escape interest charges on purchases of goods and services if you pay in full on or before the due date (about twenty-five days after the billing date).

· *My credit cards were stolen. Suppose the thief charges thousands of dollars to my accounts. Do I have to pay?*

If you notify the credit card issuers of the theft before the thief uses your cards, you have no liability. If you notify them after the cards are used, or if you don't notify them at all, your liability is a maximum of $50 for each card. These rules apply whether your cards are stolen, lost, or used without authorization.

· *I want to buy a TV set on time. I can use my credit card or I can go to a store and sign an installment contract. What's the difference?*

There are two major differences:

1. When you use your credit card, whatever you buy is yours, even before you've made a single payment. You can sell the merchandise, give it away, rent it, destroy it, or do anything you like with it. But when you buy on an installment contract, what you buy usually remains the property of the other party to the contract until you've paid off the last cent of principal and interest. Installment contracts are also known as time-purchase agreements and conditional sales contracts. (Warning: Sometimes, ownership passes to you when you make a purchase with your credit card, but the credit card company retains a lien—that is, a right to your purchase until you've paid for it. Read your agreement carefully.)
2. Should you default on an installment contract, the other party to the contract can repossess the merchandise—take it away from you. Merchandise purchased with a credit card cannot be repossessed even if you never make a single payment.

· *I've found an overcharge on my credit card statement. What's my next move?*

Don't pay it. Instead, follow the instructions in "Your Billing Rights Notice," which your credit card issuer is required to have sent you. (If you've misplaced your copy, ask for another.) Here are the highlights of the notice as they apply to overcharges. (Your rights here derive from the federal Fair Credit Billing Act; they're the same for overcharges on any kind of credit.)

● Within sixty days after the bill was sent, write or type your complaint on a separate piece of paper (never on the bill) and send it to the credit card issuer. Don't telephone; put it in writing.

- Once your letter is received, the credit card issuer cannot try to collect the overcharge, and cannot report you to a credit-reporting agency for delinquency. The overcharge, though, is likely to continue to appear on your statement.
- The credit card issuer must acknowledge receipt of your complaint within thirty days unless it has cleared up your complaint within that time.
- Within ninety days after receipt of the letter, the credit card issuer must correct the error or tell you why you were wrong in claiming an error.

· *What happens if the creditor doesn't play by the rules of the Fair Credit Billing Act?*

Then you don't have to pay more than $50 plus finance charges on the disputed item. That's a comforting thought if the overcharges ran into the hundreds or thousands of dollars. What's more, you don't have to pay more than $50 plus finance charges even if your claim of an overcharge was wrong. You can also sue for damages plus twice the finance charges, provided the finance charges are not less than $100 and not more than $1,000. Should you win, you can also collect court costs and attorney's fees. You can't, though, bring criminal charges against the violator.

· *I reported an error. For the next ninety days, the charge continued to appear on my statement* plus *interest. Can they do that?*

Yes. But you only have to pay the interest if the credit card issuer finds your claim is wrong. In that case, making the claim could be costly. Another drawback of making an overcharge claim is that during the period of investigation, your credit ceiling is lowered by the amount of the charge in question—whether you're right or wrong.

· *I bought a dishwasher on my credit card. It's a lemon. The store owner won't exchange or repair it. What shall I do?*

If you satisfy the following conditions, you may have the right *not* to pay the remaining amount due on your purchase:

- You tried in good faith to have the merchant remedy the problem.
- The purchase price was in excess of $50.
- You made the purchase in your home state or in another state within a hundred miles of your home.

Put your request to cancel further installments on the dishwasher to your credit card issuer in writing. Provide a full explanation of your request, and enclose copies (not originals) of all the relevant documents. The credit card issuer may decide that you have the right *not* to pay the remaining amount due. In a case like this, a lawyer can help the credit card issuer decide in your favor.

But remember, even when you win, all you save is the amount of the unpaid balance. The amount you've already spent on the dishwasher is irretrievable unless the merchant agrees to issue a credit to your credit card account. One exception: In California, you can get your money back from the credit card issuer. Elsewhere, if the merchant refuses to issue a credit, you'll have to bring suit to recover your money.

5

Debt: Your Right to Get Out of It

- What happens when you get into unmanageable debt
- Getting out of debt with a consolidation loan
- Getting out of debt with a reduced-payment plan
- Getting out of debt with Chapter 13 bankruptcy
- Getting out of debt with Chapter 7 bankruptcy

"Last year," reports one of the nation's leading debt counselors, Anne David, "44.4 million Americans could not meet payments on one or more of their accounts (amounting to a staggering $4.78 billion, up 10 percent over the preceding year).... Many of these people work their way out of debt, but others can't seem to find a way."

This chapter helps those others find a way out of debt from the several legal options open to them.

Our legal attitude toward debt has always been a combination of moral sense and horse sense. Our moral sense says, "Give a man who's down a chance to get on his feet again." Our horse sense says, "A man on his feet has money to spend, and that's good for everyone." The writers of the Constitution of the United States, to whom debtors' prison and involuntary servitude in payment of debt was abhorrent, and with the rehabilitation of debtors in mind, empowered Congress to "establish uniform laws on the subject of bankruptcies in the United States." Ever since, it's been part of the American Way to give the debtor the opportunity of a new start in life.

However, until just two decades ago, that opportunity was not granted without stigma and punishment. Our puritan heritage provided the stigma: not paying your debts was regarded as sinful. Our bankruptcy laws, reflecting the puritan viewpoint, provided the punishment. They relieved a man of his debts, but frequently they also relieved him of all his assets. A fresh start was possible, but too often it meant a start from scratch. Then, in 1964, something extraordinary happened that was to change all that, and create a tolerance to debtors unparalleled in the history of man and money. Since then, observed Mark Hunter and Martin Meyer, two of the more astute commentators on the financial mores of our times, "the nation has been profoundly altered by a revolution...a revolution that began... with the introduction of *free credit cards for the masses.*" (Emphasis theirs.)

"Before then," they explained, "credit cards were strictly for the Cadillac set. But in a four-year period, the nation's banks wafted out more than 100 million free credit cards in the mail. Bankers called this massive giveaway 'putting the credit cards on the air,' because the cards descended on a credit-starved citizenry like manna from heaven.

"'The free credit card,'" they quoted an anonymous banker as stating, "'established true economic democracy for the first time in America. Credit became not only available to the rich, but to all Americans of moderate income. It enabled every American citizen to get his rightful share of the consumer goods of the nation—*without waiting until his savings caught up with his desires.*'" (Emphasis ours.)

This revolution, dubbed by Hunter and Meyer "The Buying Revolution," stimulated our economy, they said, to make the U.S.A. the wealthiest nation in all history, and "has done more to heighten the middle-class standard of living than all the work of consumer advocates, social legislators and government bureaucrats put together." This is, perhaps, an overstatement; but certainly since 1964, prosperity has depended in large measure on liberal consumer credit (not only from credit cards but from other easy credit packages as well, such as check overdrafts, which eager bankers loaded onto the credit card bandwagon). Liberal consumer credit was hailed as the economic wonder drug. But since 1964, in an accelerating mode, more and more of us have suffered its most painful side effect: unmanageable debt.

By 1978, hundreds of thousands of American families were sliding beyond the debtors' point of no return. They had recourse to bankruptcy laws, but they were laws that could wipe them out, nullify them as economy-boosting consumers, and possibly place them on the already overburdened welfare rolls. With an eye to helping sustain our consumer economy and prevent dam-bursting pressures on welfare fund reservoirs, Congress enacted the Bankruptcy Reform Act of 1978 (effective October 1, 1979). For leaning over backward to relieve the bankrupt of debts without relieving them of assets, this was the Tower of Pisa of debt legislation. Although the act was tightened somewhat by Congressional revision in 1984, it remains an open sesame to debt freedom without disturbing the standard of living to which the overspender had become accustomed.

Bankruptcy, though, isn't the only legal way out of debt. The other ways are less indulgent. Bankers and merchants who suffer from the nation's slap-on-the-wrist bankruptcy law, and legislators who in 1984 voted 394 to 0 in the House and by voice vote in the Senate to add a bite to that law, say those other ways are the better ways. But the choice is yours. This chapter will help you decide.

WHAT HAPPENS WHEN YOU GET INTO UNMANAGEABLE DEBT

· *When do I get into unmanageable debt?*

If you can't pay, or can't pay in full, when your debts come due, you're in unmanageable debt. As a rule of thumb, that happens when your debt payments reach at least 25 to 30 percent of your net income. You also know you're in unmanageable debt when, after meeting your essential expenses, you can only pay the interest on your debts, not part of the principal.

· *What can I expect to happen when I stop making payments?*

You'll receive firm letters from your creditors requesting payment. If you can pay nothing at all, on receipt of the first dunning letter, contact the person who signed it and offer to make partial payments until you're on your feet again. This is a good deal all around: You get a breathing spell, and your creditor gets something rather than nothing while avoiding the cost and trouble of a collection procedure. (On page 94, you'll find a plan for offering partial payments to all your creditors.) But not all creditors will accept reduced payments.

· I've fallen behind by four installments—$126.64. Now my creditor tells me the total unpaid balance is due—$1,821.37! Is that a legal claim?

Yes, if the purchase agreement you signed specifies that on default the total unpaid balance becomes due.

· What happens if I just ignore the dunning letters?

Your debts won't go away. Eventually you'll receive a letter informing you that your account has been handed over to a debt collection agency. Debt collectors work on a commission basis. Many are highly motivated professionals skilled in the use of tested methods for extracting payment. You may be subjected to numerous unpleasant experiences.

· What protection do I have against harassment by debt collectors?

Legislation passed by the U.S. Congress controls the practice of debt collecting in the following ways:

- Debt collectors are not permitted to appear at your place of business or contact you there in any way.
- Debt collectors are not permitted to telephone you, ring your doorbell, or contact you in any way at unreasonable or inconvenient times (like three o'clock in the morning).
- Debt collectors, when making inquiries about you from friends, relatives, neighbors, or anybody else, are not permitted to embarrass you by identifying themselves as debt collectors. (But if they don't identify themselves as debt collectors, they're free to ask anybody anything about you.)

- Debt collectors, whether they identify themselves as debt collectors or not, are not permitted to question anybody about you more than once. Repeated questioning creates an undesirable atmosphere of suspicion.
- Debt collectors are not allowed to violate your privacy by querying anybody about you by postcard.
- Debt collectors are not permitted to contact you if you tell them, preferably in writing, that you can't or won't pay your debts. Then your creditor's recourse is to bring legal action against you.

· Can I call the police when debt collectors harass me by violating the rules for their conduct legislated by Congress?

Violations of these rules are not criminal offenses, so the police will not be able to help you. But if you sustain actual damage because of the actions of debt collectors (say, the loss of your job), you can bring a civil suit against them. You may deter further violations of the Congressional rules by making written complaints to the debt collection agencies, your creditors who hired them, your local Better Business Bureau, and your local office of consumer affairs.

· Can a lawyer help protect me against harassment by debt collectors?

Yes, for several reasons:

- By Congressional legislation, debt collectors are not permitted to communicate directly with you if they know you have a lawyer. All communications must be addressed to your lawyer.
- Your lawyer is familiar with state laws that offer you additional protection against abusive and unfair debt-collection practices, and knows how to make those laws work for you.
- Your lawyer has the knowledge and experience to take civil action against debt collectors in case of actual damage to you caused by their violations of federal and state debtor-protection laws.
- Your lawyer's professional clout is effective when dealing with harassment by debt collectors. A phone call or a letter

from your lawyer can bring results that you could not obtain by doing it by yourself.

· *What happens when a debt collection agency can't get a cent out of me?*

Either the debt collection or your creditor will turn your account over for legal collection. You will then receive at least one lawyer's letter requesting the amount owed plus interest and costs. At this time if you can afford to do so, it's wise to try to make a reduced-payments deal with the lawyer to prevent a lawsuit.

· *If I just send the collection lawyer a little money from time to time without making a deal, won't that protect me legally from a lawsuit?*

No.

· *What happens if I just ignore the collection lawyer's letters?*

You'll be sued. You'll know about it when you receive a summons—a device for bringing you to court to answer your creditor's claim against you. The summons can be delivered to you by a process server or it can come in the mail.

· *How can I avoid going to court when I receive a summons?*

There are several ways. You can pay up. You can make a reduced-payment deal with the lawyer. Or you can ignore the summons, which is not a wise thing to do. But be careful. When you make a reduced-payment deal, get it in writing. If you don't take these precautions, a judgment may be entered against you anyway (see next question).

· *What happens if I ignore the summons?*

A judgment will be entered against you for the amount owed plus costs and interest. A judgment is a formal entry of the court's decision that you are legally required to pay your creditor the sum awarded by the court.

· *Can I go to jail if I don't pay the judgment?*

No.

· *If my creditor gets a judgment against me, is my bank account in danger?*

Yes, if the creditor knows where you bank. Then he can issue a Bank Account Restraining Notice, which prevents you from drawing against the account, until you've paid up.

· *How can I pay a judgment if I don't have the money?*

Your creditor (now known as the judgment creditor) has the right to examine you (now known as the judgment debtor) under oath to determine your assets. (This is known as a discovery procedure or as proceedings supplementary to judgment.) The judgment creditor then may obtain from the court a Writ of Execution—a special document which directs the sheriff to seize your assets until you make full payment, or until they are liquidated (converted into cash) to pay the complete amount awarded. When full payment is made one way or the other, the judgment is said to be satisfied, and the judgment creditor has no further claim against you. A notice of satisfaction of judgment is usually sent to you in the mail. If you don't receive one, call your creditor and insist that you do.

· *I have a judgment against me, but no attempt has been made to determine my assets. I received a copy of a letter sent by my judgment creditor to the sheriff instructing him to seize all my assets. Does that mean I'll lose everything?*

If no attempt has been made to determine your assets, the sheriff doesn't know what to seize, so the instructions are of no practical value. Some sheriffs may try to bluff you into revealing your assets, but they cannot legally force you to do so. The copy of the letter of instructions to the sheriff is simply a ploy intended to intimidate you into paying up.

· *If I do reveal my assets, can my judgment creditor seize all of them?*

There's always a chance, but it's not likely. Certain assets are exempted by state laws from seizure.

· *Which of my assets are exempted from seizure to satisfy a judgment?*

That depends on the laws of the state. You can request a list of exemptions from the clerk of the court from which your summons was issued. But while some clerks are cooperative, some are not. Your lawyer can supply the information faster and fit it to your particular case better. Knowing what your exemptions are can do much to ease your mind when a judgment is issued against you.

Here is a list of some major exemptions permitted by many states:

- Your homestead (the house in which you live and the surrounding land up to a certain limit). But only up to a certain amount in some states ($10,000 in equity in New York; $20,000 if judgment is against husband and wife).
- Household goods and personal effects including wearing apparel. But wearing apparel is usually limited to necessities, and may not include a mink coat or diamond cufflinks.
- Personal property up to a fixed amount (say, $1,000). Personal property includes bank accounts, money market funds, stocks, bonds, and other investments, but not in all states.
- The tools and implements of your trade. In some states your car is considered a tool of your trade, provided it's necessary for your work. In a few states, motor vehicles are exempt even if they're not tools of the trade.
- Proceeds from your insurance and the cash surrender value of your life insurance policy
- Proceeds from your pensions

· *If my house is exempt from a judgment, does that mean my bank can't foreclose when I default on my mortgage payments?*

Your bank does not need a judgment against you to foreclose. You granted your bank the right to foreclose in case of default when you signed your mortgage contract. (But to foreclose, the bank must institute a legal action.)

• *What other properties do I stand to lose for nonpayment because of the contracts I signed?*

Your car or anything else purchased on a retail installment contract (also known as a conditional sales contract). In this type of agreement, a key line may read: "The buyer agrees that title to the goods shall remain in the seller until they are fully paid for." That means you do *not* own the goods until the final payment has been made. When you default, the buyer can retake possession (repossess) the goods.

What's more, under the conditions of some retail installment contracts, the seller can in case of default garnishee your wages. When your wages are garnisheed, a legal notice is sent to your employer directing him to pay part of your wages to your creditor instead of to you. If you have granted the seller the right to garnishee, the notice to your employer may be sent without prior notice to you.

It's wise to read your contracts carefully.

• *Can my wages be garnisheed to satisfy a judgment?*

Yes and no. It depends on what state you're in. In some states you're exempt from garnishment of wages if you're a laborer, a mechanic, a public employee, or a government worker. By federal law, seamen are exempt in all states.

Even if you're not exempt, federal law protects you against the garnishment of *all* your wages. The first $48 of your weekly earnings is exempt, and total garnishment is limited to 25 percent of your take-home pay. The protection offered by your state may be more liberal. Consult your lawyer for details on the least amount of your wages that can be garnisheed.

In some states, only one income judgment can be executed at a time—that is, if you have two or more judgments against you, your wages can be tapped to pay only one of them until the judgment is satisfied. Then your wages are tapped to pay the next judgment filed against you, and so on.

· *Can I lose my job if my wages are garnisheed?*

Federal law bars dismissing an employee for reason of garnishment for any *one* debt. The key word in the preceding sentence is *one*. If your wages are garnished for two or more debts, the law does not protect you. Also, as a practical matter, the law doesn't protect you against losing your job when just one debt results in a garnishment. Your employer can always find a legal reason to fire you.

· *I paid a judgment against me with a check for only the amount I originally owed. I did not include costs and interest. I marked the check "Paid in full." My creditor cashed the check. Then he sent me a letter requesting the costs and interest. Can he collect?*

Usually, he can't, since you marked the check "Paid in full." But some creditors simply cross out that notice. The law in a case like yours varies from state to state, so it's best to get the advice of your lawyer.

· *I've heard that some people are judgment-proof. What does that mean?*

Simply that for one reason or another, the judgment creditor can't collect. If, for example, you have no assets or your assets are exempt from a judgment against you, you're judgment-proof.

    In addition, you may be judgment-proof if you live in a "community property" state. Most states that recognize community property of spouses do not permit a judgment creditor to attach the property if a judgment is issued against one of the spouses. (Community property states are Arizona, California, Idaho, Louisiana, Nevada, New Mexico, Texas, and Washington.)

· *How can I avoid all the hassle of living with unmanageable debt?*

By getting out of debt through one of the four following options. You can take out a consolidation loan. You can work out a reduced-payment plan. Or you can seek relief under either Chapter 13 or Chapter 7 of the Federal Bankruptcy Act. The first two options are examples of preventive jurisprudence—the solution of your problem without "going to law" (in this case, without involving the bankruptcy laws). A description of each of the four options and how you can benefit from them follows.

GETTING OUT OF DEBT WITH A CONSOLIDATION LOAN

• *What is a consolidation loan?*

This is a personal loan with which you pay off all your debts. You can obtain it from a bank, a credit union, or a finance company.

• *When I take out a consolidation loan, I'll still owe the same amount of money as I did before, won't I?*

No, you won't. You'll owe more. Your debt payments will be spread out over a longer period of time, so the total amount of interest will be considerably higher.

• *Then what's the advantage of a consolidation loan?*

The single monthly payment, spread over a longer period of time than the previous payments, is smaller than the sum of the previous monthly payments. Simply stated, you pay less per month.

• *Can I get a consolidation loan even when I'm in serious debt?*

The consolidation loan was designed *for* people in serious debt. But bank and credit union consolidation loans are getting rarer and rarer. Currently, most consolidation loans are granted by finance companies whose interest rates are higher than those of other lenders. They require that the loans be secured, be guaranteed by one or more credit-worthy persons, carry insurance on your life for which you pay, and permit wage assignment. Should you find the requirements for obtaining a consolidation loan too burdensome, or if you can't obtain such a loan, then you can still choose among the three following options to get back on your feet again.

GETTING OUT OF DEBT WITH A
REDUCED-PAYMENT PLAN

· *What is a reduced-payment plan?*

It's a plan for cutting the amount of each of your monthly payments by requesting your creditors to lengthen the time for repayment of your debts. Here's how to execute the plan:

STEP 1. Draw up a list of monthly debts you have trouble paying.

Credit card	$55
Department store A	35
Department store B	35
Cash loan	75
Total	$200

STEP 2. Carefully examine your net income and total "must" expenses (rent or mortgage amount, food, clothing, medical bills, and so on), and determine how much of your income is available for monthly debt repayment. Let's say it's $100. That's 50 percent of total monthly debt.

STEP 3. Draw up a proposed schedule of repayments by reducing your monthly scheduled payments by 50 percent.

	Scheduled Payments	Proposed Payments
Credit card	$55	$27.50
Department store A	35	17.50
Department store B	35	17.50
Cash loan	75	37.50
Total		$100.00

STEP 4. Call your creditor contact on each of your delinquent accounts, and set up an appointment. The name of your creditor contact often appears on your bills, and always on dunning let-

ters. If you don't know the name of your creditor contact, call the credit department and say, "I'd like to settle my account. Whom can I talk to?"

STEP 5. When you meet with each creditor contact, tell him what your net income is, and bring a list of your "must" expenses to demonstrate that you only have $100 (or whatever sum you determine) for the monthly repayment of all your debts. Make it clear that it is your intention to use this amount to treat all your creditors equally in accordance with your proposed schedule of repayments. Give him the schedule. Emphasize that you will not add to your debt, and that you will resume full payments as soon as you can. Your creditor contact, impressed with your sincerity and willingness to pay, may go along with your plan.

· *Can certain "must" expenses be included in the proposed schedule of payments?*

If you have trouble meeting your mortgage or car payments, you can include them in the schedule.

· *How do I get help in preparing and executing a reduced-payment plan?*

Consult your lawyer, or either a credit counseling service or a family service agency. For addresses of service offices nearest you, write respectively to National Foundation of Consumer Credit, 1819 H Street, N.W., Washington, DC 10006, or to Family Service Association of America, 44 East 23rd Street, New York, NY 10010.

· *Is there any disadvantage to a reduced-payment plan?*

Yes. Interest on the unpaid balance and late charges continue, putting the debtor in a position of increasing his debt while making payments.

· *Will all creditors accept reduced-payment plans?*

Some will, but many may not. Lawyers for creditors seldom recommend a reduced-payment plan unless a substantial initial payment is made, and the debtor agrees to *a confession of judgment*—that is, an acknowledgment that the creditor holds a judgment against him.

• *I couldn't get a consolidation loan and my creditors won't agree to a reduced-payment plan. Where do I go from here?*

You still have two options open. Try Chapter 13 of the Federal Bankruptcy Act next.

GETTING OUT OF DEBT WITH CHAPTER 13 BANKRUPTCY

• *What is Chapter 13?*

Chapter 13 is a legal procedure under the Federal Bankruptcy Act to help some victims of unmanageable debt to pay all or part of their debts under the protection of the U.S. Bankruptcy Courts. (This procedure is described in Chapter 13 of the act, hence the name.) Under Chapter 7 of the act—traditional bankruptcy—you can be released from debts by paying only a fraction of what you owe, or even nothing. Chapter 13 was enacted to help honest and sincere people who want to meet their financial obligations, and to cut the estimated $1 billion annual loss to bankers and merchants from consumers who declare Chapter 7 bankruptcy even though they're able to pay off some of their debts. Under the 1984 amended Bankruptcy Code, judges will encourage petitioners for Chapter 7 bankruptcy to file for Chapter 13 instead.

• *Is anybody eligible for debt relief under Chapter 13?*

No. You're eligible only if you're a wage earner, small-business owner, or professional (unless you're a stockbroker or a commodities broker) with a regular income, and with unsecured debts under $100,000 and secured debts under $350,000. Chapter 13 was formerly called "wage earner bankruptcy," but it is not restricted to wage earners.

• *How does the U.S. Bankruptcy Court protect me under Chapter 13?*

As soon as you file—

- All legal action brought against you as a result of your debts is stopped, and any future action of this type is prohibited.
- Your creditors are forbidden to telephone you, write you, call on you, dun you, or attempt to collect in any way.
- Garnishments cannot be made against you, and those that have been made are terminated. Your wages must be paid to you without deductions to your creditors.
- Your creditors cannot contact your employer in any way.
- Late charges, service charges, and sometimes interest charges are discontinued.
- All collection attempts and garnishments against your co-signers and codebtors (if you have any) are stopped, preventing losses from hurting friends and relatives who underwrote some of your obligations. However, if your creditors make application to the court to lift this stoppage of action against cosigners, the cosigners remain liable even though you may eventually be released ("discharged") from the debt.
- Creditors cannot repossess property, or seize property put up as collateral.

· *How does Chapter 13 work?*

A trustee appointed by a federal court reviews and recommends a plan advised by you and your lawyer for your payment of all your creditors over a three-to-five-year period. A judge of the Bankruptcy Court then confirms (approves) the plan. The long payment times may decrease the amounts of your monthly payments.

If you lack sufficient net income, monthly income less monthly expenses, to pay all of your debts in full during the three-to-five-year period, the trustee arranges for you to pay only a portion of what you can. When that portion is paid, your debts are regarded as completely paid. That portion could be only a small percentage of your total debt.

· *I would prefer a five-year plan to a three-year plan. Can I request it?*

You can, but unless you can show "good cause" for extending payments over five years, the trustee will recommend, and the judge will approve, a three-year plan.

· *How do I determine how much I can pay monthly under a Chapter 13 plan?*

In much the same way as you determine how much you can pay monthly under a reduced-payment plan (page 95). The Chapter 13 plan is built around the money you have available each month for the repayment of your debts.

· *Can my creditors refuse to accept only a part of what I owe in full payment of my debts?*

No, if your debts are unsecured. Then your creditors must under law accept the payments decreed by the court, provided that under Chapter 13 they would receive more than under Chapter 7.

· *Can I receive tax-debt relief under Chapter 13?*

Some. Back and current taxes may be paid off during the life of the plan, provided they're paid in full with interest.

· *Can Chapter 13 help me if I default on my mortgage?*

Yes. Payments of arrears, which include late charges and interest, can be spread out over eighteen months to five years according to a court-approved plan, while you continue to make regular monthly payments. Permission to spread out arrears for more than three years is uncommon, but can be worked out. As long as you comply with the terms agreed on, your mortgage cannot be foreclosed.

· *Is there any other way Chapter 13 helps me pay my debts?*

Yes, when the debts include the money you owe on merchandise. If at the time you file for Chapter 13 you can prove that the value of the merchandise is less than the purchase price, you can settle your debt for the merchandise on the basis of the lower figure. But proving the value of merchandise is difficult, and this provision of Chapter 13 is seldom applied.

• *Can I arrange to have my employer deduct from my wages the amount due to the trustee, and have my employer make the payment for me?*

Yes. It's insurance against failure to pay. Sometimes, acting in your interest, the court may decree that payment to the trustee can be made *only* by payroll deductions.

• *How will the court know if I'm complying with the terms of the Chapter 13 payment plan?*

You're required to make a single payment on a regular basis to the trustee, who uses your funds to pay your creditors. If you fail to make your regular payment to the trustee, the court knows you're not complying with the plan. When you cease to comply, you lose the protection of the court, which means all your debts come due, and the debt-collecting hassle begins again.

• *What are the costs associated with Chapter 13?*

There is a filing fee of $60. To cover administrative and trustee fees, there is a charge of 10 percent of the amount paid to your creditors. Your lawyer's fee is monitored by the court. A plus: Remember, as soon as you file for Chapter 13, finance charges on your debts are stopped. These savings usually outweigh the costs associated with Chapter 13.

• *How do I get started on Chapter 13?*

Your lawyer will help you fill out some forms (they're not simple) and work out a reduced-payment plan with you. He'll file the forms. The court will then notify your creditors in writing that you have filed under Chapter 13, give them your file number, and send along a copy of your Chapter 13 reduced-payment plan. Remember that the moment your petition is filed, your creditors are prohibited by law from taking any action against you to collect the money owed them.

· What happens after I file?

You're notified by the clerk of the court to appear in court on a certain date to meet with your trustee and your creditors. At the meeting, provide certification of the market value of your house, your mortgage balance, and your take-home pay. Your trustee may ask a few questions to confirm some of the data in the forms you submitted. If there is no opposition from your creditors (there usually isn't; most creditors don't even bother to appear), the meeting is over in about five minutes. You may, depending on the practice of your Federal Court District, have to appear in court when your Chapter 13 petition is confirmed (accepted). For confirmation, all debtors must agree to the plan.

· What happens when I've complied with all the terms of my Chapter 13 reduced payment plan?

You receive an official discharge from all debts listed in your plan. You are not discharged from any other debts, nor from debts arising from alimony and child support.

· Suppose I can't meet my payments to the trustee. Are there any ways I can still get out of debt?

You have two choices.

You can request the court to approve an amended plan that reduces payments to the trustee to an affordable level.

Or you can file for bankruptcy under Chapter 7 and liquidate the remainder of your debts, provided you have already paid the equivalent of liquidation value at the time you filed under Chapter 13. Liquidation value here is defined as the market value of your assets at the time you apply for a hardship discharge.

GETTING OUT OF DEBT WITH CHAPTER 7 BANKRUPTCY

· What is Bankruptcy?

Bankruptcy—traditional bankruptcy as opposed to bankruptcy under Chapter 13—is your right under Chapter 7 of the Federal

Bankruptcy Act to clear yourself of debt and begin all over again. It's your only choice if you cannot get out of debt with the other three options open to you.

· Is there a stigma attached to bankruptcy?

Bankruptcy is your right under law to rebound from financial adversity. Whatever stigma was attached to it in the past has largely vanished. Last year about 500,000 consumers filed for personal bankruptcy under Chapter 7, and projections indicate an increase in the years ahead.

· How does bankruptcy work?

You turn over all your assets, except those that are exempt, to a trustee appointed by a federal court. The trustee converts them into cash, deducts administrative fees, and distributes the remainder to your creditors in payment of your debts. Your debts are then said to be discharged. If you have no or few nonexempt assets, your debts can be discharged without your having to pay a cent.

· What assets are exempt under the Federal Bankruptcy Act?

If you are filing jointly with your spouse, double the amounts in the following list of major exemptions:

- Your home or your personal property—up to $7,500. You can distribute this exemption in any way between your home and your personal property. If you have no home, you can apply the full exemption to your personal property.
- One motor vehicle—up to $1,200
- Household or personal property, including books, appliances, musical instruments, and animals—up to $4,000 per household
- Jewelry—up to $500
- Professional books or tools of the trade—up to $750
- Cash value of insurance policies—up to $4,000
- Health aids (professionally prescribed)—no limit
- Additional property, such as bank accounts, tax refunds, and anticipated tax refunds—up to $400

- The following forms of income: the most common kinds
of Social Security benefits, disability benefits, local public
assistance benefits, unemployment compensation, pen-
sion fund payments, profit-sharing plan payments, life insurance benefits, income from annuities, alimony, support
or separate maintenance, veterans' benefits, and any anticipated future income. Important: Not only assets and
liabilities are taken into account in determining a plan for
payment to creditors but also present income.

Some thirty-five states have "opted out" of the federal exemptions scheme, substituting their own exemption lists.
Chances are that your state's exemption checklist will be less
liberal than the federal list.

· *Knowing that I'm going to file for bankruptcy, why can't I
go on a buying spree just before I do it—and have the debts
written off?*

If you were willing to wish complicating the procedure with
charges of fraud and lack of goodwill, you could have tried, until
the passage of the new Bankruptcy Code in 1984. But that new
code prevents you from including in your petition for bankruptcy any credit card purchases made within twenty days of
filing, and any installment purchases, personal loans, or other
debts made within forty days.

· *How do I get started on Chapter 7?*

Your lawyer will help you fill out the forms. He then files your
petition for bankruptcy in the Bankruptcy Court which has jurisdiction. Your petition includes a detailed list of all your debts,
all your assets, your present income, and the exemptions you
claim. From the moment you file, it is illegal for your creditors
to make any attempt to collect their debts. You are afforded the
protection of the court in the same way as if you filed for Chapter
13 (page 97). The costs are the same as for Chapter 13 (page
100), except there's no 10 percent fee to the trustee.

· What happens after I file?

You attend a meeting of your creditors which has been set by the court for a date twenty to forty days after the filing of your petition.

The trustee appointed to your case will conduct the meeting. Be ready to answer questions from the presiding official about the papers you filed, your property, and how you got into unmanageable debt. Since there is usually nothing your creditors can do to stop the petition, they usually do not attend. In some instances, though, they may file fraud claims to object to the discharge.

After that, you cooperate with the trustee, who collects your nonexempt assets, sells them, adds your nonexempt cash which also has been seized, and distrubutes the proceeds to your creditors on a pro rata basis. Example: You owe $20,000. Your total nonexempt assets (after priority debts such as taxes have been paid and the trustee has deducted his fee from the amount he has collected) amount to $2,000. Each creditor receives 10 percent of what you owe ($2,000 divided by $20,000), or, expressed in bankruptcy jargon, 10¢ on the dollar. A debt of $8,000 is settled for $800, a debt of $2,000 is settled for $200, and so on.

You then wait about six months after you've filed your petition to receive a discharge notice from the court. You may have to attend court to receive it. The discharge notice means that all your debts listed in the petition of bankruptcy are for all practical purposes considered paid—even, in some cases, where your creditors received nothing. Legally, your debts no longer exist, and most people would say they no longer exist morally as well. But the law does not forbid you from paying off your debts (some people do).

· When my debts are discharged under Chapter 7, are my cosigners or codebtors relieved of their responsibility to pay?

No. Your creditors can collect from them.

· Can all my debts be discharged by bankruptcy?

No. Nondischargeable debts include the following:

- Alimony, maintenance, and child support obligations
- Most taxes due within the past three years unless you filed no return. Some taxes are dischargeable after a period of time.
- Debts arising from credit obtained by providing false information concerning your financial condition
- Fines or penalties payable to the government, including tax penalties and fines for traffic violations
- Payments on student loans unless they have been due and owing for five years, or unless repayment would cause substantial hardship. But in some Federal Court Districts they are dischargeable by paying a percentage of the debt.
- Other debts that the court designates as nondischargeable as the result of legal proceedings brought by the creditors

6

Contracts: Your Rights of Agreement

- The basic rules governing contracts
- How to draw up a simple contract
- What to do when a contract is broken
- What to do when a contract is breached

The following question is addressed to you. Consider your answer carefully.

· *Which of the following seven transactions are contracts?*

☐   Buying a newspaper

☐   Buying a house

☐   Getting married

☐   Using your credit card

☐   Making a phone call

☐   Taking a taxi

☐   Sharing a car pool

If you answered yes to all seven, you were right. That's because each of those transactions falls within the definition of a contract: "an agreement upon sufficient consideration to do or not to do a particular thing."

106

Here's how that definition works out in a sampling of those transactions:

When you buy a newspaper, the sufficient consideration is the price of the paper. For it the newsboy agrees to do a particular thing: hand over today's copy of the *New York Times* (or whatever paper you are buying). If you shortchange him, or if he hands over yesterday's *New York Post*, that's a breach of the contract.

When you get married, the sufficient consideration is your emotional, physical, and financial services. For it, your spouse agrees to do a particular thing: provide equivalent services for you. If she stays out of your bed for an unreasonable amount of time, or you stop contributing to the budget, that's a breach of the contract. (Marriage as a contract is a common-law concept which is now undergoing some sex-revolution refinements.)

When you make a phone call, the sufficient consideration is 25¢ in the slot (in New York). For it, the telephone company agrees to do a particular thing: put you through clearly for three minutes to the local number called. If you use a slug, or the phone company connects you to a wrong number on a line heavy with static, that's a breach of the contract.

When you share a car pool, the sufficient consideration is paying your share of the gas, taking your turn driving, showing up on time, and so on. For it, your fellow riders agree to do a particular thing: let you ride into town with them. If you show up late or they take in one of their visiting aunts one day instead of you, that's a breach of the contract.

We are by tradition and practice a society based on contractual relations—from the informal and the commonplace (switching on electric power for the TV, getting on a bus, ordering a hamburger) to the rigidly structured and significant (buying a house or car, taking out a bank loan, signing an employment contract). "Every one of our daily acts creates [a contract]," comments legal authorities M. J. and J. S. Ross. "In civil law, the contract is the basic legal concept, the foundation of all legal relations."

That's why common law considers contracts binding and enforceable in courts of law. Today's statutes on contracts, which have grown out of the common law, are incorporated in the Uniform Commercial Code (UCC), adopted by most states. Those states that have not subscribed to the UCC Code have enacted their own statutory versions of it. In all states, the law gives you the right to enter into contracts and to go to the courts, if necessary, to have them carried out or to provide redress when they're breached.

THE BASIC RULES GOVERNING CONTRACTS

· *I want to make a deal with my brother-in-law to repair my plumbing, but I want to be sure I can collect damages if he doesn't complete the job. What do I do?*

You work out a contract. Remember, that's a legally binding agreement. If your brother-in-law fails to complete the job, you can go to court to demand he recompense you for damages suffered from his breach of contract. If he does the job and you fail to pay him, he can do the same to you.

· *What are the essential elements of a contract?*

There are three: the offer, the acceptance, and the consideration.

The offer. It's a promise to do something specific (or not do something specific) in return for the other party or parties doing something specific (or not doing something specific). When you promise your brother-in-law you'll pay him X dollars to repair your plumbing if he promises to do the job by such-and-such a date, that's an offer.

The acceptance. When your brother-in-law says okay to your offer, that's the acceptance.

The consideration. When you get something in return (repaired plumbing) for what you give (X dollars), that's the consideration. It's what each party gets in return for taking on the obligations of a contract. Although there are some exceptions, without consideration for each party to an agreement, there's no contract.

These three essential elements apply whether a contract is *implied* or *expressed*. When all the terms are specifically expressed, that's an *expressed contract*. Your life insurance policy is an example. When the terms are not specifically expressed, but rather implied by the actions and behavior of the parties in certain circumstances, the law says a contract exists. That's an *implied contract*, the kind you enter into when you step into a cab.

The following subsections look at the offer, the acceptance, and the consideration in depth.

The Offer
· How do I make my offer?

Any way—orally, in writing, even by sign language—provided the person to whom you're making the offer is aware that you're doing so. If you're making the offer by mail, it's a good idea to send it certified, individual service, return receipt requested. Then you'll have proof that the person to whom you made the offer actually received it.

· Suppose I say to my brother-in-law as a joke, "I'll give you the house if you repair the plumbing," and he takes me seriously—am I stuck with a contract?

No. The law does not regard an offer made in jest as a valid offer.

· A friend of mine overheard me make an offer to my brother-in-law to repair the plumbing in my house. My friend said, "I'll do it." Does he have a contract with me?

No. The offer can only form the basis of a contract when the offer is accepted by the person to whom it was made.

· Can I make the same offer to several people at the same time?

Yes. But don't worry about being stuck with several contracts for the same thing. As soon as one person accepts, your offer to the others is automatically terminated.

· How specific must I make my offer?

As specific as you can. When you offer your brother-in-law X dollars to repair your plumbing, it's wise to also specify when the job is to be done, who pays for the supplies, when your brother-in-law will receive payment, whether payment is subject to your approval of the job, and so on. An offer that's vague about basic matters—where, who, what, when, how much—is not valid.

· *How much time shall I give a person to accept my offer?*

That's up to you. But as a practical matter, make it a reasonable time.

· *Is an offer valid if I don't set a deadline for acceptance?*

Yes. The law then assumes the deadline to be a reasonable time.

· *After I make an offer, have I the right to withdraw it?*

Yes. You can withdraw it at any time before it's accepted. If you've set a deadline for acceptance, your offer is automatically withdrawn if it's not accepted by that deadline. If you don't set a deadline for acceptance, your offer expires within a reasonable time.

· *My brother-in-law wants me to guarantee that I won't withdraw my offer before the deadline for acceptance. Is that legal?*

Yes. You can do this by giving your brother-in-law an *option*— an agreement containing all three essential elements of a contract, stating that the offer cannot be withdrawn within a specified time. When an option is part of a written offer, it is as enforceable in law as a contract.

· *My brother-in-law rejected my offer. Then a few days later, he said he'd changed his mind and he's ready to do the job. I told him, "Sorry. The offer no longer stands." He says it does. Who's right?*

You are. A rejection terminates an offer. It doesn't, however, terminate the possibility of an eventual contract. Let's say your brother-in-law turned down the job because of a condition you could remedy: not enough money. You and he could negotiate a price satisfactory to both of you, and arrive at a contract.

Contract negotiation is basically a matter of offers and counter-offers.

• *Does my offer, once it's accepted, automatically become part of the contract?*

Not necessarily. An offer covers only basic terms (subject of the contract, price, and so on). It need not include all details, as anyone who has ever bought a house knows. Amendments to the offer can appear by mutual consent in the eventual contract.

The Acceptance

• *My brother-in-law wants his plumbing fixed, and he's made me an offer. How do I accept the offer?*

That depends on the type of contract that can be created by the offer.

Should your brother-in-law say, "I promise to pay you X dollars if you promise to repair my plumbing by such-and-such a date," he's offering you a *bilateral contract*—an exchange of mutual promises. You can accept a bilateral contract in any way that clearly communicates assent—a handclasp will do; so will a nod or a grunt.

But should your brother-in-law say, "I'll pay you X dollars when you finish repairing my plumbing," he's offering you a *unilateral contract*—one which becomes binding only on performance of a specific action (or actions). You can accept this kind of offer only by completing the action (or actions) called for—in this case, repairing the plumbing.

• *On the basis of my brother-in-law's offer to pay me X dollars when I've repaired the plumbing, I began the job. Now he wants to take me off the job and give it to somebody else. Can he do it?*

No. On a unilateral contract, such as this one, the person who makes the offer cannot withdraw it once the party to whom the offer has been made has begun to perform.

• *I want to accept an offer, but I want to make some changes. Okay?*

Not okay. Your changes constitute a rejection. You'll have to negotiate with the person who made the offer, and come to mutually acceptable terms to create a contract.

• *I had two weeks to accept an offer from my brother-in-law. I rejected it after a week. But a few days later, I changed my mind and accepted. Since I got in my acceptance before the deadline, I think I have a contract. My brother-in-law says no. Who's right?*

Your brother-in-law. Once you've made your rejection, the offer is no longer open, even though the deadline for acceptance has not been reached.

• *My brother-in-law withdrew his offer while my acceptance was in the mail. Where do I stand?*

If his offer came to you by mail, then your acceptance becomes effective the day you mailed it, not the day he received it. Your brother-in-law may not like it, but he has a contract.

On the other hand, if the offer did not come to you by mail, your acceptance only becomes effective on the date he receives it. Since he withdrew his offer before that date, there's no contract.

The Consideration

• *Does the consideration have to be money?*

No. It can be almost anything, even just promises made by each party. "I promise to teach you how to play chess if you promise to teach me how to play PacMan" contains the element of consideration necessary to create a contract.

• *Can consideration be created by mutual promises* not *to do something?*

Yes. "I promise not to smoke if you promise not to use salt in your diet" creates consideration.

• *Does consideration have to have a minimum value set by law before it's valid?*

No. Whatever you and the other party or parties to the contract agree on is sufficient consideration in the eyes of the law.

• *You say that consideration can be "almost" anything. What things are not regarded as consideration?*

There are three major types of *quid pro quo*—the legal term for "something in return for something"—that the law does not look upon as consideration.

1. An illegal *quid pro quo*. If your brother-in-law promises you X percent of the take if you promise to stash a shipment of marijuana in the plumbing you're repairing, there's no consideration.
2. A *quid pro quo* arising out of a moral obligation. If you promise to do something for your brother-in-law because he's done something for you for nothing, like taking your kids to the ball game, there's no consideration.
3. A *quid pro quo* involving the payment of a debt to a third party without receiving some benefit from that party. If your brother-in-law promises to repair your plumbing in return for your paying off part of his debt to the finance company, and you gain in no way from the finance company, there's no consideration.

• *My brother-in-law agreed to repair my plumbing for nothing. A few weeks after he finished the job, he asked for X dollars for his work. I say I don't have to pay. He says I do. Who's right?*

You are. Consideration must be created at the same time a contract is made—not after and not before. Without consideration in this instance, you have no contract, and you don't have to pay.

• *I understand there are some kinds of contracts that are valid without consideration. What are they?*

There are two such kinds of contracts.

1. Contracts which alter any agreements concerning real or personal property ("real property" means real estate). Example: You have a contract with your brother-in-law

to repair all the plumbing in your house (which is real property). You decide the plumbing in the kids' bathrooms needs more work than the contract called for. You persuade your brother-in-law to do it at no extra cost, and sign a modified agreement to that effect. No consideration was created but the modified agreement is a valid contract.

2. Contract under seal. In some states, no consideration is necessary when the seals of the parties are affixed to a written contract. Since most of us don't have our own seals, the initials L.S. on documents can replace them. L.S. stands for the Latin *locus sigilli*, which means "the place of the seal."

In addition, some states presume consideration to be present in most contracts. Consult your lawyer about whether that's the law in your state in case you want to draw up a contract without consideration.

HOW TO DRAW UP A SIMPLE CONTRACT

· *Must a contract be in writing?*

No. But putting it in writing helps prevent misunderstandings. Also keep in mind that there are some kinds of contracts that are not valid unless they are in writing.

· *Why are certain kinds of contracts required to be in writing?*

Let's say it's several hundred years ago and you're a small landowner in England. Your neighbor has an eye on your property. He goes to court and swears that you had agreed orally to sell the property to him for only a small fraction of its value. He produces a half-dozen witnesses who testify under oath that they heard you make the agreement. In the face of the evidence, the court rules you and your neighbor had entered into a valid contract, and you're forced to sell the land at a tremendous loss.

The truth is that you had never even spoken to your neighbor about the sale of the land. He and his witnesses had concocted a fraudulent contract, perjured themselves, and gotten away with it.

To stem a rising tide of such fraudulent and perjurious claims based on nonexisting oral contracts (and some even on existing ones), the English Parliament in 1676 passed a law stating in effect that to be enforceable legally certain kinds of contracts had to be in writing and signed by the parties to the contract. With some modifications, this law, which became known as the Statute of Frauds, still determines which kinds of contracts are required to be in writing in both England and the United States.

· What kinds of contracts have to be in writing?

The list may vary from state to state, but the major ones are:

- Contracts for the sale of goods over a certain price (usually $500)
- Contracts which by their terms are not to be performed completely within a certain period of time (usually one year). Example: If that certain period of time in your state is one year, a contract calling for complete performance in eleven months could be oral; but one that calls for complete performance in thirteen months, and cannot by the terms of the contract be performed in less than twelve months, must be written.
- Contracts which by their terms require performance to the end of a lifetime. Example: a contract with a nursing home for lifetime care.
- Contracts to sell interest in real property (real estate), or to leave real property in a will, or to create a real property trust
- Contracts for the lease of real property for more than a specified amount of time (usually a year, but in some states three years)
- Contracts to create personal property trusts
- Contracts to assume another person's obligations
- Premarital and marital contracts

There are others. So before you say okay to a word-of-mouth agreement, consult your lawyer. You may have to put it in writing.

· Can I draw up a written contract myself?

Yes, if it's simple. But after you draw it up, it's a good idea to have your lawyer look it over. If the contract is complicated, don't even think about doing it yourself.

· How do I go about drawing up a written contract myself?

An easy way is to put it in the form of a business letter. Prepare it in duplicate.

If your name and address is not printed on your stationery, write that information on the top or bottom of the page.

Then address the letter to the other party.

Mr. George Simon
4414 Lake Shore Drive
Milltown, OH 17241

Include the following six essential elements:

1. A definite offer

Dear George:
I want you to inspect the plumbing in my house, located at the address on this letter, and make the necessary repairs. I want this work to be completed in 10 business days, commencing on May 17 of this year, during the hours from 10 A.M. to 4 P.M.

2. Consideration

In return for material and labor supplied by you, I will pay you X dollars when you begin the job, and another X dollars when you finish it.

3. Duration of offer

I will hold this offer open for 31 calendar days from the date of this letter. Should you fail to accept by that date, the offer will be automatically withdrawn.

4. Provision in case of partial performance or nonperformance

In the event you do not begin the job on the date specified in this letter, the contract will be void. In the event you begin the job but do not finish it, the down payment is returnable to me on demand, and you will receive no further payment.

5. Other provisions

Should any of the plumbing become defective within two years after you make your repairs, you will make additional repairs at no cost within three business days after I notify you of the defects.

6. Manner of acceptance

If you agree to the terms set forth in this letter of agreement, kindly sign the attached copy and return it to me by mail or by hand.

> *Cordially yours,*
> *[your signature]*

Agreed:

_____   Date:_____

George Simon

WHAT TO DO WHEN A CONTRACT IS BROKEN

· *Are there any legal ways a contract can be broken?*

Yes. A contract is legally invalid under the following conditions:

- When any of the three essential elements of a contract—offer, acceptance, or consideration—is missing.
- When the purpose or subject matter of the contract is illegal or contrary to public policy or morals.
- When any of the parties to the contract signs under duress or undue influence. "Under duress" means the signature was obtained by force or threat of force. "Under undue influence" means the signature was obtained by psychological pressure.

- When any of the parties to the contract signed as a result of fraud or misrepresentation. "Fraud" is intentional deception. "Misrepresentation" is a false statement which may or may not be intentional.
- When the signature of any of the parties to the contract is a forgery.
- When there is a misunderstanding shared by the parties to the contract concerning the subject matter of the contract. In law, this is called a "mutual mistake."
- When at the time the contract was signed any of the parties to the contract was insane, intoxicated, or under the statutory age of consent. However, some minors have the legal right to sign contracts under some conditions.
- When any of the parties to the contract cannot live up to his responsibilities under the contract for reasons beyond his control.

· *My brother-in-law didn't live up to an essential provision in our contract. Must I still live up to the provisions dealing with my responsibilities?*

No. Your brother-in-law breached the contract, and it is no longer in effect.

· *My brother-in-law sold the contract he had with me to a friend of his. Is that a breach of the contract?*

Yes. What your brother in law did was to *assign* the contract— pass on his contractual rights and obligations to another person. It's not legal to assign contracts for personal services. Your brother-in-law's breach invalidated the contract.

All other types of contracts can be assigned. But assignment can be prevented by including a provision that the contract cannot be assigned unless all parties agree to it.

WHAT TO DO WHEN A CONTRACT IS BREACHED

Your first step is to try to straighten the matter out with the person who breached it. If you can't, call your lawyer. A lawyer's letter and a follow-up phone call often has pay-off clout. It's sometimes astonishing how fast your contract dispute can be cleared up without going to court—and usually in a manner satisfactory to both parties—once your lawyer enters the picture.

• *What happens when my lawyer is unable to settle my contract dispute out of court?*

If the contract calls for a settlement of disputes by arbitration, he'll start the arbitration process for you, and act on your behalf during it. If no arbitration is involved, your lawyer will commence litigation. Since your claim is a civil action, the burden of proof will be on you; but remember, a contract is binding and enforceable by law, and if your evidence can convince a jury, you can recover damages for breach of contract. If a small amount of money is involved, as in the example in this chapter, you or your lawyer may bring your claim to a small claims court.

• *What's the best advice you can give me about contract disputes?*

Have your lawyer prepare your contract for you. A properly prepared and executed contract decreases the likelihood of contract disputes and violations. And in the event that a breach of contract does occur, the properly prepared and executed contract will serve as a base for securing damages.

7

Your Home:
Your Rights When You Buy or Rent

- How to get your rights in the purchase
  agreement for your house
- How to get your rights in the contract for sale
- What you should know about your basic rights
  when you buy a condo or co-op
- What you should know about your rights as a
  tenant

A distressed young couple came to us. They had just bought a house. Everything had been fine—until it rained. Then a part of the roof fell in. Their children's bedrooms were flooded and their lovely new rugs were ruined. Could we help them?

We examined the contract of sale. Legally speaking, there wasn't a thing we could do. The contract left the seller off the hook. Nevertheless, we telephoned the seller—a lovely older woman—and she volunteered to pay a good part of the damages, thanking us for the opportunity to help set things right. Sometimes lawyers succeed by being good friends to both parties.

But that's not the point. The point is: had the young couple sought legal advice *before* they signed the contract of sale, they never would have had to worry about their right to collect from the seller when the roof fell in. A real estate lawyer could have insisted on making the right to recover damages in case of structural defects a provision of the contract. (Although this kind of right usually would not be in effect after the house has become legally yours—that is, after you've "closed"—unless the house is new.)

Most of your rights when you buy a house (or the new kinds of dwellings, the condo and the co-op) are written into the contract. They're the results of negotiations between you and the seller, and of setting them down in a manner that fulfills the legal requirements of a contract. The contract of sale is your bill of rights when you buy a house. That's why a description of that contract occupies the major part of this chapter.

But the very existence of that contract expresses a more fundamental right: the right to *own* your home. Behind the iron curtain, there is no such right. Here you can sell your house, rent it, borrow against it, and do what you like with it within limits. There you can't. The right to own property—and that includes real property (real estate)—is fundamental to the American way of life. Without that right, so the men who gave us this nation's Constitution believed, there can be no liberty. In this country, a government authority can take your property away from you—exercise its right of eminent domain—only when the property is needed for public use, and only with due process of law and reasonable and just compensation.

But the right to own a house is meaningless if you don't have the money to buy it. The right to earn that money is in the warp and woof of the basic laws of the land. But the right to borrow that money, for the great majority of people, didn't come until well into the nineteenth century. What happened was this:

From its birth a nation of homeowners, the United States going into the third decade of the 1800s had developed a population of workers, farmers, petty officials, small merchants, and doctors and other professional men who could not afford the soaring cost of a home. In the Eastern states, where most of this population was clustered, the cost of a modest dwelling was more than ten times a man's annual income (as contrasted with only up to three times these days), and it was payable on the barrelhead. One man's story is typical. Unable to provide a home for his family in the East, he led them into the wilderness of Kentucky, staked out a land claim, and with his own hands built a log cabin from timber he had cut himself. That man was Thomas Lincoln, the father of Abe.

The legislation that made it possible for men like Thomas

Lincoln to buy their own houses legalized a special kind of bank: the savings and loan association. It was an association of members of the community who pooled their savings to supply funds on loan to its members for the purchase of a home. The loan was paid back with interest in installments. The contract that established the terms of the loan was a mortgage—and still is. Today there are about five thousand savings and loan associations in the nation, and they provide the bulk of the nation's mortgages.

Later, legislation increased the availability of home financing by granting savings banks and other financial institutions the right to issue mortgages. But all mortgages were short-term, about four to five years, which made for heavy monthly payments; and interest rates, a laughingly low 4 to 6 percent by modern standards, were a burden for all but the well-heeled. When the Great Depression walloped the nation in 1929, hundreds of thousands of families found the onerous mortgage terms far beyond their means; homes were lost as mortgages were foreclosed, and home purchases crashed to an all-time low. Once more, legislation provided the right to borrow money to own a home—this time, on affordable terms.

In 1934, under the banner of Franklin D. Roosevelt's New Deal, Congress enacted a group of laws designed to help not only the homeless but also the banks that issued the mortgages. The keystone of that legislation was the establishment of the FHA, the Federal Housing Administration. The FHA had two major purposes: to encourage banks to make mortgages by insuring the loans; and to encourage consumers to take out mortgages by providing easy payment terms. The new mortgages were long-term—thirty to thirty-five years—with happy-days-are-here-again low monthly payments and interest rates well below the banking norm. Today, the FHA-insured mortgage, although much harder to get, remains one of our economy's biggest bargains.

The FHA, Department of Housing and Urban Development, 451 7th Street, S.W., Washington, DC 20410, will inform you about current FHA-insured mortgages. And for facts and figures on other federally legislated low-cost mortgage plans write if you're a veteran to VA Mortgage Division, Veteran's Administration, Washington, DC 20420; and if you're a farmer to FmHA, Mortgage Division, Farmers Home Administration, Washington, DC 20250. All government-insured mortgages are available only if you qualify, and that means, among other things, an acceptable credit rating.

Exercising your right to borrow for a home—obtaining the mortgage that's right for you—is something you can do yourself, although your lawyer and accountant can help. But obtaining your contractual rights when you buy a house is something you're not likely to do right without a lawyer. Here's the basic information on those contractual rights, so you can work better with your lawyer to get your dream house without a nightmare.

Many people find it desirable, for personal and economic reasons, to rent rather than buy. Included in this chapter is a summary of tenants' rights.

HOW TO GET YOUR RIGHTS IN THE PURCHASE AGREEMENT FOR YOUR HOUSE

· *My wife and I have decided on the house we want. What next?*

To show that you're in earnest about making the purchase, you put up a modest amount of money called earnest money; and to bind the deal, you may also sign a binder. Now you've made the first legal step toward buying the house of your choice, but you still have a long way to go before it becomes yours.

Warning: Under no circumstance make an oral agreement. The law requires that all real estate transactions be in writing.

· *Is the binder a purchase agreement?*

Maybe. A purchase agreement can be an agreement to sign a contract of sale, or the contract itself. In some states the binder can be either, and hence a purchase agreement. In other states it's neither, just a receipt for the earnest money—a loose bond that can be dissolved with the return of the money. Be careful: You may think you're signing a receipt, but it could be a purchase agreement. Ask your lawyer before you sign anything.

· *Is there any way I can get out of a purchase agreement after I've signed it?*

You can get out only when the purchase agreement states specifically that you have the right to cancel under certain conditions. It's up to you to spell out those conditions (inability to secure a mortgage is one; subject to your lawyer's review is another), and persuade the seller to include them in the purchase agreement.

· *When I cancel a purchase agreement, do I get my earnest money back?*

That depends on the cancellation terms you and the seller agree to write into the purchase agreement. Ordinarily, when the seller grants you the right to cancel, your earnest money is refunded when you exercise that right. When the seller does not grant you the right to cancel but you cancel anyway, the seller as a practical matter usually keeps your earnest money in exchange for releasing you from your obligation to go ahead with the terms of the agreement (which could mean having to buy the house).

· *How can I be sure the seller will return my earnest money even if he agrees to do so?*

Place the money in escrow. That means the money is held in custody by a third party, and neither the seller nor you can touch it until the deal goes through or falls through. The third party may be the real estate broker, your lawyer, or a bank; but it's usually the seller's attorney.

· *Who draws up a purchase agreement?*

Your lawyer should. If, instead, the real estate broker presents you with a printed purchase agreement form, read it carefully, agree with the seller on the changes and additions you want to make, then write them in on all copies. Be sure they're initialed by you and the seller.

· *What items are included in the purchase agreement?*

If the purchase order is an agreement to sign a contract for sale, most of the items that appear in the contract are included, but not necessarily in as great detail. If the purchase order *is* the contract, then all necessary items, fully detailed, are included. Those items are covered in the following section.

HOW TO GET YOUR RIGHTS IN THE CONTRACT FOR SALE

· *Does the contract of sale spell out how and when the purchase price is to be paid?*

Yes. The contract usually states that the purchase price of X dollars shall be paid as follows:

Cash deposit	$_____
Cash on closing	_____
Mortgage	_____
Existing liens assumed	_____
Deferred payments	_____
Total	$_____

Here's what each of those lines means:

Cash deposit. That's normally your earnest money, but it may include an additional deposit as well.

Cash on closing. That's the amount of cash to be added to your deposit to make up your down payment if you're buying the property with the aid of a mortgage, or your full payment if you're buying for cash. A certified check is usually accepted in lieu of cash. *Closing* is a legal ceremony in which the deed and title to the property pass from the seller to the buyer.

Mortgage. That's a method of financing the purchase of your house by putting up the property as security. The full amount of the mortgage is payable to the seller, and you repay the mortgage periodically. Should you fail to make your payments, the mortgagee can claim your property—a procedure known as foreclosure. The mortgagee can be a bank, a finance company, or an individual. Not infrequently the seller is the mortgagee.

You can take a mortgage on your own, or you can take over the seller's existing mortgage if permitted under the conditions of that mortgage. If you do the latter, be careful: If the contract reads you're "assuming the mortgage," there may be trouble in your future. "Assuming the mortgage" makes you personally liable *for the full payment* (in installments as set forth in the mortgage). If in the event of foreclosure your house is sold by the mortgagee for less than the balance due on the mortgage, you could be held responsible for the difference. Preferably, your contract should read you're "taking subject to the mortgage," in which case you're only responsible for making payments when due. In case of foreclosure, you owe nothing more.

Existing liens assumed. A lien is legal claim against property, usually as the result of a debt. To assume existing liens usually means to become personally liable for some or all of the seller's debts which resulted in those liens. The amount of the debt assumed is considered a part of the total purchase price.

Deferred payments. You can defer some of the cash due on closing by making an arrangement with the seller.

· *I can afford to buy the house only if I get a mortgage or sell my present house. Can this condition be included in the contract for sale?*

It had better be. If it isn't, and you fail to come up with the cash at closing, you've breached the contract. The seller is then free to sell the house to someone else, and you may be liable for any loss the seller may incur as a result of your action.

Usually the seller will agree in the contract for sale to give you a specified time to obtain a mortgage and/or sell your present house; and should you be unable to do so, the contract is considered terminated by mutual consent. The seller is then free to sell the house to someone else, but you are not liable for any loss the seller may incur as a result of your action.

· *The only mortgage I can get is too expensive for me. If I refuse it, do I breach the contract for sale?*

Not if you've taken the precaution to specify in the contract for sale that the contract is terminated by mutual consent if you can't get the kind of mortgage acceptable to you. You can specify the interest rate, the amount of the monthly payments, and the number of years the mortgage is to run. If you're unacquainted with the kinds of mortgages available to you, you might want to study the Federal Trade Commission's *Mortgage Money Guide*. It's free from the Federal Trade Commission, Washington, DC 20402.

· *In the contract for sale, can the property be identified simply by the street number?*

No. In addition to the street number (or the section, block, and lot number if your property is a subdivision), the property may also be described by "metes and bounds"—that is to say, as a surveyor would describe it in terms of accurate measurements. The description should include the location of the boundaries and of all structures on the lot (house, garage, swimming pool, and so on). The contract of sale should provide for the seller to furnish you with a description of the property based on a current survey.

· *Why is a current survey of the property necessary?*

Because the description based on the previous survey may no longer accurately represent the facts. Between the time of that survey and the time your contract for sale is being negotiated, the following changes may have occurred:

- Neighbors may have made encroachments on your property. An encroachment is something, such as a part of a building or a fence, that intrudes illegally on a neighbor's property.
- The seller may have made encroachments on a neighbor's property.
- The seller may have made improvements on the house, or added other structures to the property, that do not comply with local laws dealing with the placement of such structures. For example, a swimming pool may not be set back far enough from the road.

Should you buy the property unaware of these changes, you could pay for more property than you receive, be liable to legal action from your neighbors, and face the possibility of having to move structures that have been positioned contrary to local law (and, perhaps, pay a fine as well).

• *Who pays for the survey?*

Usually the purchaser, although it's negotiable.

• *I assume that when I buy the house, the carpeting, draperies, and garden statuary automatically go with it. Right or wrong?*

Wrong. What you're buying is "real property"—that is to say, all the items which are part of the land or affixed to it. Carpeting, draperies, and garden statuary—as well as other furnishings and appliances—are "personal property." If you wish to acquire some of the seller's personal property as part of the sale, be sure to list it in the contract for sale.

Warning: Sometimes the distinction between real property and personal property can be fuzzy. For example, a divider wall between two rooms is real property, and a bookcase is personal property. But what is a divider wall that's also a bookcase? In an actual case, a dispute arose between a seller who regarded the divider wall/bookcase as personal property and wanted to take it with him, and a buyer who regarded it as real property and wanted it to remain in the house. The dispute was settled when lawyers for both parties pointed out that since the divider wall/bookcase was really a part of the house, and not a separate fixture, it was real property and could not be removed by the seller. If you're not sure whether an item is real property or personal property, consult your lawyer.

• *How do I know that the seller really owns the property?*

Under the terms of the contract for sale, the seller must furnish you with an *abstract of title*. "Title," as it refers to real property, is usually a legal document which contains all the necessary facts to prove the right to possession and ownership of a property. An abstract of title is a short summary of the legal history of the title over the years. It shows whether the seller has a clear claim to the title or whether the title is "clouded" by other claims—that is to say, whether the seller has undisputed ownership of the property, or whether other people may have a right to all or part of it.

The abstract of title is made as a result of a title search, usually conducted by a title company, a professional organization skilled in the examination of public records. A claim against the title is called a *defect of record* or an *encumbrance*.

• *What happens if the abstract of title indicates the title is clouded?*

The contract for sale requires that the seller supply you with a "good and marketable" title. A "good" title is one which gives you the right to own, occupy, and use the property free from the legal claims of others. A "marketable" title is one which gives you the right to mortgage or sell the property without legal restrictions by others. In the event the abstract of title shows legal claims (encumbrances, or defects of title) against the property, the seller must remove those claims by the time of closing in order for the title to be good and marketable.

• *Is the abstract of title always accurate?*

Not always. The title searcher may have made an error. Besides, there may be "hidden" claims which the searcher is not able to detect. These may result from forged deeds, typographical errors in the records, missing heirs, and numerous other causes. According to the Federal Housing Administration (FHA), there are about a thousand different claims that can be made against your property.

• *If the abstract of title doesn't protect me against claims against the property, what does?*

Title insurance. In general, if there are claims against the title once it passes to you, the insurance company will defend it in court and pay all legal expenses; and if you lose, the insurance company will pay the claimant. For title insurance, there's only one premium, and it's paid at the time of closing. Usually it's the responsibility of the purchaser, but you can try to get the seller to pay for it.

Be careful: Title insurance does not always give you complete coverage. A policy usually insures against claims against the property with such exceptions as encumbrances revealed by the survey; recorded easements (rights granted to another property owner to use your land for certain purposes, say for power lines); and unfiled liens for labor and material. *Read* the policy. If you have difficulty understanding the language, ask the insurance agent, or better still your lawyer, to translate.

Many financial institutions and the FHA demand title insurance before they'll okay a mortgage.

• *I'm no expert. How do I know the house I'm about to buy isn't termite-infested or unsound in other respects?*

Try to have the contract for sale require the seller to supply you with an up-to-date termite inspection report, plus up-to-date reports from experts on the condition of the roofing, plumbing, electrical and heating systems, the house in general, and so on. It's customary, though, for the purchaser to pay for having these reports made. (For guidance on what should be inspected, refer to *Basic Housing Inspection*. It's free from HEW, Room 1587, Parklawn Building, 5600 Fisher's Lane, Rockville, MD 20852.) Should these reports indicate infestation or structural defects, insist that the contract for sale require the seller at his own expense to make corrections within a certain period of time. Also insist that the working parts of the house—such as appliances, heating, air conditioning, electricity, plumbing, and so on—be put in working order at the seller's expense by a specified time. That time is usually closing or possession, whichever comes later.

• *It seems there are a lot of expenses in connection with the sale of a house. Does the seller pay all of them?*

No. Those expenses are a matter for negotiation between you and the seller, and not a matter of law. But as a matter of custom, the purchaser usually pays for the abstract of title, the title insurance, termite and other inspections, and recording the deed. The seller usually pays the real estate agent's commission on the preparation of the deed, and for the revenue stamps on the deed. Whether you or the seller pays for the up-to-date survey and the mortgage company's transfer fee (in the event you're taking over the existing mortgage) depends on your negotiating skills.

· *What are escrowed funds?*

These are funds delivered to an escrow account administered by the mortgage lender, or sometimes by a lawyer. From this fund, the mortgage lender after the sale pays periodic expenses related to the property, such as real estate taxes and homeowner insurance (hazard insurance). This is a condition of most mortgages to ensure the payment of these expenses to avoid major creditors' claims on the property in the event of foreclosure. (Don't confuse this escrow fund with the earnest-money escrow fund, page 124.)

· *I'm taking possession of the house on October 1, but the seller's escrow funds cover the final quarter of the year. Does that mean for that final quarter I don't have to pay real estate taxes, homeowner insurance premiums, and other periodic debts that come due?*

Of course not. The contract for sale usually calls for these periodic expenses to be prorated between you and the seller— that is to say, divided proportionately depending on how long during the year each of you occupies the property. In this case, expenses for the year would be prorated so that you paid only for one-quarter of the periodic expenses.

To carry out this arrangement, the contract for sale usually calls for the seller to transfer all escrow funds to you, and for you to reimburse the seller at closing. At that time the periodic expenses would be prorated. Since in this case your prorated share is one-quarter of the total year's expenses, you would reimburse the seller with an amount equal to the amount held in escrow for the last quarter.

· *How do I know the property is really mine?*

When you receive a deed—a legal document that transfers title to the property from the seller to you. You get the deed at closing in return for payment.

There are several kinds of deeds. The best kind is the *full covenant and warranty deed.* Bernard Meltzer, a leading consumer expert specializing in real estate, explains why: "In this deed, the seller says [in essence], 'I promise and guarantee that you will enjoy the ownership of this property, and you can use it as you see fit within the limitations of the deed, and no one will dispute your rights, and no one will interfere with them. If anybody makes a claim on the title, I'll be financially responsible for any loss or damage to you.' You can understand why this document is called 'the deed of quiet enjoyment.'"

The most commonly used deed, though, is the "Covenants against Grantor's Acts." It relies on title insurance to protect you in the event a claim is made on your property.

· *What are the "limitations of the deed?"*

Recorded legal restrictions, regulations, and easements common to the neighborhood which in effect limit your right of ownership. Existing mortgage and current taxes are also regarded as limitations.

· *Suppose between the time I sign the contract for sale and get the deed, the house is hit by flood, fire, storm, or vandals—am I stuck with a damaged house?*

Until you receive the deed at closing, the house remains the property of the seller. The contract for sale should state specifically that the seller shall deliver the house in substantially the same condition as on the date the contract for sale is signed, except for promised alterations. If the property is partially damaged before closing, the contract for sale usually grants the seller a certain period of time to restore the property at his own expense; and the closing date is extended. If the seller does not fulfill this condition, the contract for sale is terminated and your deposit is returned in full.

· *Is the date of closing the date I move in?*

It could be, but it may not be. The date of closing is the date
the house becomes yours, but you may elect to move in at a
later date. Both the closing date and the date you move in are
fixed in the contract for sale.

· *I'm purchasing the house with my husband. Are both our
signatures required on the contract for sale?*

Yes. There are three ways you can purchase a house (or any
property) jointly. You'll find them described beginning on page
177. With the advice of your lawyer, select the one that's best
for you, and include your decision in the contract for sale. If
the seller owns the house jointly, the signatures of the joint
owners are required.

· *What are closing costs?*

All costs other than the cost of the house itself. These include
"points" (mortgage discount fees), and fees for termite and structural inspections, recording and surveys, title and abstract, and
insurance. These costs, which also include realtor and legal
feels, are payable at closing.

WHAT YOU SHOULD KNOW ABOUT YOUR BASIC RIGHTS WHEN YOU BUY A CONDO OR CO-OP

· *What is a condo?*

A condo, or condominium, is a multiunit dwelling project in
which each unit consists of a dwelling plus an undivided interest in the areas and facilities designed for common use. "Buying a condo" ordinarily means buying a unit, not buying the
multidwelling project.

· *How do I buy a condo?*

The same way you buy a house. As a matter of fact, some condos
are houses. They're units of a cluster of houses, either attached
or unattached. But most condos are apartments.

· *In a condo what are the areas and facilities designed for common use?*

They include parking space, recreational facilities (from a cinema to a golf course), commercial facilities (many condos have their own stores), and community facilities (a meeting hall is an example), as well as lobbies, halls, utility systems, roofs, floors, stairways, elevators, main walls, driveways, and the land area of the project.

· *If I buy a condo, what interest would I have in the common areas and facilities?*

You can figure it out with this simple formula: Divide the value of your unit by the total value of all units. For example, your unit is worth $250,000. The total value of all units is $250,000,000. Your interest in the common areas and facilities is $250,000 divided by $250,000,000 or 0.1 percent. (Some other formula may be used, so check with you lawyer.)

· *Who pays for the maintenance of the common areas and facilities?*

You do, and so do the other unit owners. Your share is equal to the total cost of maintenance multiplied by your interest in the common areas and facilities. If the total annual cost of maintenance is $8,000,000 and your interest is 0.1 percent, then your share of maintenance for that year is $8,000 ($8,000,000 × 0.1 percent). These charges are included in your monthly maintenance bill, which also includes the cost of maintaining your unit.

· *In the condo I'm thinking of buying, there are six tennis courts and a swimming pool. I don't play tennis and I don't swim. Must I pay my share for the maintenance of facilities I can't use?*

Yes.

· *Do I have a vote in the management of the condo project?*

Yes, you have a vote in the condominium corporation equal to the value of your unit divided by the value of the total units.

The condominium corporation, which is financed by the unit owners, sets up by-laws—rules and regulations—with which all owners have to comply, and manages the project through a board of directors.

· *Are there national laws governing condominiums?*

No, the laws are set by each state, and they can be complicated. Before you buy a condominium, see your lawyer. Before you see your lawyer, it might be a good idea to read through the *Condominium Buyer's Guide.* It's available free from the National Association of Home Builders, 15th and M Streets, Washington, DC 20005.

· *What is a cooperative?*

It's a multidwelling project in which stock ownership in the corporation that owns and manages the project gives you the right to live in an apartment and use the areas and facilities designed for common use.

· *What does "co-op" mean?*

It's short for "cooperative," and it can mean either a dwelling unit or the multidwelling project.

· *Can a co-op be a house?*

Although it's a theoretical possibility, it never is. Co-ops are apartments.

· *What's the difference between ownership of a condo and of a co-op?*

In simplest terms, you own a condo, but you don't own a co-op (you just own a share in the co-op corporation).

When you buy a condo, you receive a deed and take title to your property. You can mortgage your condo, lease it, sell it, will it, or do anything else you like with it (subject to some possible restrictions by the condo corporation).

On the other hand, your share in the co-op corporation only entitles you to a lease on your apartment (it's called a proprietary lease), which prohibits you from altering, disposing of, or doing almost anything with your co-op without the approval of the board of directors of the co-op corporation.

· *How do I "buy" a co-op?*

If it is a new unit, you start by signing a subscription agreement (it shows your intent to buy) and making a deposit in the shares. Otherwise, your money is held in escrow until you've signed the contract, arranged for financing, and received the shares and the proprietary lease.

· *If I don't "own" my co-op, how can I finance it?*

One way is through participation in the cooperative corporation's mortgage, which covers all apartments. The drawback of that method of financing is that if the co-op corporation defaults on its mortgage payments and the mortgager forecloses, you could lose your interest in the corporation and your apartment.

Another way is to obtain a bank loan with your share in the co-op corporation as collateral (you'll need the approval of the co-op corporation's board of directors). Should you default, your collateral is forfeited, and you lose your apartment. So this kind of financing works out much like an individual mortgage.

· *Who runs a co-op?*

As a shareholder, you have a vote in determining how the co-op is managed, and in electing directors and officers. In practice, the day-to-day activities of the co-op are usually conducted by professional managers. In some co-ops, each shareholder has an equal vote; in other co-ops, the value of a shareholder's vote is proportionate to the number of shares held.

· *Since I don't own a co-op, do I have to pay taxes on it?*

Not in the same way that you pay taxes on a condo or a house, but you do have to pay your share of the taxes on the cooperative project. It's included in your monthly maintenance fee, which is paid to the co-op corporation. The maintenance fee also includes expenses for the upkeep of your apartment and the building as a whole, and can include mortgage payments as well.

· *Are state laws governing co-ops as complex as those governing condos?*

Yes. A wise co-op purchaser investigates with his lawyer the subscription agreement, contract, and possible pitfalls of co-op living *before* he signs anything.

WHAT YOU SHOULD KNOW ABOUT YOUR RIGHTS AS A TENANT

· *Are laws governing tenant-landlord relations uniform throughout the country?*

No. They vary from state to state and usually from locality to locality. What follows is information about tenant-landlord relations as they apply to the area of highest rental-unit density, New York City. Since there is no situation involving tenants rights that does not occur in the Big Apple, New York City's tenant-landlord statutes, regulations, and codes are frequently models for their counterparts throughout the nation. Here is a practical guide to the rights of a tenant in New York. They may be similar to your rights as a tenant where you live, or they may give you a frame of reference when you talk to your lawyer.

· *What are my general basic rights as a tenant?*

1. You have the right to a lease. A lease is a contract between a landlord and tenant, specifying the tenant's rights and obligations. It must be written in plain language.
2. You have the right to a safe, well-repaired, livable apartment and apartment house.
3. You have the right to complain to your landlord and superintendent.
4. You have the right to organize tenant meetings, and hold them in your lobby.
5. You have the right to be free from retaliatory eviction for organizing tenants or participating in organized tenant activities.
6. You have the right to go on a rent strike. (But remember, we're talking about New York City, so be sure to check with your lawyer about your right to strike in your community.)

· What are my specific rights as a tenant?

1. You have the right to emergency repairs. The landlord is required to provide you with a twenty-four-hour emergency-repair phone number, and a phone number within fifty miles of the city at which the owner can be reached at all times. In addition, the landlord must provide you with the name and address of someone authorized to make emergency repairs who lives or works in the city.

2. You have the right to live in a clean apartment house. The landlord is required to keep every part of the building (halls, stairs, cellar, roof, stoop, and so on) clean and free of trash and garbage, and to keep all outside areas (sidewalks, private park or other common enclosure, parking lot, and so on) free as well of dirt, litter, ice, and snow. The landlord, though, is not responsible for the cleanliness of your apartment.

3. You have the right to live in a vermin-free apartment house. The landlord is required to provide exterminating service to keep all parts of the building, inside and out, including your apartment, free from rats, mice, roaches, and other insects. Moreover, the landlord is required to give you advance notice of the date and time exterminators are to be in the building.

4. You have the right to daily garbage disposal. The landlord must provide this service by means of an incinerator or compactor, or sufficient number of sealed plastic garbage bags or covered garbage cans.

5. You have the right to adequate heat. The landlord must provide heat from October 1 to May 31 in accordance with the following formula: The temperature in your apartment must be at least 55 degrees between 10:00 P.M. and 6:00 A.M. whenever the outside temperature is below 40 degrees; and at least 68 degrees between 6:00 A.M. and 10:00 P.M. whenever the outside temperature is below 55 degrees. Temperature is measured in degrees Fahrenheit.

6. You have the right to hot water. The landlord must maintain hot water at no less than 120 degrees Fahrenheit between 6:00 A.M. and midnight.

7. You have the right to live in a well-maintained apartment house. The entire building, inside and out, should

be kept in good repair, walls, ceilings, floors, windows, facade, plumbing and sewage systems, electric circuitry, elevators, safety and fire-protection systems, and so on. The walls and the ceilings of public areas must be painted periodically.

8. You have the right to have appliances installed by your landlord in your apartment in good repair. This right applies to stoves, air conditioners, doorbells, refrigerators, sinks, showers, and so on. If any landlord-installed appliance cannot be repaired, it must be replaced by the landlord at no cost to you. However, if you request a new appliance in place of an appliance in good repair, you may be required to pay a percentage of the cost.

9. You have the right to have your apartment painted. If your building has three or more apartments, each apartment must be painted at least once in every three-year period at no charge to the tenants. In rent-stabilized apartments (page 140), tenants renewing their leases for less than three years may have to pay a "painting deposit." For a one-year lease, this amounts to two-thirds the cost of painting; for a two-year lease, one-third. The deposit is refundable upon renewal of the lease.

10. You have the right to have your security deposit placed in a separate account, and to be informed by the landlord of the name of the bank holding that account. A security deposit covers one month's rent, and can be claimed by the landlord in case of default. If your apartment house has at least six apartments, you must be paid the interest on your security deposit annually. When a lease is not renewed, the security deposit becomes payment for the last month of residency. (This is not legal, but most landlords do it.)

11. You have the right to have the landlord purchase and install at least one smoke detector in your apartment (provided your apartment house has more than three apartments). You are required to permit the landlord to make the installation, and pay him $10 in a single sum when billed or in monthly installments over the course of a year.

12. You have the right to janitorial service. If your apartment house has at least nine apartments, this service must be

supplied by a superintendent who lives in the building or within a one-block radius, or by a twenty-four-hour janitorial service. When the super does not live in the building, a prominently placed sign must display his name, address, and phone number. When two or three buildings are connected, one superintendent can service them, provided there are no more than sixty-five apartments in all.

13. You have the right to window guards if you have children ten years or younger living with you. Request window guards from your landlord in writing by certified mail, return receipt requested. Your charge, provided your apartment is rent-controlled or rent-stabilized (see following question), is only $10 per guard, which can be paid at the rate of 25¢ per guard per month.

· *What is a rent-controlled apartment? What is a rent-stabilized apartment?*

A *rent-controlled apartment* is one with a maximum base rent (MBR) which can never be exceeded. If the rent is lower than the MBR it can be raised 7.5 percent a year until the MBR is reached, provided the apartment house is properly maintained. Rent increases are also permitted to compensate for the cost of new improvements (a new boiler, for example), rising fuel costs, and profit levels lower than allowed by rent-control guidelines. An apartment is designated as a rent-controlled apartment when the tenant has been living in the apartment house since before February 1947, and in the current apartment since before June 30, 1971. Rents for apartments in this category are the lowest in the city. Rent-controlled apartments are regulated by the city's Office of Rent Control, which establishes the MBR.

A *rent-stabilized apartment* is one with a rent that can be raised on the renewal of a lease, or the issuance of a lease to a first-time tenant, in accordance with rent-rise formulas determined annually by the city's Rent Guidelines Board. Rent increases are also allowed, as they are for rent-controlled apartments, to compensate for the cost of new improvements and for profit levels lower than that permitted by rent-stabilization guidelines. But rising fuel costs are passed along to the tenant as surcharges, and not as part of the rent.

An apartment is designated as rent-stabilized when it is in a building of six or more apartments built between February 1, 1947, and January 1, 1974. An apartment is also rent-stabilized if the apartment house was built prior to February 1, 1947, and the tenant moved in after June 30, 1974. Rent-stabilization designation has also been given to tenants residing in tax-abated buildings built after January 1, 1974, but only for the duration of the tax abatement (about ten years). The rents for rent-stabilized apartments, although considerably lower than those for free-market apartments, are considerably higher than those for rent-controlled apartments.

· *What's my recourse when my rights as a tenant are violated?*

It depends on the nature of the violation. Some examples:

If your property is destroyed because of the landlord's negligence (say, your sofa is ruined by a water-pipe leak), you can bring suit in small claims court (page 32).

If your deposit money is not kept in a separate account or if annual interest on it is not paid you, you can complain to the New York State Assistant Attorney General, Consumer Fraud Bureau.

If your landlord refuses to comply with the window guard requirement, your complaint should be addressed to the Health Department, Central Complaints Bureau.

If there are violations under the rent-control program, the place to take your complaints is the District Rent Control Office.

If there are violations under the rent-stabilization program, complaints should be made to the office of the Rent Stabilization Association.

If there are chronic violations of tenants' rights throughout the building (vermin infestation, lack of adequate heat or hot water, poor or no maintenance, and so on), you can join with other tenants to remedy the condition in the following ways:

- Take an HP action. This is simply initiated by obtaining an Order to Show Cause from the clerk of the Housing Court, and sending it with other necessary papers to both the landlord and the city's Housing Department (HPD). The order requests the landlord to "show cause" why violations exist and why fines should not be imposed. This results in an inspection of the building by the HPD; and, provided the inspection proves out your complaints, it can be used as a basis for requesting the judge of the Housing Court to sign an Order of Repair, mandating that the landlord correct all violations within a specified time, usually fifteen to ninety days. But the HPD inspection may not confirm all your complaints; and even if it does, the judge, for any of a number of technical reasons, may not sign the Order of Repair. Then—

• Hold a rent strike. "A rent strike," asserts the City of New York Commission on Human Rights, "is one of the most powerful weapons that a tenants association can use." In a rent strike, the tenants as a group withhold rents until the landlord has corrected all violations. (The rents are deposited with the tenants association, and held in a special account.) Rent strikes require a strong tenants association, experienced leadership, expert legal advice, and bulldog tenacity. You can win a rent strike—other tenants organizations have—but can lose. If you do, then—

• Initiate a 7A proceedings. Under Article 7A of the Real Property Actions and Proceedings Law of New York, one third of the tenants in the building can request the court to appoint an administrator to run the building until all violations have been corrected and the building is back in shape. But unless you can prove to the satisfaction of the court that the landlord has chronically ignored requests to make repairs, has abandoned the building, has shown no capacity to manage a building, or has created conditions hazardous to life, health, and safety, your chance of winning a 7A proceedings is poor.

No matter what remedial actions you contemplate, whether alone or as part of a tenants group, it is wise to take none until you've discussed the matter with your lawyer.

• Can I be evicted?

Not for tenant-organization activities, but you can for other reasons. To evict you, the landlord must first obtain a judgment from the Housing Court. You are then served with a Notice of Eviction (a Dispossess Notice), ordering you to vacate the apartment in a specified time—sometimes as little as seventy-two hours. If you fail to vacate, the city marshal is empowered to remove you and your belongings from the apartment.

· When can I be evicted?

When you violate the lease, when the landlord needs the apartment for himself or his immediate family, and when an eviction plan is an element of the conversion procedure to a co-op or a condo. However, there are exceptions to each of these grounds for eviction, as you will see in the answers to the following three questions.

· What are the exceptions to eviction as the result of violating a lease?

By statute, courts are directed to give tenants judged to be in violation of the lease ten days to correct the violation. If that's done, the order to evict is canceled.

In addition, violations of the following clauses of a lease are *not* considered cause for eviction.

- The "home office clause," which states that the apartment can be used only for residential purposes. In a decision that is certain to have national impact, a New York State Appellate Court in 1984, ruling on an eviction case concerning a psychiatrist who saw fifteen patients a week in her apartment, said: "Most people engage in a certain amount of business in their homes. What is crucial is not whether a tenant conducts some business in his or her apartment, but that the extent of that undertaking is kept within reasonable bounds. [This particular business] is inherently quiet, unobtrusive, harmonious with a residential setting, and of undoubted social usefulness." If yours is, too, you can't be evicted.
- The "live-in-friends and lovers clause," which states that occupancy is limited to the tenant and his immediate family, and makes occupancy by live-in friends and lovers grounds for eviction. The New York State Legislature in 1984 by statute made that clause unenforceable, arguing that if it were enforceable "thousands of households throughout the state composed of unrelated persons who live together by reasons of economy, safety and companionship may be placed in jeopardy." The statute provides

the tenant with the right to occupy the apartment with his immediate family *and* one other person and that person's dependent children.
• The "no pet clause" prohibits the keeping of any kind of pet in the apartment. But a City Council bill signed into law in 1983 provides that if the tenant "openly and notoriously keeps the pet for [three months], the landlord loses the right to sue under the lease to evict the tenant for his pets."

• What are the exceptions to eviction when the landlord needs the apartment for himself or his immediate family?

Tenants over sixty-two, permanently disabled tenants, and tenants who choose to stay on as rentors in a noneviction-plan co-op or condo are exempt from this "personal use" eviction. Administrative red tape makes it extremely difficult for a landlord to make a "personal use" eviction from a rent-controlled apartment.

• What are the exceptions to eviction in an eviction-plan co-op or condo?

When a rental property is converted to a co-op or a condo, tenants who elect not to purchase are permitted to stay on as rental tenants (noneviction-plan conversion) or they are evicted (eviction-plan conversion). Nonpurchasers in an eviction-plan conversion, though, may stay on indefinitely as renters if they're over sixty-two or permanently disabled; and all others may stay on as renters for three years.

8

Your Business:
Your Rights as an Entrepreneur

- Your rights and obligations as a sole proprietor
- Your rights and obligations as a partner
- Your rights and obligations as a corporate stockholder

Inseparable from the American way is your right to pull yourself up by your bootstraps, win your way to the top, start from next to nothing, and build an empire. The launching pad to that American dream can be a small business.

Take Roy Kroc, who started with a single hamburger stand, built it into a $500,000,000 fortune for himself, and made McDonald's a household world worldwide.

Take Julia Phillips, an $8,000-a-year editorial assistant on a magazine, who started a one-woman motion-picture-script business and took home as her share of just one movie, *The Sting*, $2,500,000.

Take Victor Potamkin, who propelled himself from a single car dealership on borrowed money to become the multimillionaire owner of the largest chain of car dealerships in the world.

Take Curtis LeRoy Carlson, who zoomed his shoestring stamp-trading company into a conglomerate of hotels and businesses dealing with property development, sales incentives, food retailing, showrooms, catalogs, and real estate valued at more than $500,000,000.

Aside from its Aladdin's-lamp promise, small business provides a comfortable-to-affluent livelihood to millions of owners.
Small business is not only the mom-and-pop store, it's the high-
tech subcontractor; not only the boutique, but the small pub-
lisher; not only the home-based mail-order house, but the independent film producer. Small business does everything, is
everywhere, and, surprisingly, contributes a major share to the
nation's prosperity.

"America is small business," President Ronald Reagan said,
celebrating Small Business Week in 1983. "Small firms account
for nearly half our jobs; they create some 60 percent of new
jobs; and they're on the cutting edge of innovation, providing
products and ideas for the future." Small business people, the
President added, are the "forgotten heroes" of America.

If you're thinking of joining their ranks, you should know
your rights. Your basic rights to do business are built into the
fundamental laws of the land. They're the rights to own property
and to own patents, the right to personal freedom, and the right
to act competitively. Without those basic rights no business, big
or small, could exist. From pioneer days to well into the nineteenth century those rights were virtually free of government
interference; and the nation spread from sea to shining sea under the banner of free enterprise.

But with the growth of industrial giants and their threats to
the free enterprise of others, as well as to the general welfare,
new federal and state laws imposed restrictions on business's
almost unbridled freedom. Today our economic system, although freer than any other, is no longer a free-enterprise system; it's a limited free-enterprise system. From local ordinances
to Federal Trade Commission (FTC) regulations, government
controls so many business activities that it would be self-de-
feating for anyone to start a business without the guidance of a
lawyer.

But the rights that remain legally yours when you start a small
business are the foundations of success for millions of people,
and can be for you. To begin with, there are three legally acceptable forms for setting up a business: a sole proprietorship,
a partnership, and a corporation—and you have the right to
choose the one that's best for you. This chapter, by highlighting

the basic rights you have in each of these forms, can help you make your choice.

YOUR RIGHTS AND OBLIGATIONS AS A SOLE PROPRIETOR

• *What's sole proprietorship?*

Individual ownership. The business is yours. You have nobody to answer to but yourself. You're the boss. If the business makes money, it goes into your pocket; if the business loses money, it comes out of your pocket. When you own a sole proprietorship you're referred to as the sole proprietor or individual owner.

• *Is there red tape involved in starting up a sole proprietorship?*

There's red tape involved in starting up any form of business. You have to comply with local, state, and federal laws and regulations. You may have to be licensed, carry insurance, obey zoning restrictions, file a business certificate, and so on. Remember, ignorance of the law is no excuse; if you violate any of the laws governing setting up a business, you could be penalized. For information on getting a new business started, contact your local Small Business Chamber of Commerce, your local Chamber of Commerce, your local IRS office, the Small Business Administration (see your White Pages or call 202-653-6365 in Washington), your accountant, and your lawyer.

• *I'm starting a phone-answering service. It's a sole proprietorship. I want to call it Tingle Bells. Any problem?*

Not legally. But since the business is a sole proprietorship, "Tingle Bells" is regarded by law as your assumed name; and if your state has an "assumed names act," you must file both your assumed name and *your real name* with county and state authorities. The reason for filing your real name is so that anybody who has a complaint against Tingle Bells will know whom to target. You can find out if your state has an assumed names act, and if so how to file under it, by calling the clerk of your county clerk (see your White Pages) or consulting your lawyer.

· *Suppose Jane Consumer brings a suit against my company, Tingle Bells, and gets a judgment. Am I personally off the hook?*

No. The complaint will read: "Jane Consumer, Plaintiff, against [your name], doing business under the firm name of Tingle Bells." *You* have full responsibility, not your firm.

· *If Tingle Bells can't pay its debts, am I personally liable?*

Yes, since Tingle Bells is a sole proprietorship. If you can't come up with the cash, you could, as a result of a suit, have a lien placed on your home, your bank account, and all of the rest of your assets. A lien gives your creditor the right to hold on to your property until you settle his claim against you. The major drawback of a sole proprietorship is personal liability. Like other sole proprietors, you may elect to carry high-cost business liability insurance to protect yourself.

· *I have a sole proprietorship I want to close down. Do I need to go through any legal procedure?*

No. Just close down. But first pay off all the debts incurred by the business, and settle the firm's obligations.

YOUR RIGHTS AND OBLIGATIONS AS A PARTNER

· *What's a partnership?*

It's an arrangement by two or more persons to conduct a business, sharing profits, losses, and expenses in a manner agreed on by all partners. There are two kinds of partnerships: general and limited. They're discussed separately in the following subsections.

The General Partnership

· *What's a general partnership?*

A partnership in which each partner is responsible for the actions of the others, is liable for all business debts, and may be obliged to satisfy partnership-incurred debts from his own assets.

· *My boss announced that I've been promoted to partner in the firm. I have my reasons for not wanting to be a partner. Does my boss's announcement make me a partner anyway?*

No. You can't become a partner without your consent. Partnership is a voluntary state, and it cannot be forced on you.

· *Can a partnership be a handclasp agreement?*

Yes. But it has the weakness of all nonwritten arrangements in that memory lapses, misinterpretations, and, in some cases, deliberate misrepresentations may result in disputes.

· *I'm in a handclasp partnership. My partner and I are in dispute over my rights. How can I straighten out this matter?*

In most states, when there is no written agreement, state partnership statutes set the rights and obligations of partners. Consult your lawyer. Another way to settle the dispute is for both parties to agree to submit to arbitration (see page 29).

· *What kind of written agreement must I enter into when I form a partnership?*

A specific kind of contract, called a partnership agreement. It must contain all the essential elements of a contract to be enforceable legally (see page 108).

· *Can I make up my own partnership agreement?*

Yes. But if you do, it's wise to have your lawyer's approval before signing; and it's even wiser to have the agreement drawn by your lawyer in the first place. A printed partnership agreement form can be purchased in a stationery shop handling legal forms.

· *I'm thinking of starting a two-partner firm. What should the general partnership agreement contain?*

The following nineteen essentials.

1. Your name and address and your partner's.
2. The name of your firm. The partnership does business in the firm's name and not in the names of the partners, unless the names of the partners constitute the firm's name.
3. The type of business in which you're engaged.
4. The address of your firm.
5. The date the partnership becomes effective.
6. How long the partnership is to last. Ordinarily, a partnership lasts until it's terminated.
7. How the partnership can be terminated. Some common conditions for termination are a partner's death, mental or physical incapacity, incompetence, improper conduct, and bankruptcy. The partnership also may be terminated by mutual consent, and, in a two-person partnership, by the retirement of one of the partners. (It's a good idea to agree on the acceptable age of retirement to prevent one of the two partners from breaking up the partnership without the consent of the other by retiring at an early age.)
8. A description of each partner's investment in the partnership. A partnership does not require equal dollar investments. In some cases, one partner may put up all the capital, and the other all the goods and/or services. Often, too, specialized knowledge, skills, or experience are considered as an investment instead of money. But whatever investment arrangement you and your partner agree on, be sure to describe it accurately.
9. How profits, expenses, and losses are shared. All these items are shared equally unless another arrangement is made by mutual consent. As a partner, you cannot receive a salary or another form of compensation for working for the partnership. You can receive, however, a weekly or monthly draw against profits.
10. What each partner does in the business. Neither of the partners may do anything, preferring to hire people to carry on the business. But in most cases, each of the

partners has specific job responsibilities which are spelled out in the partnership agreement.

11. Who makes what decisions concerning management and operations. It's up to you and your partner to come to a meeting of minds. If both of you have equal rights in the management and operation of the business, you may agree that every decision must be made by mutual consent. But since that could create troublesome situations, most partners agree to delegate to each other the decision-making function in specific areas of the business. *Caution*: Whatever your partner does in relation to the business binds you—and, of course, vice versa. Your choice of an efficient and trustworthy partner is a keystone to your partnership's success.

12. How each partner can check on each other concerning money coming in and money coming out. It's prudent to provide that (a) the books of the partnership shall be kept in the place of business, (b) that the books shall be available for inspection by each of the partners at any time, (c) that the books shall be balanced periodically, and that an accurate accounting statement shall be made available to each partner, and (d) that the books shall be audited annually, and statements supplied to each partner. Consult your accountant about setting up a bookkeeping system.

13. How funds are to be deposited and withdrawn. Specify the name and address of the bank in which your firm will make deposits, and whether one signature or two are required on checks drawn against your firm's account.

14. How the rights of each partner to make major financial transactions are limited. Since each partner is bound by the actions of the other, a loss incurred as a result of a major financial transaction made by one partner would, in the absence of any agreement to the contrary, be shared equally by the other. Therefore, it is prudent to curb the right of each partner to make such transactions as follows:

- No partner shall take out a loan or act as cosigner on behalf of the partnership without the consent of the other partner.

- No partner shall release in any way a debt to the partnership without receipt of full payment, except with the consent of the other partner.
- No partner shall buy any property on behalf of the partnership, except property normally bought in the operation of the business, without the consent of the other partner.
- No partner shall dispose of any of his interest in the partnership, or of any of the assets of the partnership, without the consent of the other partner.

15. The partners' rights to engage in another business. Usually, each partner agrees not to engage in any competitive business for the duration of the partnership, but each partner reserves the right to engage during that period in any noncompetitive business.

16. The buy-sell arrangement. If for any reason one of the partners ceases to be a partner, the buy-sell arrangement gives the other partner an option to buy the former partner's interest or share in the business within a specified period of time, and obligates the former partner to sell that interest or share to the other partner.

    The financial arrangements concerning the sale—the purchase price of the share and how it is to be paid— should be worked out in detail. Usually, the purchase price is equal to the "book value" of the share. The book value is the dollar figure set for your partner's share by standard accounting practice applied to your firm's books. The purchase price is usually paid in cash, or in installments at a specified rate of interest.

17. The right to the name of the partnership. In the event one partner severs his connections with the partnership, it is usually agreed that the other partner may continue the business using the name of the partnership.

18. Settlement of disputes. It's a good idea to agree to have unresolved disputes between you and your partner settled by arbitration in accordance with the rules of the American Arbitration Association. This could avoid burdensome and expensive litigation.

19. Witnessed signatures of the parties, and the date of the agreement. In some states, if a partner is a married man, the signature of his wife is required. To find out if this requirement applies in your state, consult

the County Clerk's Office (see your White Pages) or your lawyer.

• *There are two partners in my firm. I want to bring in a third, even though my present partner objects. Can I do it?*

No. Mutual consent is necessary.

• *My partner and I want to bring in a third partner. How do we do it?*

Terminate your current partnership, then prepare a new agreement of partnership including the third partner. Your firm's name and operations can continue as before. In this way, as many partners can be added to the firm as agreed upon by the existing partners.

• *I plan to become a partner in an already existing partnership. Do I become liable for the existing debts of the partnership?*

No. Your liability begins once you become a partner. But your investment can be used to help pay off those debts with or without your consent.

• *I plan to resign from a partnership. Will that free me from the debts contracted by the partnership while I was a partner?*

No. And you may be liable for debts contracted by the partnership even after you leave, unless you send a written notice to all creditors announcing that you're no longer a partner.

• *How can a partnership go out of business?*

Meet all your obligations, then close your doors. It's a good idea, to let your customers and suppliers know you're going out of business. Remember: If the partnership is unable to pay off its debts when you decide to call it quits, you and your partner personally must come up with the money before you *can* call it quits. And if your partner can't come up with his share, or is judgment-proof (see page 93), *you* are stuck with the whole debt.

The Limited Partnership

· What's a limited partnership?

It's a partnership in which the liability of some of the partners is limited to the amount of their investments. Those partners are called "limited partners." A limited partnership also includes general partners who have liability similar to that of partners in a general partnership.

· Can the limited partnership be used for any type of business?

Yes. Its use is particularly widespread in theatrical and motion picture production.

· In a limited partnership, what are the functions of the general partners and the limited partners?

The general partners are responsible for the operation of the business, and are not permitted to render services of any kind to the partnership.

· What investments are made by the limited and the general partners?

The limited partners ordinarily supply all the risk capital for the enterprise. The general partners supply knowledge, experience, and management skills, but seldom make cash investments.

· What share of the profits do the general partners and the limited partners receive?

That depends on the specific limited partnership agreement, but the general partners usually receive the lion's share. In a typical limited partnership agreement for a theatrical production, the general partners receive 50 percent of the profits, and the limited partners together the remaining 50 percent. Each limited partner then receives a portion of that amount proportionate to his investment. Ordinarily, as a limited partnership earns money the limited partners are repaid their investments before profits are distributed.

· I want to invest in a Broadway show as a limited partner. I don't want my wife to know about it. Can I keep it a secret?

No. New York State's limited partnership law requires that a certificate of limited partnership be filed in the County Clerk's Office. The contents of that certificate include the names, home addresses, amount of investment, and share of profits of each limited partner. What's more, the law requires that the contents must be published in a newspaper in the county in which the limited partnership conducts its business. Check with your lawyer about filing and disclosure requirements in your state.

· Must the names and home addresses of the general partners also appear in the certificate of limited partnership?

Yes. And they also appear when the contents of the certificate are published in a newspaper.

· Can I draw up a limited partnership agreement myself?

Although you can buy a limited partnership agreement form in stationery stores handling legal forms, and adapt it to your needs, the relationships between the general partners and the limited partners can be complex. When you're setting up a limited partnership agreement, don't do it without your lawyer. And to be certain you're complying with your state's limited partnership law—especially when you solicit limited partners, amend the agreement, or terminate it—be sure you act on your lawyer's advice.

YOUR RIGHTS AND OBLIGATIONS AS A CORPORATE STOCKHOLDER

· What's a corporation?

It's a business regarded by the law as a person. Like a person, it has certain legal rights (it can buy, sell, and inherit property, for example), and certain responsibilities (if, for example, it commits a crime, it can be tried and punished).

The important thing is that a corporation is a *different* legal person than the people who own it. That means that as an owner or part owner of a corporation you are normally immune from the acts of the corporation, and are not personally liable for its debts (except up to the value of your investment). This protection is not afforded you as a sole proprietor or a general partner.

· *How is a corporation created?*

By the state, usually through granting a charter which endows the corporation with specific powers (including those described in the preceding answer). Since a corporation is regarded legally as a person, it is often said to be a "creature of the state." One former best-seller on corporations was called with dramatic appropriateness *Frankenstein, Inc.* For details on how to have the state create a corporation for you—that is to say, how to incorporate a business—see page 158.

· *Are there different kinds of corporations?*

Yes. Here is a list of the more common ones and their functions.

- A *public corporation* acts for the benefit of the public. The Port of New York Authority is an example.
- A *municipal corporation* carries on a function of a city government or an incorporated village. The Pawnutuck School Board Corporation is an example.
- A *membership corporation* runs some nonprofit organizations. Since members of nonprofit organizations cannot profit from them, no stock is issued. Scientific, religious, and charitable corporations are examples.
- A *professional corporation* or *P.C.* practices a specific profession while limiting the liability of its shareholders. However, in case of malpractice, an individual shareholder, rather than the corporation, may be liable. Legal and medical corporations are examples.
- A *nonprofit corporation* is a private enterprise that conducts a business not for profit. Charitable corporations are examples.
- A *business corporation* is a private enterprise that con-

ducts a business for profit under the protection afforded
a corporation. Also called a stock corporation, it's the kind
of corporation discussed in the remainder of this section.

· What's the structure of a business corporation?

It's composed of *shareholders* or *stockholders*, who own the
corporation; *officers*, who operate the corporation; and the *board
of directors*, which sets the policy and makes major management
decisions.

· How are the directors of a corporation chosen?

By a majority vote of the stockholders. Not infrequently, each
stockholder has a number of votes determined by multiplying
the number of his shares by the number of directors to be elected.
If you have a hundred shares, for example, and ten directors
are to be elected, you have a thousand votes (100 times 10). You
may distribute your votes in any way you choose among the ten
candidates, casting more or up to all of your votes for any one
candidate. The voting is conducted at a stockholders' meeting
which you can attend; or you may choose to cast your vote
through a proxy—a person whom you authorize in writing to
vote in your place.

· How are the officers of a corporation chosen?

They're elected by the board of directors. The officers of a corporation are the president, the secretary, the treasurer, and one
or more vice-presidents. The president must be chosen from
among the directors, but other officers need not be directors.
No officer need be a stockholder. One person can hold two
offices—say, vice-president and treasurer.

· Who really controls a corporation?

The stockholder or stockholders who control a majority of the
votes, since that majority selects the directors, who in turn select
the officers.

Several minority stockholders can band together to form a
voting majority. One way of accomplishing this is for a group of
stockholders to transfer their shares to a trustee for a certain

period of time for the sole purpose of providing that party with voting rights to their shares. The trustee is usually an expert in corporate management, who is capable of selecting a board of directors who can implement his objectives. More than one trustee can be appointed, and the trustee can be another corporation as well. This method of controlling a corporation is known as a *voting trust.*

• *I'm a minority stockholder, so I really have no control over the corporation. How do I know I'm getting a fair deal?*

Most corporate statutes provide you with the right of access to corporate books, records of stockholder and board of directors meetings, as well as relevant information about other stockholders and their shares. If you wish to exercise this right, put your request in writing to the president of the corporation.

• *I want to form a corporation. But there will be only two stockholders. Can I do it?*

In some states, only one stockholder is sufficient to form a corporation. In other states, two or three is the minimum requirement. Check with the office of your state's secretary of state (see your White Pages) or your lawyer for the requirements in your state. Although corporations are often regarded as large organizations in the perception of the general public, there are many times more small corporations in this country than large ones. Those of five stockholders or less are known as "close corporations," and are usually family businesses.

• *Should I incorporate my family business?*

It is advantageous from the liability viewpoint, but not always from the tax viewpoint. That's something your accountant and lawyer should help you decide. Since both you and your corporation are subject to taxes, you may pay more than if your business were a partnership. One way of avoiding excessive taxation is to register your corporation with the IRS as a subchapter S, in which case your corporation is taxed as if it were a partnership.

• *In what state should I incorporate?*

Ordinarily, in the state in which you do the bulk of your business. However, corporate statutes differ from state to state; and for your kind of business, incorporating in a state other than the one in which you do the bulk of your business may have statutory advantages. Consult your lawyer.

• *When I incorporate a business, do I have to make "Incorporated" a part of its name—like Tingle Bells, Incorporated?*

It depends on the state in which you incorporate. Some states require that either "Incorporated," "Corporation," "Limited," or their abbreviations "Inc.," "Corp.," or "Ltd." be part of the corporate name. Other states okay "Company" or "Co." For the rule in your state, check with the office of the secretary of state (see your White Pages) or consult your lawyer.

• *I plan to convert my sole proprietorship, Tingle Bells, to a corporation. Can I do it myself?*

Yes. Write to your secretary of state (see your White Pages) and tell him that you would like to form a corporation in the name Tingle Bells, Inc. If no other corporation in the state bears that name or a similar one, the secretary of state will permit you to incorporate under that name. If the secretary of state refuses your request to incorporate under Tingle Bells, Inc., write again with a suggested list of about five names. Chances are one or more will be acceptable. Choose the acceptable name you prefer.

Next, purchase certificate of incorporation forms from a stationery store handling legal forms, fill them out, and send them, accompanied by the fees called for, to the secretary of state. Provided you've filled out the forms correctly, you'll receive your certificate of incorporation within a short time.

Caution: Many people who start their corporations on their own find they're faced with numerous legal problems they can't answer, such as: How many shares shall be issued? To whom? What shall the by-laws contain? It's prudent to have your lawyer handle your incorporation. That way, you'll have the answers you need to launch your corporation without difficulties.

· Can my corporation expand into all kinds of business?

In general, most corporations have the right to engage in any kinds of acts an individual could perform. But your certificate of incorporation may not provide for expansion, and there may be statutory restrictions in your state on the kinds of business into which your corporation can expand. Consult your lawyer.

· How long can a corporation last?

Forever, unless its life is limited by state statutes. The death, withdrawal, or disability of the stockholders need not affect the corporate life span.

· Can I terminate my corporation just by closing my doors?

No. The dissolution of a corporation must comply with state laws. To terminate, take the following three steps:

1. Obtain unanimous consent of all your stockholders to the dissolution of the corporation.
2. Write to your secretary of state (see your White Pages) for information on what legal requirements you must meet to dissolve your corporation.
3. Obtain a dissolution form from a stationer that handles legal forms. Fill it out, and send it to the secretary of state.

There is also a slower way. Don't pay your franchise tax for two consecutive years. Your corporation is then usually involuntarily dissolved by the secretary of state.

Caution: Problems are likely to account for your desire to terminate your corporation. If that's the case, handling the dissolution by yourself could create more problems. One way to help solve all your termination problems is to have your lawyer handle them for you.

9

Wills: Your Right to Determine the Distribution of Your Property After Your Death

---

- Why you should have a will, and what happens when you don't
- What you can include in your will
- How to make a will
- How to change your will
- What happens to your will after your death
- How to avoid probate

From *Webster's New International Unabridged Dictionary*:

> *Will* (wĭl), n....a legal declaration of a person's mind as to the manner in which he would have his property or estate disposed of after his death; a written instrument legally executed by which a man makes disposition of his estate to take effect after death. [This definition applies to women as well as men.]

Looks simple, doesn't it?

But did you know that your will can be worthless if you punch loose-leaf holes in it? If you don't have the right number of witnesses? If you don't go through a ritual when you sign it? If you place instructions after your signature? If you don't comply with every single requirement of your state? And the list of such requirements is long.

Are you aware that you can't disinherit your spouse, but you can come pretty close? That you can disinherit your children, except in two states? That there's one kind of will that in many states is valid without witnesses? That you can't change your will just by writing in new instructions? That under some circumstances you don't have to put your will in writing?

Can you tell the difference between the words in the following pairs of will-related terms? Testate and intestate; reciprocal wills and mutual wills; right of dower and right of curtesy; executor and executrix; general legacy and specific legacy; holographic will and noncupative will.

Are you familiar with what you can and can't put into a will? What legal language is sometimes necessary to validate a will? What happens to your will after you're dead? What grounds are required for contesting a will? What possessions you can pass on without a will? What you can do to avoid probate—and whether it is worth doing?

Here are the answers to these, and many more, questions about wills. This information could be among the most important you'll ever receive. Your will is the only legal procedure that grants you the right, with certain limitations, to pass on your possessions the way *you* want to pass them on. It is a right enforced by statute in each of the fifty states.

You also have the right *not* to make a will. But if you choose that right, you not only lose your freedom to dispose of your property your way, but you could also bring distress and unhappiness to your loved ones. When you don't make a will, the state, in effect, makes it for you. Are you willing to have the cold, rigid formulas of the "statutes of descent" determine who gets what? To have impersonal bureaucrats control the welfare of your family? To have your spouse and children wait for months and months before the state releases *your* property to them? If you haven't made a will, now's the time to do it.

This chapter is a simple briefing on what you should know before you ask your lawyer to draw up your will. It will help you work with him faster, more easily, and more effectively.

WHY YOU SHOULD HAVE A WILL, AND WHAT HAPPENS WHEN YOU DON'T

· *Aren't wills only for rich people?*

Of course not. No matter how few your personal possessions are, you have the right to dispose of them as you wish (with certain limitations). Besides, if you take the time to write down all the property you possess, you'll find you're richer than you think. Consider too this fact of life, however unpleasant: Each year about fifty thousand Americans are accident fatalities. Insurance compensation for your accidental death could be substantial. You might be able to distribute some of it your way with a will.

· *What happens to my possessions if I die without a will?*

They're distributed by the state under its statutes of descent—written laws governing the disposition of an individual's property after death. When you die without a will, you are said to die intestate.

· *If the state distributes my possessions for me when I die intestate, why should I bother with a will?*

When you make a will:

- *You* can dispose of your property as you wish (with certain restrictions), not as the state decrees.
- *You* can name the person to administer your estate—the executor, if a man; the executrix, if a woman. (In some states, "executor" applies to both men and women, or the term "administrator" is used.) Should you die intestate, state law, not you, determines who qualifies. Your estate consists of your property at the time of your death which must be distributed in accordance with either your will or the intestacy laws of your state.
- *You* can spare your loved ones the additional costs of administering your estate when you die intestate; and you can leave more of your estate to them by applying legal

methods for lowering estate and inheritance taxes, which no state will do for you.

In short, when you make a will, you gain maximum control over the distribution of your property at minimum expense.

· If I die intestate, how will the state distribute my possessions?

It will vary from state to state, but there is no variant likely to correspond to what you have in mind. Some examples:
You die intestate, but—

- You would like your spouse to receive all or the bulk of your estate. However, in most states, your spouse receives only one-third to one-half of your estate. In some other states, your spouse and your children share equally; so if you have three children, your spouse receives only one-quarter of your estate. And in still other states, your spouse may have to share a substantial part of your estate with your parents.
- You would like your children to share in your estate. However, in some community-property states (see page 178) your spouse receives the bulk of your estate, and your children receive nothing.
- You would like a larger part of your estate to go to your handicapped child than to your normal children. However, no state makes provisions for special treatment of handicapped offspring; all children share equally in the estate.
- You would like your spouse to manage the shares of your estate that go to your children under eighteen years of age. However, in some states, the court may appoint a guardian who is not your spouse to handle that financial management. The guardian could be a stranger, or a member of the family whom you distrust. In most instances, though, a parent of the child, who could be your spouse, is appointed guardian.
- You would like your spouse, in the event he or she is appointed by the court as guardian of your minor children, to manage your bequests to them without interference by anybody. However, in most states, your spouse, as guardian, would have to obtain permission from the court before

spending any portion of the children's share of the estate on their behalf—even when the expenditures are for essentials such as food, clothing, and education. Moreover, the court would require an annual accounting of the money earned from your children's share of the estate, and the money spent. In essence, your spouse would be permitted to manage your minor children's share of the estate only under the scrutiny and approval of the court.

- You would like part of your estate to go to relatives other than your immediate family, or to friends, charities, and educational and other institutions. However, no state normally makes this kind of distribution.
- You would like your estate to be distributed as rapidly as possible to provide funds for your survivors. However, it normally takes longer for distribution to be made when you die intestate than when you die testate (with a will).

· My husband died intestate in an auto accident. His estate was paid $100,000 in liability insurance. According to state law, I will receive only one-third of that. The rest of the money will be divided among my four children. I'm fifty-five, and have no employment skills, and my husband left me nothing. Can I obtain an exception to the law, and have the state distribute most of my children's share to me?

Intestacy laws are rigid, and no exceptions are granted except in rare cases. The chances are the court will not consider your case rare. Had your husband made a will leaving all or the bulk of his estate to you, this sad situation might have been avoided. However, had you lived in another state, with your children not dependent on you, you would have received the full $100,000 even if he died intestate.

· I'm a homemaker. My husband has a will. Why is it necessary for me to have one?

For these reasons:

- You have property—jewelry, furs, clothing, heirlooms, and more—and if you die without a will, the state will distribute that property, not you.
- You will inherit at least a portion of your husband's prop-

erty, and you need a will to distribute that property according to your wishes. If you wait until after your husband's death to make a will, you risk the chance of dying before you do so.

- You and your husband may die simultaneously (in an auto accident, for example), and if you are the sole beneficiary of your husband's will and leave no will of your own, the situation is the same as if your husband had died intestate: You will not have control over the distribution of the assets.

- You would like to choose the guardian for your minor children in case of your death—your husband or any other person you select. When you make a will, *you* may be able to do it. When you don't make a will, the state may appoint a guardian not of your choice.

Every adult, man or woman, married or single, should have a will.

WHAT YOU CAN INCLUDE IN YOUR WILL

· *Are there any of my assets I can pass on without a will?*

Yes. Common ones include benefits from your life insurance policies and from pensions that continue after your death, U.S. Savings Bonds, and most jointly held property. These assets pass directly to the designated beneficiaries, or, in case of most jointly owned property, to the survivor. For other ways of passing on your possessions without a will, see the section on avoiding probate, beginning on page 177.

· *Can any of my assets that I don't have to include in my will be included?*

Yes, you can include benefits from your life insurance policies. Do so on advice of your attorney and accountant to gain a tax advantage.

· *Is it legal for my wife and me to leave everything to each other?*

Yes. You can draw up a will designating her as your sole beneficiary; and she can reciprocate by drawing up a will designating you as her sole beneficiary. These wills, called reciprocal wills, are executed at the same time. Reciprocal wills often specify that the children shall share all of the estate when the surviving spouse dies.

· *My wife and I have reciprocal wills. Can she make a new will after my death, disinheriting the children?*

Usually, yes. Normally, anyone can change his own will anytime before his death. If, however, both parties to a reciprocal will make an agreement, in writing, not to change the will, then the will becomes a mutual will, or joint will, if combined in one document. If you had a mutual will, your wife *could* make a new will, but the children could contest it, and very likely win. Courts have decided repeatedly that one party cannot alter the intent of mutual wills without the consent (usually written) of the other party.

· *Can I cut my wife out of my will?*

Maybe, if she has abandoned you (and, in some states, you've been subsequently divorced), and under certain other circumstances in accordance with state law. When these circumstances do not occur, you cannot completely disinherit your wife. Here are your wife's rights to your estate after your death:

If you're in a state that recognizes the *right of dower*, your wife is entitled to the use of at least one-third of your real estate as long as she lives. Right-of-dower states include Alabama, Delaware, Massachusetts, Ohio and Wisconsin. Check with your attorney.

In most other states, your wife is entitled to choose between her inheritance as prescribed in your will or one-third to one-half of your estate. This is called a *right of election*.

However, if you're intent on minimizing the legacy to your wife, you can under the 1981 federal tax law set up a qualified terminal interest property trust (a QTIP), which grants your wife only the income from the fund (and still takes advantage of the marital deduction for estate tax purposes). After your wife's death, the principal then goes to a beneficiary designated in your will.

Such a trust might satisfy your wife's minimum rights in your estate.

· Can I cut my husband out of my will?

Yes, in much the same manner as he can cut you out (see preceding question). In most states, your husband enjoys the same rights of dower or election as you do. In other states, he enjoys the *rights of curtesy*—an interest in your real estate after your death, provided you and he together have had a child during your marriage. The amount of that interest varies in each of the rights-of-curtesy states: Alabama, Arkansas, and Vermont.

· I'm a man in my late fifties. I'm planning to marry again, but I want to preserve my estate for my children. Can I do it in a will?

No, but you can with a premarital agreement. Have your spouse release all rights to your property while you're living and after your death. If your spouse is well off, she's likely to request a similar release from you. If she's not well off, she may ask you to provide in the agreement for a lump settlement and/or guaranteed periodic payments. (Remember, a premarital agreement is not limited to property. It can include all aspects of married life.)

· Can I cut my children out of my will?

Yes. Except in Louisiana, you don't have to leave your children anything. However, if you don't expressly state in your will that your children are excluded from your bequest, the court may presume the exclusion was an oversight, and the children could make a claim on your estate. When excluding children from your will, it is prudent to include a sentence like this:

"I intentionally make no provision for my children whether living now or born after the execution of my will."

The phrase "or born after the execution of the will" is important because "after-born" children in most states inherit as if you had died intestate; a portion of your estate goes to them unless you indicate otherwise.

· I have collected many trinkets and items of jewelry over the years, and I would like them to go to several different people. Does every item have to be listed in my will?

Usually, if you want someone to have a particular item, you must so specify in your will. In some states, however, you may keep a list of smaller items with your will with specific instructions about them, and mention only the list in your will. This is called *incorporation by reference.* Before you attempt to do this, consult your lawyer to make sure your state allows this procedure.

HOW TO MAKE A WILL

· How old must I be before I can make a will?

You must be at least fourteen in Georgia, sixteen in Louisiana, and nineteen in Alaska. Almost all other states require that you be at least eighteen. But some states make exceptions to these age requirements if you are under the specified age and married, or have personal property (not real estate) you would like to dispose of after your death.

· Can I draw up my own will?

Yes, if it's simple. But it's prudent to have your will, no matter how simple, drawn up by your lawyer, since failure to comply with a single technicality may invalidate it. It is especially important to consult your lawyer if you wish to disinherit a spouse or child, designate a guardian of your child other than the child's parent, or include unusual provisions or instructions in your will. What's more, some states make probate easier and quicker when a lawyer prepares your will.

· Is there a special form for making a will?

No, except in California, Maine, and possibly in the state of Louisiana. All that is necessary is that you express your instructions clearly. Your will need not be phrased in legal language. However, the use of specific legal phraseology which has been accepted by the courts over the years is advisable. This is another sound reason for having your lawyer draw up your will.

· *How do I prepare a simple will?*

This paragraph-by-paragraph outline can help you.

PARAGRAPH 1. Identify yourself by giving your name and address. Then declare that you are old enough to make a will, that you are sane and in control of your faculties, that the document is your last will and testament, and that you revoke all previous wills and codicils (amendments or additions to your wills) if you have made any. *Example:*

"I, George Stevens, residing at 3049 South Hayworth Boulevard, Santa Monica, California 90035, being of full age and sound mind, declare this document to be my last Will and Testament and at this time revoke all my previous wills and codicils."

PARAGRAPH 2. Direct your executor or executrix to pay promptly your undisputed debts, taxes, the cost of administering your estate, and your funeral expenses. You may also provide instructions concerning your funeral. *Example:*

"I direct my executrix, whom I name later in this document, to pay my undisputed debts, taxes, the costs of administering my estate, and my funeral expenses as soon after my death as is practical. I direct that my remains be buried in the Stevens family plot at the Fairlawn Cemetery in Los Angeles, California."

Keep this in mind: The expenses specified in the foregoing paragraph have first claim against your estate. Your executor regards all of your estate (cash and other property) as a single pool of assets and makes the first-claim payments from it (unless you give other specific instructions). The assets that remain after payment of first-claim expenses are then distributed according to your wishes.

PARAGRAPH 3. Give detailed instructions concerning specific bequests, including whether you desire your estate to assume any of the taxes associated with the legacy which your beneficiary otherwise might have to pay. *Example:*

"I give and bequeath the following: 1. To my only son, Eugene Stevens, 1212 Old Plantation Drive, New Athens, Georgia, who is of full age, the sum of $10,000. So that he will receive this amount in full, I charge my estate with the payment of all estate and transfer taxes associated with this legacy, and I direct that the payment be made from my residual estate. 2. To my sister-in-law, Alice Parker Stevens, 378 Central Park South, New York, New York, 500 preferred shares of International Electronic Medical Supplies, Inc."

Keep this in mind: In this example, the first bequest is known as a general legacy, since the money can be drawn from any part of your estate. The second bequest is known as a specific legacy, since it comes from a particular part of the estate. General and specific legacies are ordinarily paid before residual legacies. Residual legacies are paid from your residual estate—the remaining assets after first-claim expenses and general and specific bequests have been paid. Since the residual estate usually goes to your principal heir (your spouse, for example), it is prudent to limit the amount bequeathed in general and specific legacies to avoid sharply reducing your residual estate in the event of financial reverses.

PARAGRAPH 4. Provide instructions for the disposition of your residual estate. Keep this in mind: You can direct that all taxes be paid from your residual estate. That will permit all specific and general legatees (the persons receiving a legacy), as well as all persons receiving joint or trust property (see page 177) to receive the full amount you provide for them. *Example:*

"All estate, inheritance, and other death taxes of any nature, payable by reason of my death, shall be paid out of my residual estate as an expense of administration. I further give and bequeath my residual estate to my wife, Amelia Prescott Stevens, 3049 South Hayworth Boulevard, Santa Monica, California, for her absolute use forever."

PARAGRAPH 5. Appoint the executor or executrix of your estate, and direct that no bond be required to assure proper handling of the estate by him or her (otherwise, your estate would bear the cost of the bond). *Example:*

"I appoint my wife, Amelia Prescott Stevens, as executrix of this will, and I direct that no bond or security shall be required of her."

Keep this in mind: The job of the executor or executrix is to gather your disposable assets and distribute them in accordance with the terms of your will. But this job can be carried out by a nonprofessional only if your will is simple. For advice on appointing a professional executor or executrix to handle a complicated will, and the fee involved, consult your lawyer.

PARAGRAPH 6. Indicate that you know the contents of the will, add the date, and sign the document. *Example* (it is advisable to use the following legal language):

"In witness whereof, I have hereunto set my hand and affixed my seal this eighteenth day of May, 1985. George Stevens [signature].

PARAGRAPH 7. This is the *attestation clause*, a statement by witnesses that they heard you say the document you are about to sign is your will, that you requested them to be witnesses, that they saw you sign the document in the presence of all witnesses, and that each witness signed the document in your presence and in the presence of all the other witnesses. The addresses of the witnesses are given. *Example* (it is advisable to use the following legal language; the term "testator" which appears in this example means "the person making the will"):

"Signed, sealed, published, and declared by the above named Testator, George Stevens, as and for his last Will and Testament, in the presence of each of us, who, at his request, in his presence, and in the presence of each other, have hereunto subscribed our names as attesting witnesses, the day and year last written above. Charles Legree [signature], 1001 Shirley Street, Santa Monica, California 90035; William Eagle [signature], 61–B Aldergate Road, Santa Monica, California 90035; Mary Carr [signature], 43–27 East Plainview Place, Santa Monica, California 90035."

Keep this in mind: Since the witnesses will have to be identified after your death when the will is probated, it is advisable, but not legally required, to print or type the names of the witnesses below their signatures. Also, the attestation ceremony described in Paragraph 7 must be adhered to without deviation: You must say in the presence of all the witnesses that this is your will; you must request them to be witnesses; you must sign the document in the presence of all the witnesses; and each witness must sign the document in your presence and in the presence of the other witnesses. If there are several pages to your will, each page must be initialed by you and your witnesses during the same ceremony. Finally, do *not* sign more than one document. If you do sign more than one, all must be found and submitted to the court in order to admit your will to probate.

· *How many witnesses do I need?*

Most states require two, the others three (Connecticut, Louisiana, Maine, Massachusetts, New Hampshire, South Carolina, and Vermont).

· *Are my witnesses required to know the contents of my will?*

No. But they must know that the document is your will.

· *I don't want a typist to know the contents of my will. Can I write it out in longhand?*

Certainly. But make sure it is legible. And don't include any typewritten, printed, or stamped materials. That could void the will. A will made out in your own handwriting is called a holographic will. It is valid without the required witnesses in the following states: Alaska, Arizona, Arkansas, California, Idaho, Kentucky, Louisiana, Mississippi, Montana, Nevada, North Carolina, North Dakota, Oklahoma, South Dakota, Tennessee, Texas, Utah, Virginia, West Virginia, and Wyoming.

· *Can't I just* tell *people how I want my possessions to be distributed after my death without all the red tape of writing out a will?*

You can make a valid oral will (called a noncupative will), but only under the following conditions:

- If you're terminally ill, limit your bequests to a small amount of personal property, and make your statement to two witnesses. (Your statement must then be put into writing in from three to thirty days, and signed by the persons who witnessed your statement.) Although about two-thirds of the states recognize a will made under these conditions, this kind of will so severely restricts your right to make bequests (maximums range from $50 to $500 according to the state) that it cannot be regarded as a realistic substitute for a written will.

- If you're a member of the armed services in possible-risk duty (such as going overseas), or a member of the merchant marine at sea, and make your statement to two witnesses. A will made under these conditions is recognized by most states and may be used to distribute all your property, but it has drawbacks similar to those of oral wills made by terminally ill civilians.

HOW TO CHANGE YOUR WILL

· *How long do I have to change my will?*

As long as you live. Your will does not go into effect until you die.

· *How many times can I change my will?*

As many times as you like.

· *Can I change my will by just writing in new instructions?*

No. In some instances that could make your entire will invalid (even though in some other instances it would have no effect whatsoever). The same holds true if you do any of the following:

- Cross out, erase, or alter the text in any way
- Replace a page with a new one
- Delete a page
- Rearrange the position of pages
- Place any instructions after your signature
- Make stray holes in the document

In short, any attempted alterations to the original document may be disastrous.

• *Is there a specific legal way to change my will?*

To make a valid change, you must add a codicil (amendment) to your will in a manner approved by the court. Here's an example:

"CODICIL TO WILL. I, George Stevens, residing at 3049 South Hayworth Boulevard, Santa Monica, California 90035, declare this to be a Codicil to my Last Will and Testament, dated the eighteenth day of May, 1985.

"PARAGRAPH 1: At this time, I revoke Paragraph 3 of my Will, and direct that the property described in that paragraph shall go to The Society for Nutritional Research, Inc., 1023 Avenue of the Americas, New York, New York 10020.

"PARAGRAPH 2: In all other respects, I confirm the provisions of this Will. In witness whereof, I have hereunto set my hand and affixed my seal to this Codicil to my Last Will and Testament this third day of January, 1987. George Stevens [signature]

"The foregoing Codicil, consisting of this page, was this third day of January, 1987, signed, sealed, and declared by the Testator as and for a Codicil to his Last Will and Testament dated the eighteenth day of May, 1985, in the presence of each of us, who, at his request, in his presence, and in the presence of each other, have hereunto subscribed our names as attesting witnesses. Sally Hallman [signature], 3 West 4th Street, Santa Monica, California 90035; Mary Lou Asner [signature], 3 West 4th Street, Santa Monica, California 90035; Mary Carr [signature], 43–27 East Plainview Place, Santa Monica, California 90035."

Keep this in mind: The "attestation ceremony" for a codicil is the same as for a will. Although the number of witnesses required for a codicil is the same as for a will, the witnesses need not be the same people who witnessed the will. However, since it is easier for your executor or executrix to locate when necessary during probate three witnesses rather than four, five, or six, the use of the same witnesses for both documents is preferable.

• *When do I write a codicil to a will, and when do I make a new will?*

You could write a codicil if the changes are few or minor. If they're extensive or major, write a new will that revokes the old. It also may be advisable to make a new will if the witnesses have disappeared or died. Consult your lawyer.

WHAT HAPPENS TO YOUR WILL AFTER YOUR DEATH

· *Shouldn't my will be easily accessible in case of my death?*

Yes. Keep it in a safe place known to your executor or executrix, or to a trusted friend or member of your family. In some states it's not wise to keep it in your safe deposit box, even if your spouse has keys to it as well, because your box may be sealed on your death, and may only be opened when your executor or executrix obtains a court order—a time-consuming procedure. You may also consider having your lawyer file it in the surrogate's court. Keep this in mind: Except in very rare circumstances, only the original document with the original signatures may be used in court.

· *How is my will processed after I die?*

Your lawyer submits it to the proper court with proof (your witnesses' testimony) that it has been executed properly. The court then decides whether the will submitted is your final, authoritative, and official will; and whether it complies with the statutory requirements of the state.

This procedure is known as probate. Once the validity of the will has been established by the court—that is to say, once the will has been probated—your executor or executrix has the legal power to act. The instructions contained in your will are then carried out.

· *Suppose my daughter regards her legacy as unfair. Is there anything she can do about it?*

When a will is submitted for probate, the heirs, next of kin, and beneficiaries under a previous will can contest it. The court then holds a hearing and decides whether the will is legal. In this case, "unfairness" is no grounds for having the will ruled illegal. Your daughter would have to show that your will is invalid because of your mental inability to make one, because of the way it was made, or because of mistake, fraud, or undue influence. In any event, contesting a will can be a costly, long-drawn-out affair no matter what the result. But there are ways lawyers can minimize the chances of a will contest; if you think one might arise, consult your lawyer.

• How long does it take to probate an uncontested will?

About six months on the average, although some probates can take a year. If you're in a state that operates under the Uniform Probate Code (check with your lawyer), your will may be probated in from two to six months.

• I'd like my beneficiaries to receive their bequests rapidly. Can I avoid probate?

Yes. Other reasons some people would like to avoid probate are to cut court costs and to avoid publicity (probate records are available to the public). In the following section, you'll find out how you can avoid probate.

HOW TO AVOID PROBATE

• What's the basic strategy for avoiding probate?

Once a will is made, it must be probated to become effective; so the basic strategy for avoiding probate is to make use of devices for passing on your possessions *without a will*. Here is a description of those devices—joint tenancy, gifts made before your death, and trusts—and how you can put them to work for you.

Joint Tenancy

• What is joint tenancy?

It's a legal term for two or more people holding property together. There are three kinds of joint tenancy: *joint tenancy with the right of survivorship, tenancy by the entirety*, and *tenancy in common.* (Tenancy by the entirety applies only to real estate.)

· *After my husband dies, does joint tenancy pass the house to me without the need of a will?*

That depends on the kind of joint tenancy under which you took title to your house. Both joint tenancy with the right of survivorship and tenancy by the entirety pass the house to you without the need of a will. But in the absence of a will, tenancy in common passes your husband's share of the house to his heirs-at-law, with distribution determined by the state. Unless you're the only heir-at-law, you're not likely to become the sole owner. (But you would have at least one-third to one-half the estate.)

· *Since our house passes to me on the death of my husband whether we took title under joint tenancy with the right of survivorship or tenancy by the entirety, does it matter which form of tenancy appears in the deed?*

Yes it does.

Under *joint tenancy with the right of survivorship,* your husband while he's alive can dispose of his interest in the house without your consent. You could end up with only your interest in the house. However, should your husband dispose of his interest, the house would remain in your physical possession after his death. (You have the same right to dispose of your interest in the house while you're alive as your husband has to dispose of his.)

Under *tenancy by the entirety,* your husband while he's alive *cannot* dispose of his interest in the house without your consent. You're assured of becoming sole owner on his death. (Similarly, while you're alive you cannot dispose of your interest in the house without your husband's consent.)

· *Tenancy by the entirety seems like the best kind of joint tenancy for passing on our house to each other without a will. How do we acquire that kind of tenancy?*

In some states, the joint tenancy of a house (or any real estate) by husband and wife is regarded automatically as a tenancy by the entirety.

But in community property states, and in many other states, tenancy by the entirety has been abolished. In some of those states, the house passes to you. But in some others, only your interest in the house does; and your spouse's interest is disposed of by will or the statutes of intestacy. Ask your lawyer whether the state in which you live has abolished tenancy by the entirety; and if it has, whether your state's statutes permit the house to pass directly to you without probate. (Community property states are Arizona, California, Idaho, Louisiana, Nevada, New Mexico, Texas, and Washington.)

• *My husband and I jointly own a bank account and some stocks and bonds. Can they be passed on to each of us without a will?*

Depends. If your bank account is in a savings bank, usually yes; if it's in a commercial bank, usually no. Whether you can pass on your stocks and bonds depends on the wording on the paper. Check with your broker. *Caution*: The listed joint owner of a joint account has every right to use the money in the account, and has the absolute right to the funds after your death. So never list a joint owner on your account if you only want that person to help out should you be "unable to get to the bank."

• *We regard all our household property as jointly owned. Will it pass to me on my husband's death?*

No. That property is held by you as tenants in common. Should your husband omit instructions for the distribution of household property in his will (or should he die intestate), you may have to share that property with other members of your family. Your husband would find himself in the same situation should you die before he does.

• *How would you evaluate joint tenancy as a means of avoiding probate?*

Through joint tenancy you can pass on some of your estate without a will. But if you desire all your wishes concerning your estate to be carried out after your death, joint ownership is no substitute for a will.

Gifts Made Before Your Death

· *Instead of making my bequests in a will, I plan to give the money away before I die. Any drawbacks?*

Just one. But it's a big one. The federal tax laws, and the tax laws of several states, regard such bequests as gifts, and gifts may be taxable (if they're large enough). Moreover, it's you—not the recipient—who pays the gift taxes. If your estate is large, you may pay more in gift taxes than in estate taxes. (However, done properly, gift giving may reduce estate taxes. Work it out with your lawyer and accountant.)

· *But can't I give some gifts tax-free?*

True. Under federal tax laws, you're permitted to give away up to $10,000 a year tax-free to each of as many individuals as you choose. If you and your spouse are making the gifts, the tax-free ceiling is $20,000 to each recipient. You're also permitted to give gifts tax-free without a ceiling to any individuals for school tuition or medical expenses, provided you pay the school, doctor, hospital, or other medical service directly.

· *Are bequests made before death a realistic way to avoid probate?*

Whether you want to lose control of some of your assets while you're still alive is a decision you must make. Certainly you're not likely to give away all of your assets; and those that you do retain should be covered by a will. Before you make bequests during your lifetime, have a talk with your lawyer.

Trusts

· *What is a trust?*

It's a device for transferring your assets (title to your property) to another person or other persons to hold in trust for you or any other person or persons you designate (your beneficiaries).

· What is a trustee?

The person or company you designate to hold your assets in trust. The trustee invests your assets and otherwise manages them for the best advantage of your beneficiaries.

· How can a trust be used to avoid probate?

You can set up a trust in your lifetime (called a *living trust* or *inter vivos trust*) naming a beneficiary or beneficiaries to inherit the trust after your death.

· Don't I lose control of my assets during my lifetime when I set up a living trust?

Yes and no.

Yes, when you set up an *irrevocable* living trust. This is an agreement which cannot be broken, and you have no say in the management of your money.

No, when you set up a *semirevocable* living trust or a *revocable* living trust. A semirevocable living trust can be canceled after a certain length of time and under specified conditions— and that gives you some control of your assets. A revocable living trust can be canceled or changed any time—and that gives you a great deal of control over your assets.

· I want to set up a living revocable trust to avoid probate. How do I do it?

Follow these three steps:

1. Have your bank (or trust company) set up the trust for you.
2. Appoint the bank (or trust company) as trustee.
3. Include a provision in the trust stating that on your death, the assets are to pass to your beneficiary or beneficiaries.

· Can I appoint myself trustee of a living revocable trust and retain complete control of my assets?

In some states the courts have ruled that a trust over which you have complete control is not a trust at all. It is regarded as a will and must go through probate. Consult your lawyer concerning whether appointing yourself trustee to your own living trust is acceptable in your state.

· *A living revocable trust looks like a sound way to avoid probate. Any drawbacks?*

Yes.

- If you have to rely on a bank or trust company as a trustee, you'll have to pay a fee. In about five or six years, the fee could equal the costs of probate; and after that, your living revocable trust could be more expensive than probate.
- A living revocable trust can be challenged in court just as a will is challenged. Should the court find evidence of mental incompetence, fraud, duress, or undue influence, the trust can be set aside.
- Your beneficiaries can experience delays in receiving their inheritance. In most states, creditors have six to eight months to make claims against your estate; and banks will not ordinarily release your assets until all debts have been paid.
- You gain no tax advantage with a revocable trust. (But irrevocable and semirevocable trusts can have significant tax advantages.)
- Some of your property cannot be included in the trust (your clothes, your personal effects, and your car, for example). A will would be necessary to cover your nontrust possessions.
- Semirevocable and revocable living trusts may be regarded as gifts and taxed accordingly. What's more, if you retain sufficient control over the gifts, they may also be regarded as part of your estate and taxed as such.

· *Is there any trust other than a living trust with which I can avoid probate?*

Yes. It's called a *Totten trust* or a *bank-account trust*. When you set up a bank account, indicate to the bank officer that you would like it to be "in trust to" and the name of the beneficiary to whom your account will pass upon your death. (This type of account is sometimes called a P.O.D. or Pay on Death account; it is frequently used with deposits of U.S. Savings Bonds.)

Advantage: You can control your money completely during your lifetime. Disadvantage: You can't place all your estate in a bank account.

• *Do I need to set up some sort of trust to soften the impact of estate taxes?*

Not if you're leaving everything to your spouse. Under the 1981 federal tax law the marital exemption is 100 percent—that is to say, none of the assets you leave your spouse are taxable by the federal government. (The state may impose a tax.)

Moreover, you can leave substantial amounts free from estate taxes to beneficiaries other than your spouse. When the marital exemption does not apply, the amount of your estate exempt from federal tax in 1985 is $400,000; in 1986, $500,000; and in 1987, $600,000.

Should you have an estate valued higher than the tax-exempt ceiling, or if you contemplate your surviving spouse having such an estate, irrevocable and semirevocable trusts as well as testamentary trusts can help cut estate costs. Testamentary trusts are those that become effective after your death, and instructions for setting them up must be included in your will. (There is a large variety of testamentary trusts, and the selection and application of the right ones for you is best left to your lawyer, accountant, and estate planner. When you opt for a testamentary trust, you can make sizable tax gains, but you cannot avoid probate.)

• *I wish to avoid probate with a living trust. Can I set one up so that my daughter who is now sixteen receives only the income from the trust until she is thirty-five, and then the principal?*

Yes, and you can do it with a testamentary trust as well. Just include your specific instructions in the trust agreement. Your lawyer, your banker, or an officer of the trust company can help you.

• *Can my lawyer arrange for me to avoid probate?*

Yes, your lawyer can combine elements of joint tenancy, gifts before death, and trusts to pass on your estate without a will.

· *Should I avoid probate?*

Ask your lawyer the following questions, then decide:

- Is avoiding probate practical? (You may have to give away your car and your jewelry before your death.)
- Will I save money? (When you count up all the fees involved, probate may be cheaper.)
- Will I speed up the distribution of my assets? (Without probate, the distribution may take longer than with probate.)
- Will I avoid publicity? (Yes. But even though probate records are public, it's not likely that your probate record will be published in your local newspaper.)
- Will I bypass estate taxes? (No. Avoiding probate does not avoid estate taxes, nor does it even lower them except when certain trusts are applied.)

You may find that probate isn't so bad after all—and that a will is the best way to dispose of your property after your death.

10

Man and Woman: Your Rights in Marriage and When You Live Together

- What you should know about getting married
- What you should know about being married: rights and obligations, who owns what, children, the battered wife
- What you should know about breaking up: annulment, separation, divorce
- What you should know about living together unmarried

Legal attitudes in a democracy reflect changing social attitudes. "You've come a long way, baby," joyously proclaims a long-running national ad which extols the triumphant progress of female liberation. It's a liberation that, among other things, elevated women in this nation to an equal sexual status with men, and, as a consequence, revolutionized our legal attitudes toward marriage and divorce, and toward "living in sin," a phrase now as archaic as petticoats, corsets, and maidenly blushes.

The basic changes have been profound.

Take marriage. Just a few decades ago, statutes set rigorous and extensive patterns of rights and obligations for the married couple, with rights heavily weighted toward the husband, and obligations toward the wife. Today the balance has been so equalized that in many states the words "husband" and "wife" have been replaced in statutes with the unisexual "spouse." Spousal rights, no longer the exclusive domain of state legislatures, are now largely determined by the married couple themselves—friends, lovers, and, in the eyes of the law, equal partners. In fact, in the eight community property states, statutes sanction marriage *as* a partnership. In other states it's a relationship by contract, always implied, and now with increasing frequency expressed in formal contracts drawn up by lawyers and enforceable in the courts.

Take divorce. "Young people cannot imagine the lurid aura that once surrounded a woman who was a 'divorcée,'" comments Marvin Mitchelson, a celebrated lawyer who specializes in man-and-woman relations. "Adultery was the only possible ground [for divorce in some states]....Proving adultery meant hiring private detectives to shadow the suspected wife or husband, then breaking into the errant spouse's love nest with a photographer to snap compromising pictures. In other states even if there were no requirements to prove adultery, there was still the legal problem of determining who was 'at fault'—the decisive factor affecting the amount of alimony and the division of property.... The [present] easy grounds [for divorce] and no-fault system of divorce [in some states] mean that anyone can go to court and get a divorce with very little effort. Not only is it easy, but there's almost no stigma attached."

Mitchelson's statement may exaggerate the ease of divorce (it is still not easy in states requiring one of the partners to be "at fault," and even in no-fault states, there may be complications), but by and large, it is certainly easier to break the ties of wedlock now than it ever has been. Witness the sharply rising divorce rate since the onset of easier divorces in the 1970s. Today about one out of two marriages end in a divorce.

Take living together. Unheard-of before the 1960s, and regarded then by the mainstream population as a scandalous aberration of the hippie generation, it is now a way of American sex life practiced by more than a million couples. In theory, living together is a design for living for two equal and independent people of the opposite sex who have made a moral—not a legal—commitment to stay together for sexual companionship. But in practice, most live-in partners are not equal; the man usually has the better or even the dominant income. They are not independent; the woman, who usually has the lesser income or no income at all, is dependent on the man. And they're not bound by the moral commitment, which turns into a no-strings-attached arrangement when one of the partners wishes to leave. A dependent woman live-in partner is frequently left not only emotionally but financially bereft. Understanding that, the landmark decision in California's *Marvin* v. *Marvin* palimony case held that if there was a contract—the equivalent of a marriage contract—between the live-in partners, the deserted partner can bring suit to enforce it. The contract could be implied.

This chapter introduces you to your legal rights in marriage and living together from the first yes to the final breakup *as of today*. Those words are emphasized because the law, as it is affected by, and as it affects, the sexual revolution is in a state of flux. But the basics presented here are not likely to suffer any more than superficial changes, and they can remain your guide, in tandem with your lawyer's advice, to your marital and live-in problems.

WHAT YOU SHOULD KNOW ABOUT GETTING MARRIED

• *From the legal point of view, what's a marriage?*

It's a special kind of contract. It's a *contract* because it specifies certain rights and obligations to both parties according to state law. It's *special* because other contracts can be dissolved by mutual consent of the parties involved, but marriage can be dissolved only by the sovereign power of the state—that is to say, through a divorce or annulment.

• *Do I have to sign a contract when I marry?*

Not in the ordinary sense, but in general you are required to go through certain formalities, which taken together constitute the marriage contract. These formalities include applying for a marriage license in a marriage license bureau, circuit court, or other local agency, and signing the application form; meeting the state's age and other requirements for obtaining a marriage license, including in most states certification by means of a blood test that both parties are free of communicable syphilis; obtaining the license; and solemnizing the marriage within a certain time with a ceremony conducted by a qualified clergyman, a judge, or a person appointed by the court (a clerk in the marriage license bureau, for example).

You can also enter into the more familiar form of contract. This is done mainly to help prevent future property disputes by putting in writing just who is going to own what in your marriage. It can also contain provisions concerning all aspects of your marriage, even including who sleeps where and when. Such a contract drawn up before marriage is called a premarital or antenuptial contract; after marriage, it's called a postmarital or postnuptial contract.

· *What are some of the provisions commonly found in premarital contracts?*

- Agreement on keeping each spouse's property and income separate
- Agreement on sharing expenses for child care and home maintenance
- Agreement on a predetermined financial settlement in case of a divorce
- Agreement on child custody and visitation rights in case of divorce
- Agreement to divide household and child-care chores
- Agreement to full disclosure of each spouse's sex experiences prior to marriage
- Agreement to negotiate living arrangements prior to marriage (for example, how many times a month to have in-laws for dinner)
- Agreement on disposition of the estate after death of either spouse

Postmarital contracts contain similar provisions.

Marital contracts should be drawn by lawyers representing each partner, after each party has made full financial disclosure.

· *As a practical matter, can prenuptial contracts be enforced in the courts?*

So far as prenuptial contracts determine the day-to-day activities of the couple, *no*.

So far as prenuptial contracts determine the terms of the divorce settlement, *maybe*. Terms concerning child care and custody in particular are subject to modifications by the court.

So far as prenuptial contracts determine inheritances (such as a husband waiving his rights to his wife's estate), *yes*.

This answer applies to postmarital contracts as well.

· *What states do not require blood tests?*

Georgia, Maryland, Minnesota, Nevada, New York, South Carolina, and Washington.

· *Do state regulations prohibit certain kinds of marriages?*

Yes. Homosexual, incestuous, and bigamous marriages are prohibited in all states. Some states forbid the marriage of mental incompetents, alcoholics, drug addicts, and habitual criminals. Most states base their prohibitions on minimum age requirements and the results of mandatory blood tests. Thirty-two states prohibit marriages between first cousins.

· *How old must I be before I can get a marriage license without parental consent?*

If you're a man, the minimum age is sixteen in Colorado and Wyoming; seventeen in Mississippi and Oregon; twenty-one in Missouri, Oklahoma, and Utah; and eighteen in the other states.

If you're a woman, the minimum age is fifteen in Mississippi; sixteen in Minnesota and Rhode Island; seventeen in Oregon; twenty-one in Florida; and eighteen in other states.

· *With parental consent, how old must I be before I can get a marriage license?*

If you're a man, there is no minimum age in Mississippi. The minimum age is fourteen in Kansas, Massachusetts, Rhode Island, South Carolina, and Texas; fifteen in Idaho and Missouri; sixteen in Colorado, Connecticut, Hawaii, Illinois, Maine, Maryland, Minnesota, New York, North Carolina, Oklahoma,

Tennessee, Utah, Virginia, and Wyoming; seventeen in Washington; and eighteen in the other states.

If you're a woman, there is no minimum age in Mississippi. The minimum age is twelve in Kansas, Massachusetts, and Rhode Island; fourteen in Alabama, New York, Texas, and Utah; fifteen in Idaho, Missouri, and North Dakota; sixteen in Alaska, Colorado, Connecticut, Delaware, Florida, Georgia, Hawaii, Illinois, Louisiana, Maine, Maryland, Michigan, Minnesota, North Carolina, Ohio, Oklahoma, South Carolina, South Dakota, Tennessee, Vermont, Virginia, West Virginia, and Wyoming; seventeen in Oregon and Washington; and eighteen in other states.

· *In my state, we have to wait three days after we get the marriage license before we can marry. Do all states require such a long waiting period?*

Some states like yours have legislated "cooling-off" periods during which you and your intended can think things over.

But in the following states you can marry the moment your marriage license is in your hands: Alabama, Alaska, Arizona, California, Colorado, Idaho, Illinois, Iowa, Michigan, Nevada, South Carolina, South Dakota, Texas, Utah, Virginia, and Wyoming.

The lengths of time you have to wait in cooling-off states are: one day in South Carolina; one to four days in Delaware; two days in Maryland; three days in Arkansas, Florida, Georgia, Hawaii, Indiana, Kansas, Kentucky, Mississippi, Missouri, Nebraska, New Jersey, New York, Pennsylvania, Tennessee, Washington, and West Virginia; four days in Connecticut; five days in Maine, Massachusetts, Minnesota, Montana, New Hampshire, Ohio, Vermont, and Wisconsin; and seven days in Oregon.

· *I want to keep my maiden name after I'm married. Is that legal?*

Yes. In forty-eight states, all you have to do is continue to use it. But in Alabama, if you wish to use your maiden name after marriage, you'll have to fill out a special form; and in Hawaii, you'll have to sign your marriage certificate with the name you intend to use after marriage.

· *I'm about to be married. My maiden name is Turner; my fiancé's is Brown. After marriage, can I call myself Turner-Brown?*

Creating a new name on marriage by hyphenating, or otherwise combining, the birth names of husband and wife is generally permissible. Just assume the new name after the wedding and continue to use it.

· *If after I've taken my husband's name I want to change back to my maiden name, is there any legal action I must take?*

Not in most states. Just change your name on all your IDs and notify interested parties. In some states, you may have to go to court to have your name changed. If you run into difficulties, get in touch with the Center for a Woman's Own Name, 261 Kimberly, Barrington, IL 60301, or consult your lawyer.

· *I'm thinking of marrying a man who's in debt. I'll be bringing a considerable amount of money and property into the marriage. Will his creditors be able to seize any part of it?*

No, thanks to the Married Women's Property Acts. What's more, you won't be liable for any debts your husband incurs after your marriage, unless your funds and your husband's are commingled, or you've guaranted any of his debts. You may also be responsible for charges you've made on his credit cards.

· *I'm in debt for about $10,000. I've got about $10,000. Can I avoid payment by getting married and handing the money over to my husband?*

No. He's liable for your premarital debts up to the amount of money you give him. If you give him nothing, though, he's not liable for any of those debts.

· *We lied to obtain our marriage license, but since we were married in church we regard our marriage as valid. Are we right?*

You may not be. If you violated any of the state laws concerning establishing a valid marriage, even though a ceremony is conducted by a clergyman or other qualified official, you may not be legally married. Should your violation be brought to the attention of the court (by your spouse or your parents, for example), your marriage could be annulled. It's a good idea to check with your lawyer about *your* state's laws in this kind of case.

· *Is it true that even though we have a marriage license and go through with the ceremony, we're not married until we have sex relations?*

No. You're married after the completion of the ceremony.

WHAT YOU SHOULD KNOW ABOUT BEING MARRIED: RIGHTS AND OBLIGATIONS, WHO OWNS WHAT, CHILDREN, THE BATTERED WIFE
Rights and Obligations

· *What are my sexual rights in marriage?*

One spouse cannot deny sex to the other without good cause; but although it's the law, it's not enforceable (however, depending on the state, it may be grounds for divorce). Moreover, if you force sex on an unwilling spouse, that is considered rape in some states, and assault and battery in others. If you opt for adultery—sexual relations with someone other than your spouse—you're breaking the law in some states; but those states no longer enforce that law. Sex or no sex, fidelity or adultery, the law assumes that you will live with your spouse; but even *that's* not enforceable.

· *I'm a woman. What are my nonsexual rights in marriage?*

To begin with, the same civil rights as you have as an unmarried adult. Marriage does not curtail those rights. You can as an individual, for example, own property, obtain credit, negotiate and sign contracts, carry on business activities, and retain your earnings. In addition, marriage grants you certain rights in all states to your husband's estate after his death; and you have the right to share half of his assets acquired after marriage in community property states (see page 178). A man's nonsexual rights in marriage are the same as yours.

· *I'm a man. What are my nonsexual rights in marriage?*

Theoretically, the same as a woman's. But some legal experts contend that practically the law still grants the man a "financial upper hand."

· *After my marriage, I want to take care of my home, my husband, and my kids—period. Do I have an obligation to go to work to help support my family?*

No. The law recognizes your right to choose to be financially dependent on your husband. You're then known as a "dependent spouse," and you have no obligation to provide for your family's financial support as long as he continues to be the breadwinner. Similarly, if your husband chooses to play "Mr. Mom" and maintains the home while you go out and work, he becomes the dependent spouse, and you have to support him financially.

· *I'm a homemaker. My husband makes an excellent salary, but he scrimps on me. Is there anything I can do legally?*

There's a chance that the court may order your husband to maintain you in a style consistent with his financial ability. But there's an equal, and often a better, chance that the court will permit your husband to set his own standard of living for his family. Actually, all the law demands of your husband as far as you're concerned is that he prevent you from becoming a public charge (going on welfare, for example). The law is now sexually neutral, and would treat you in the same manner if you were the scrimping breadwinner and your husband the dependent spouse.

· *We both work. Since I share the financial burden with my husband, is he obligated to share the housekeeping burden with me?*

Not legally. That's something you have to work out together.

· We both work. I make more than my husband. Do I have to pay more of the expenses than he does?

The law simply says you have to support each other. How you do it is left up to you.

· Legally, who owns what in a marriage?

The question ordinarily doesn't come up unless there is a divorce. Then, there's no definitive answer until the parties agree on the division of property (they do this with a written statement called a *stipulation*) or the judge decides (he does this with an *order of judgment*). But, in advance of divorce, here are the broad outlines of who owns what as they apply in states either with or without community property laws (see page 179).

Who Owns What in States Without Community Property Laws

· I've always believed that the bride owned all the wedding presents. But my husband says we own them fifty-fifty. Who's right?

Neither you nor your husband. If your husband receives a present from his relatives that only he can use, he owns the gift; and if you receive a present from your relatives that only you can use, you own the gift. All other gifts are owned jointly.

· We've just been married, and we plan to buy a house. Can I sell half of it without my husband's consent?

It depends on which of the three types of joint tenancy is specified when you take title to your house. The answer is yes under joint tenancy with the right of survivorship or joint tenancy in common. It is no when you take title under tenancy by the entirety unless you obtain your husband's permission to sell. (For an explanation of these types of joint tenancy, see the discussion beginning on page 177.) Your husband's right to sell is also dependent on the type of joint tenancy under which you take title. The usual type of joint tenancy for a married couple is tenancy by the entirety.

• *The house is in my name. I want to sell it. My husband says I can't do it unless he agrees, and he won't agree. Can he stop me from making the sale?*

Yes, in some states. If the house is in both your names, it may be necessary to bring an action to partition the house to force a sale.

• *I brought my own furniture into the marriage. My husband says he owns half of it anyway. Is he right?*

No. Whatever property you bring into a marriage is yours. The same rule applies to the property your husband brings into a marriage.

• *My husband couldn't pay the rent. I paid it. I told him I want the money back from him when he can afford it. He says no way. Can I collect?*

No. When you (or your husband) use your money to pay a family expense, the law regards it as making a gift to the family. Gifts are not repayable.

• *My wife has run up some large bills for luxuries. Do I have to pay them?*

No, unless you gave her the right to incur debts in your name. If your wife is a chronic overspender, pay off her outstanding bills; then notify your credit sources that you are no longer responsible for her debts; and, where required by local laws, publish a notice to that effect in your local paper. A wife can take the same protective action against a spendthrift husband.

• *My wife runs an unincorporated business from our home. She contracts for services and supplies. Recently, she fell behind in payments and her creditors billed me. Must I pay?*

No. Neither spouse is responsible for the contractual obligations of the other unless they're for the purchase of items necessary for the family or home.

• *Suppose I'm convinced my husband is holding on to property that is rightly mine. Can I sue him?*

Yes. Any partner in a marriage can sue the other to establish property rights.

Who Owns What in States With Community Property Laws

• *What is "community property"?*

It's property, including earnings, acquired *after* marriage by the work and efforts of you or your spouse, or you and your spouse together. Each of you own an undivided half. ("Undivided" means neither spouse can individually sell, give away, or otherwise dispose of the property except in the event of divorce or the death of the other spouse.) Community property is recognized only in the eight community property states: Arizona, California, Idaho, Louisiana, Nevada, New Mexico, Texas, and Washington.

• *In a community property state does all property acquired after marriage become community property?*

Only the property, including earnings, acquired by the work and effort of you or your spouse, or you and your spouse together. Inheritances and gifts are, therefore, considered the property solely of the individual who receives them.

• *What about property acquired before marriage—can I retain it?*

Yes. It does not become community property.

• *Is there any way we can each own our own property in a community property state?*

Yes. You can separate the community property into individual property by means of a premarital or postmarital contract. But be sure to have your lawyer draw up the contract.

Children

· *Can I choose to use contraceptive devices without my husband's consent?*

Yes. It's your body, and in the opinion of many legal experts you can do what you wish with it. But warning: If you choose not to have a child, and your husband wasn't aware of your decision before you were married, he could have the marriage annulled.

· *Can I choose not to use contraceptive devices without my husband's consent?*

If you want a child, you have the right to bear one.

· *I want my husband in the delivery room when I have my child. He says no, and he says the hospital backs him up. What can I do?*

You can't force him to appear in the delivery room, even if it's in your prenuptial contract. As far as the hospital is concerned, once you've consented to specific treatment, the hospital and your doctor have the right to determine the procedures that are best for you and your child. They may admit your husband or they may not.

· *I want to have my baby at home with the help of a midwife, not a doctor. My husband objects on "legal grounds." Can he stop me?*

He can't stop you. But in some communities, if anything goes wrong during delivery, you may be charged with child abuse. If your midwife is not a doctor or a nurse, she may be charged with practicing medicine without a license. By and large, the law would like your baby to be delivered in a hospital by a doctor or by a nurse midwife (preferably licensed) working under the supervision of a doctor.

· *Our child was born before we married. Is she legitimate?*

Generally, only a child born after marriage is considered legitimate, even though it was conceived before marriage. Legitimacy is important if your child is to be entitled to his legal rights including financial support and inheritance. However, these days the courts tend to honor the claims of an illegitimate child as they would those of a legitimate one, as long as the husband admits to paternity.

· *My illegitimate child by another man is living with us. My husband says he doesn't have to support her. Is that true?*

That's true. As the natural mother, it's your responsibility to support and care for your child (an obligation you share with the natural father). In your case, it would have been a good idea to have your husband agree in a premarital contract to support or adopt your child.

· *Does an adopted child have the same rights as a legitimate child?*

Yes, provided the child is adopted legally. Adoption means "to take into one's own family *by legal process* and treat as one's own child."

· *We want to adopt a child. We've heard we must apply to an adoption agency. What's that?*

An agency that has children available for adoption. You make application to such an agency, and if you meet its standards of acceptance, which are high, you may be able to adopt a child. The agency takes care of all details. But according to the Washington-based National Committee for Adoption, there are more than ten requests for every child available from an agency. About fifty thousand adoptions were made in the U.S.A. in 1983.

· *Do we have to go to an adoption agency to adopt a child?*

No, independent adoptions can be set up by a lawyer, a doctor, or some other intermediary who deals with the natural parents or parents of the child. In New York, lawyers handling independent adoptions on a regular basis must be licensed as an adoption agency.

• Can we adopt a foreign child?

Yes, by either independent adoption or going through an international adoption agency. The babies must be okayed physically by a U.S. embassy physician in the child's native country. A visa must be obtained for the child, and the adoptive parents must petition the Immigration and Naturalization Service for the child to enter the country as an immediate relative. To adopt a foreign child, both parents must be U.S. citizens. Currently, there's a substantial pool of accessible orphans in Korea and Colombia.

• We've been having trouble adopting a child. We've been offered a child for a considerable amount of money. Is that legal?

No. It *is* legal to pay the natural mother's medical expenses, and to pay legal fees. But to pay more than that is illegal. Buying and selling children is a criminal offense.

• My wife has three children from a previous marriage, two of whom are adopted. Am I responsible for all those children?

The law makes no distinction between your wife's natural child and her adopted children. In most states, you're not responsible for any of her children by a former marriage. In some states, you're responsible for all of them when you take them into your home. In the states in which you have no responsibility for the children, it's the legal duty of your wife and her former husband to provide for the children's support.

• I hold a job and so does my husband. I feel it's up to the man to support the kids. He says it's up to both of us. Am I right?

You were right before the passage of unisex laws. Now you are as responsible for the support of your children as your husband.

• Who's responsible for the care of our children—myself or my husband?

Both you and your husband. In an undisrupted marriage, both parents have joint custody of the children. Custody involves the duty to care for the children with love and kindness, provide reasonable financial support, and see that they are educated in either public or private schools.

• *My husband can't work because he's physically incapacitated. Am I responsible for the support of our children?*

Yes. You're also responsible in case he leaves you or in case he dies. You're also responsible for *his* support. He would be responsible if the situation were reversed. (Your children may be entitled to Social Security or disability benefits because of your husband's condition.)

• *My youngster skips school frequently. My wife says it's the job of her teachers to make her show up. I say it's my wife's job. Who's right?*

Neither of you. Both parents have the responsibility for the attendance of their children in school.

• *Who is responsible for disciplining my children—my husband or me?*

Both of you. You can use "reasonable force." A good old-fashioned spanking is not considered child abuse. You can also dictate who your children can associate with at home, and away from home. You can set the moral standards. The law, however, can't enforce those rights for you.

   Caution: The use of unreasonable force is child abuse, and so is disciplining by excessive deprivation. If the evidence is clear and convincing that you're abusing your child, the state can take your child away from you. Also, if you use excessive force on a child resulting in an injury, the child can bring a civil suit against you despite your parenthood—and some teenagers have done just that.

• *My five-year-old tore up a sizable patch of my neighbor's lawn while my husband was asleep in the hammock. Now my neighbors are threatening to sue my husband and my five-year-old. Can they?*

The law assumes that a child of that age was not aware of the nature of his act and did not know it was harmful, so he can't be sued. Ordinarily, neither can your husband, unless he knew what your child was doing and didn't stop him or encouraged the child to do it. But even without your involvement in the tort (a civil wrong which interferes with somebody's personal rights), some courts may hold not only your husband but you liable. The changing attitude of the law toward harmful civil, as well as delinquent, acts of children is placing more and more responsibility on the parents.

• *My twelve-year-old does things like scaring old people on the street, and threatening younger kids who come into the neighborhood. Whom does the law hold responsible for his behavior—my husband or me?*

What your kid is doing is delinquency—an infraction of the law, not a crime. In some states, if your kid's acts are willful and malicious, both you and your husband are held responsible; and some states hold both of you responsible even if the acts are not willful and malicious.

• *My fourteen-year-old works part-time in a supermarket. Who has the right to his earnings—my son, my husband, or me?*

You do. A parent has the right to a minor child's earnings provided the parent requests them from the employer. The child's consent is not necessary.

• *My sixteen-year-old daughter is a model. She's moved into her own home and supports herself. My husband insists he still has the right to control her life because she's not of legal age. Is he right?*

Maybe not. Since she supports herself in her own home, the court may decide she's "emancipated"—that is to say, she's regarded as an adult even though she's not yet reached adult age—and as an adult she's free of parental control. Another way an underage child can become a legal adult is by marrying. A child normally becomes an adult on reaching statutory legal age—eighteen or twenty-one in most states.

The Battered Wife

· *What does the law consider a battered wife?*

A wife who's been beaten by her husband. To be beaten in the legal sense is to be the victim of battery or assault. *Battery* means inflicting substantial harm—any injury requiring medical care. *Assault* means threatening substantial harm while demonstrating the ability to carry out the threat. A husband menacing his wife while wielding a baseball bat is committing assault.

· *My husband treats me roughly, shoves me, yells at me, sometimes slaps me. Am I a battered wife?*

You're an abused wife, but not a battered one. You're only battered when he commits battery or assault as defined in the preceding question.

· *If I'm being beaten by my husband, what can I do?*

Call the police if you can, or call them as soon after the beating as possible. You'll get immediate protection, but not permanent protection. The police, as a rule, do not interfere with domestic quarrels. And they will not arrest your husband unless you file criminal charges. In New York, a wife can obtain an Order of Protection, which directs the police to imprison the husband if there is a future assault.

· *I'm a battered wife. What options are open to me?*

You can file criminal charges. You can file a civil suit. You can file for a legal separation and divorce. You can just leave.

· *What happens when I file criminal charges for wife beating?*

To begin with, don't do it without the advice of your lawyer. He'll ask you for evidence that your husband committed either battery or assault. The evidence could include a police report (that's why it's a good idea to call the police), a medical report of your injuries, names and addresses of witnesses to the beatings, and photographs of your injuries. Remember, though, your husband will be out on bail, and even if convicted and sentenced, he's likely to be paroled—and when he's free, he could beat you again.

• *What happens when I file a civil suit against my husband for wife beating?*

Actually, you'll be suing for redress for battery or assault. Your lawyer should handle this for you. You'll have to supply the same kind of evidence as for a criminal action. Civil actions are costly and long-drawn-out, and unless your husband has the assets to pay the award, a verdict in your favor is meaningless. And you could lose. During the lengthy legal process, moreover, your husband is free, and can beat you again. You can help prevent that by obtaining an Order of Protection, which forbids your husband to contact you in any way on penalty of a fine of imprisonment.

• *What happens when I file for legal separation or divorce on the grounds of wife beating?*

In no-fault divorce states (see page 209), you don't need grounds for separation or divorce. In most other states, physical cruelty is sufficient grounds. When you've separated, the judge can issue an order (called a Restraining Order or Cease and Desist Order) that calls for your husband to stay away from you. Failure to comply could mean a fine or imprisonment. If you've filed for divorce, the courts can grant you "exclusive possession" of your home, which gives you the legal right to exclude your husband (if he comes banging on your door, you can call the police), and/or can order your husband to post a "peace bond"— money which is forfeited if he bothers you.

• *What happens if I just leave my husband because he beats me?*

You have the legal right to leave him in these circumstances; it is not desertion. If you have no safe place to go, there may be a shelter for battered wives in your community. A call to your local police station or to your lawyer should get you the address. The American Bar Association advises: "The consensus among those who've studied this problem [of battered wives] is that spouses who beat their spouses will continue doing so. If your spouse beats you and you do not leave him or her, you are risking your health and possibly your life."

• *When I separate, divorce, or leave my husband because he beats me, can I take the children with me?*

Yes. There's no likelihood that a court would grant custody of the children to a proven wife beater.

WHAT YOU SHOULD KNOW ABOUT BREAKING UP: ANNULMENT, SEPARATION, DIVORCE
Annulment

• *What's the difference between an annulment and divorce?*

A divorce dissolves a legal marriage. An annulment declares that there never was a legal marriage. When a marriage can be annulled (because at least one spouse is not bound to the other legally), it is said to be voidable; when a marriage is annulled it is said to be void.

• *What are the grounds for an annulment?*

The major grounds are, depending on the state, incest; bigamy; underage at time of marriage; insanity, idiocy, or sexual incapacity at time of marriage; a lifetime prison sentence; communicable loathsome disease; force; the threat of violence; and fraud.

• *What are some fraudulent acts that can result in an annulment?*

Here are several:

- Reneging on your promise to go through with a religious ceremony after the civil ceremony
- Keeping secret your intent not to have children or to live with your spouse
- Concealing serious health conditions, including venereal diseases
- Failing to reveal your previous marriages
- Misrepresentation of your sexual morality before marriage
- At the time of your marriage, hiding from your husband your pregnancy by another man

· *How do I get an annulment?*

You can bring a court action based on any of the grounds for annulment recognized in your state. But warning: If annulment is based on fraud, the court usually will not grant a decree of annulment if you have had sexual relations with your spouse after the discovery of the fraud.

· *My marriage was annulled, and that left me without support. Is my former husband required to help me?*

Some state statutes provide for maintenance payments if you can show need. But generally, after an annulment you're back on your own.

Separation

· *How does a separation differ from a divorce?*

When you're divorced, your marriage is dissolved. When you're separated, you're still married but you live apart.

· *I've decided to move out. Is that considered a legal separation?*

There's no law that forces you to stay with your spouse, so moving out is legal. But a "legal separation" is usually regarded in most states as one that is court-approved or based on an oral or, preferably, a written agreement between the spouses.

· *Must a legal separation be court-approved?*

No. If you and your spouse agree to separate voluntarily, the agreement you work out with your spouse is sufficient.

· *I want a separation. My husband doesn't. What's my next move?*

Initiate a lawsuit for "formal judicial separation." In some states you need grounds similar to those for divorce. If you cannot prove grounds, no separation will be ordered. If you can, the judge sets the terms of the separation agreement. The court then orders your husband to comply with the terms whether he likes them or not. You're bound in the same manner. Of course, your husband has an equal right to apply for a formal judicial separation from you. He can also contest your lawsuit.

· *Can my husband and I draw up a legal separation agreement ourselves?*

You can. But the aid of a lawyer is advisable, particularly these days when family law is in a state of flux.

· *What should my husband and I include in our legal separation agreement?*

Don't try to make up your own agreement unless you and your husband can come to a friendly meeting of minds. If you can, then prepare a preliminary memo of agreement for your lawyer as follows. Each of you should have a separate lawyer.

Start by stating that because of the differences and disputes between you and your husband, each of you desires to settle your mutual marital rights and obligations in the following categories:

Right to live apart. State that you have the right to live anyplace you choose, without molestation, interference, or harassment from your spouse, and that your spouse has the same right.

Spousal support. Formerly, this was called alimony, and was payable to the wife. Spousal support is now also known as maintenance, and is payable to either you *or* your husband. Work out between you who gets how much and for how long.

Child custody. Decide on who gets custody of the children, remembering that in some states you and your husband can retain joint custody.

Visitation rights. If you have custody of the children, you can arrange with your husband to visit and be visited by your children at *reasonable* times and places, or at *specific* times and places. If your husband has custody, he can make similar arrangements with you. It's a good idea to plan visitation rights for grandparents, aunts, uncles, brothers, sisters, and other close relatives. Almost all states now permit grandparents to seek visitation rights legally when denied them, and some states extend this right to other relatives.

Child support. Decide on the child's needs and the ability of each of you to meet those needs. Remember, it is no longer the obligation of the husband alone to provide child support.

Medical and dental expenses. Work out a division of responsibility between you and your husband for such expenses, including insurance covering each member of the family. Remember to allocate funds for medical/dental expenses not covered by insurance.

Children's education. Determine how much you and your husband are willing and able to contribute and for how long. Do take into consideration the cost of private school, college, and professional school fees, room and board, books, and so on.

Disposition of property. When arriving at an agreement with your husband about who gets what, keep in mind the following state provisions governing the distribution of real and personal property in separation (and divorce) agreements:

- In South Carolina, Mississippi, and West Virginia, property belongs to the title holder.
- In four community property states—California, Idaho, Louisiana, and New Mexico—property is divided equally.
- In the other four community property states—Arizona, Nevada, Texas, and Washington—property is divided equitably, according to certain formulas. "Equitable" means "fair," but not necessarily "equal."
- All other states provide guidelines for a fair distribution

of the property regardless of who holds title, or grant the judge the right to distribute the property equitably. These states are known as the equitable distribution states.

Debts. Come to a meeting of minds about who pays what debts when. Add that you and your husband will "indemnify and hold each other harmless" from any claims resulting from your or your husband's failure to pay the debts you agreed to pay. "Indemnify" means to secure you against loss or damage. "Hold harmless" means to protect you against any legal action.

Life insurance. Decide who will carry life insurance policies and for how much and name the beneficiaries.

Income tax. Decide on whether you wish to file a separate or a joint tax return; and if you decide on a joint return, agree on how refunds, deficiencies, and penalties are to be shared.

Inheritance rights. Each of you may agree to waive benefits from your wills, including the rights of dower and curtesy (see pages 167 and 168), or you may grant certain inheritance rights to each other.

Income and assets. You and your husband must certify that as a basis for the settlements in the separation agreement, you have made a full disclosure of income and assets to each other. Less than a full disclosure may invalidate the agreement.

Divorce. The separation agreement usually states that nothing in it shall prevent either you or your husband from filing for a divorce. It further states that either the provisions of the separation agreement are to be incorporated into a divorce decree, or are not. It's up to you and your husband to decide which.

Other provisions. Add any agreements you and your husband make together other than those already included. You may, for example, if your husband has custody of a child, wish to have periodic reports on the child's health and educational progress.

You and your husband should sign and date the agreement, and have your signatures witnessed.

· *Can I include basic provisions of a separation and subsequent divorce agreement in a premarital agreement?*

You can, and more and more couples are doing just that. It's a prudent action to help relieve the tensions in the event of separation and divorce.

Divorce

· *I moved out and I started divorce proceedings. My husband came to my apartment and forced me to have sex with him. Isn't that rape?*

Yes, in about half the states in the union. In the other states, your husband continues to have the right to have sex with you until your marriage is dissolved.

· *How long must I be a resident of a state before I can apply for divorce?*

There is no minimum residence requirement in Louisiana and Maryland. It is six weeks in Idaho and Nevada; sixty days in Arkansas and Wyoming; six months in California, Oklahoma, Vermont, and Washington; two years in New Jersey, Rhode Island, and Wisconsin; and one year in all the other states, except in Massachusetts, where the minimum residence requirement is variable, and New York, which requires two years when only one party resides in the state. (Most states make exceptions to minimum residence requirements.)

· *What's the difference between a "fault" divorce and a "no-fault" divorce?*

A fault divorce is granted on the premise that one of the parties is at fault. A no-fault divorce is granted without either of the parties being at fault. (A no-fault divorce in some states is not even called a divorce. It's referred to as a "dissolution of marriage.")

Fault is the traditional grounds for divorce. But now, as a result of the revolution in family law which began in the 1960s, only two states, Illinois and South Dakota, limit divorce to traditional grounds.

· *What are the traditional grounds for divorce in Illinois and South Dakota?*

In Illinois: adultery, bigamy, cruelty, desertion or abandonment, drunkenness or drug addiction, felony or imprisonment, incapacity or impotence, attempt on spouse's life, communicable venereal disease.

In South Dakota: adultery, cruelty, desertion or abandonment, drunkenness or drug addiction, felony or imprisonment, insanity, nonsupport or willful neglect, separation.

· *What are the traditional grounds for divorce in general?*

They vary according to statutes passed by each state's legislature. Here is an alphabetical list of the major statutory grounds for divorce and the states in which they apply.

Adultery. All states except California and Iowa.

Bigamy. Arkansas, Delaware, Florida, Illinois, Mississippi, Missouri, Ohio, Pennsylvania, and Tennessee.

Cruelty. All states except Alabama, California, Iowa, Maryland, North Carolina, Vermont, and Virginia.

Crimes against nature (sexual perversions). Alabama, North Carolina, and Virginia.

Desertion. All states except California, Florida, Iowa, and North Carolina.

Drunkenness or drug addiction. All states except California, Iowa, Maryland, New Jersey, New York, North Carolina, Pennsylvania, Texas, Vermont, and Virginia.

Felony or imprisonment. All states except California, Florida, Iowa, Maine, New Jersey, North Carolina, and South Carolina.

Fraud or force. Connecticut, Georgia, Kentucky, Ohio, Oklahoma, Pennsylvania, and Washington.

Incapacity or impotency. All states except California, Connecticut, Delaware, Hawaii, Idaho, Iowa, Kansas, Louisiana, Montana, New Jersey, New York, North Dakota, South Carolina, South Dakota, Texas, Vermont, West Virginia, and Wisconsin.

Insanity. All states except Arizona, California, Illinois, Iowa, Louisiana, Maine, Massachusetts, Michigan, Missouri, New Hampshire, New Jersey, New York, Ohio, Pennsylvania, Rhode Island, South Carolina, Tennessee, Virginia, and Wisconsin.

Marriage to a relative. Florida, Georgia, Mississippi, and Pennsylvania.

Other causes: Membership in a religious cult that opposes marriage in Kentucky and New Hampshire; attempted murder of a spouse in Illinois, Louisiana, Tennessee, and Vermont; wife's prostitution in Virginia; and if a spouse is a fugitive from justice in Louisiana.

· *What steps must I take to obtain a fault divorce?*

There are seven major steps. Take them with a lawyer.

1. Establish the statutory grounds for divorce.
2. Decide which party is at fault; then have the other party bring suit for divorce.
3. File the suit with the clerk of the state supreme court.
4. Start the action by having a summons served on the party at fault. The summons is accompanied by a complaint which specifies the grounds for the action.
5. Attend a hearing before a judge. (There may also be a hearing before a conciliation board. The object is to try to save the marriage.)
6. Try to settle your differences and come to an agreement that's fair to both parties prior to trial. You can never be sure just how a judge may determine your rights. Pretrial agreements make so much sense that very few divorce cases ever come to trial.
7. If no pretrial settlement can be reached, attend a trial, at the end of which the judge will decree a settlement. But settlements can be made by agreement between the parties even after a trial has begun.

· *Are there grounds for a no-fault divorce?*

Yes. They are mutual consent, living separate and apart for a certain time, incompatibility, and irretrievable breakdown of a marriage (the only no-fault grounds in several states). Many states require a combination of no-fault and fault grounds. In some states, you can obtain a no-fault divorce only when you and your spouse agree on all provisions of the divorce agreement. Since grounds for no-fault divorce are subject to change, ask your lawyer for the current grounds in your state.

· *Can I obtain a no-fault divorce without a lawyer?*

Some states make it easy for you to do so with a *summary dissolution procedure*, provided you've been recently married, you're childless, and you and your spouse agree to a simple financial settlement. Then all you do is:

1. Fill out certain forms. (They can be obtained in many stationery stores, particularly those near the courthouse.)
2. File the forms with the clerk of the state supreme court.
3. Appear in court for a trial—usually within two months after filing. Answer some routine questions, and your marriage is dissolved.

If you do not qualify for a summary dissolution procedure or if that procedure is not offered in your state, you can still obtain a no-fault divorce by yourself by following the instructions of the clerk of the state supreme court.

Caution: Even though a no-fault divorce is simpler than a fault divorce, it's still wise to have a lawyer handle your case.

· *Can I collect alimony from my ex-wife?*

Yes, but the courts now prefer to call alimony "spousal support" or "maintenance." If you need the money and your ex-wife can afford it, the judge will award you maintenance.

· *Is maintenance payable to me for the rest of my life?*

Theoretically, yes. But the courts like to award maintenance only long enough for either spouse to become self-sustaining. However, if your marriage was a lengthy one, the court may still award maintenance "until death or remarriage."

· *My wife and I are in dispute about the property settlement. How can we work it out?*

In one of two ways. Your lawyer and your spouse's can come up with a compromise settlement subject to the approval of both of you, or you can go to mediation. That's a process by which a neutral third party works out the settlement. Mediation is available through state and independent services. Refer to the *Dispute Resolution Program Directory*, available from the American Bar Association, 1800 M Street, N.W., Washington, DC 20036.

• *Is mediation available solely for property settlement disputes?*

No. It's available for all types of disputes associated with a divorce. Some states make mediation mandatory in child custody disputes. "Divorce mediation" has become a new legal service that helps couples form their own separation agreements with the aid of professionally trained mediators, usually lawyers and psychologists.

• *Is it true that the mother gets custody of the children nine times out of ten?*

The statistics are accurate, but there's a growing tendency for the court to award custody to the father or to the parents jointly. In some states rigorous guidelines have been established for awarding custody, sometimes requiring judges to obtain psychological reports on the parents and the children.

• *Do our children have anything to say in a custody dispute?*

When a child reaches an age at which he's mature enough to choose the parent he wants to live with, the child's wishes are generally taken into consideration when the court makes an award of custody. What that "mature" age is varies with the court. In some states children of all ages can be represented by a lawyer or guardian. Such representation is mandatory in Wisconsin and New Hampshire.

• *My husband was awarded custody of our daughter. I intend to take her across state lines to live with me. Can I do it?*

You could have done it in the recent past, because states were not obligated to honor the custody awards of other states. But that has changed. Now a custody award made in any state is honored in all other states with the exception of Massachusetts. What's more, "child snatching" is now regarded as a form of kidnapping—and that's a crime. For a detailed account of your child custody rights refer to *Interstate and International Child Custody Rights*, available for $10 from the National Resource Center for Child Advocacy and Protestation, American Bar Association, 1800 M Street, N.W., Washington, DC 20036.

• *Who pays for child support after a divorce—I or my wife?*

In most states, you *or* your wife, or you *and* your wife, depending on your respective financial capabilities.

• *Can I go to jail if I don't pay child support ordered by the court?*

Yes, in many states the court could hold you in contempt, and that could lead to a jail sentence.

• *I have a child support provision in my divorce decree. Can I be sure my husband will live up to the agreement?*

Up until 1984, you couldn't. The system of collection was, according to Representative Marge Roukema, Republican of New Jersey, "costly and ineffective.... In 1981, according to the latest Census Bureau data available, only 53 percent of custodial parents received the court-ordered payments that were due their children. Twenty-eight percent received nothing." She and other supporters of legislation strengthening efforts to collect child support payments estimated that about two million children were being cheated out of an estimated four billion dollars annually in such payments.

Legislation passed by Congress in August 1984 "puts the federal government on record that child support is not a voluntary commitment, but a legal as well as a moral obligation," Roukema said. The key provisions of the new legislation which apply to all families are:

- Mandatory withholding of wages from parents thirty days late in making payments
- Imposition of property liens when payments are in arrears
- Interception of state and federal tax refunds of delinquent parents and deducting child-care payments in arrears
- Reporting of child support delinquencies to consumer credit agencies
- Interstate enforcement of child support orders

· After my divorce, how long must I wait to get married again?

Sixty days in Alabama, Kansas, and Oregon; three months in Delaware, Utah, and Vermont; six months in Massachusetts, Minnesota, Nebraska, Oklahoma, Rhode Island, and Texas; one year in Iowa and Wisconsin. There are variable time restrictions in Louisana and New Hampshire. There are no waiting periods for marriage in the other states.

WHAT YOU SHOULD KNOW ABOUT LIVING TOGETHER UNMARRIED

· Is common-law marriage the same as living together?

No. One is marriage, the other isn't.

In common-law marriage, you live together and tell people that you're married. No license, no ceremony—but you *are* married. You have all the legal rights and obligations of a married couple. You can even separate and divorce. Drawback: Common-law marriages are recognized only in the following states: Alabama, Colorado, Idaho, Iowa, Kansas, Montana, Nebraska, Ohio, Oklahoma, Pennsylvania, Rhode Island, South Carolina, and Texas.

Living together is an alternative to marriage. None of the traditional rights and obligations of marriage necessarily apply. Legally, the relationship is governed by a contract, implied or expressed, between the two parties. Living together may be said to express a desire of young people to break away from traditional marriage rules, and create their own.

· *Is living together legal?*

No state specifically prohibits two unrelated people of the opposite sex from living together. However, not being married has its disadvantages in some states when it comes to obtaining joint credit, funding living quarters, collecting maintenance from a former spouse, retaining custody of your children from a former spouse, or having a hospital accept your signature as next of kin. You also may find you're paying more taxes than a normally married couple; and under some circumstances you could lose Social Security benefits should you eventually decide to marry.

· *Are my living-together children legitimate?*

No. But there are three ways to legitimatize them: have the father declare his paternity in writing, have the father as well as the mother place their names on the birth certificate, or bring an uncontested paternity suit.

· *What is contained in a living-together contract?*

Expressed or implied, just about everything that's contained in a premarital contract. An expressed contract in writing (an expressed contract *can* be oral) when prepared by lawyers has a good chance to stand up in court. An implied contract—one in which the terms are never precisely expressed—has at the best only an iffy chance of legal enforcement; and we don't know of any that has ever been enforced. When you draw up a contract, have one lawyer represent you, and another lawyer represent your live-in partner.

· *Can I put this provision in my live-together contract: "For every sexual favor, I will be paid the sum of $50"?*

You can put it in, but don't expect to be able to enforce it in the courts. To receive payments for sexual favors is illegal in all states. Moreover, such "illegal consideration" is invalid in a contract, and may invalidate the whole contract.

· *Can I put this provision in my live-together contract: "In return for my services as a lover, mother, and homemaker,*

*you will support me and our children as long as you shall
live, whether we're together or apart"?*

Yes. The idea is good, but you'll need a lawyer to sharpen the
terms. One reason the idea is good is that it provides for you
and the children should you split with your live-in partner. You
should also, in that event, provide specifically for the custody
of the children and the disposition of property.

• *What's palimony?*

Essentially, it is alimony paid to a live-in partner or "pal"—
hence, palimony. The term was coined by the attorney for the
plaintiff, Marvin Mitchelson, in the landmark suit *Marvin* v.
Marvin. The plaintiff, Michelle Triola (she used the name Marvin during the trial), had lived with the actor Lee Marvin for
six years, without benefit of marriage or a written living-together
contract. He left her to marry another woman—and left her
broke. Triola claimed that she had a verbally expressed contract
with Lee Marvin, guaranteeing her a share of his assets and
income.

The suit led to two significant decisions. First, the court ruled
that a contract between living-together partners is valid. Second,
it ruled that should a contract exist, the partners may have to
share their incomes and assets.

Triola lost because she could not prove the existence of a
contract. But a precedent had been set. The unbridled freedom
to walk out of a live-together relationship with no strings attached had suffered a major blow.

11

Negligence: Your Rights When Somebody Injures You Accidentally

- What you should know about negligence
- When you can sue for negligence
- How negligence is handled in car accident cases: fault and no-fault systems

"One of the most common areas of litigation occurs when a person believes he or she has been the victim of an injury, negligently inflicted by another," writes Judge Leon Katz, former Chancellor of the Philadelphia Bar Association. Yet, he adds, "many...wrongfully injured parties...are deprived of their right to compensation [because they're unaware] of their basic legal rights in personal-injury cases [and how to] help themselves make their cases more likely successes."

This chapter helps close that awareness gap.

It is intended for *you*, even though you may not have had a serious accident in your life and don't anticipate one. Face the facts: Among the ten leading causes of death for our total population, accidents other than car accidents rank fourth, and car accidents rank sixth. For every accident fatality there are about ten injuries. Car accidents alone account yearly for about 50,000 deaths and 500,000 injuries. One out of twenty-five of us is likely to be an accident casualty this year. And with odds that short, that one could be you.

Your injury could come from a fall, from a defective product, from the carelessness or incompetence of a doctor, a dentist, or a mechanic, from a car or construction accident, or from any mishap. The result could be minor—a sprain, a slight limp, a half-dozen stitches, a lost tooth—or you could be permanently crippled, disfigured for life, lose limbs, eyesight, or hearing, sink into a deep psychosis, even die. But whatever the injury or its magnitude, if it was caused by some other person's negligence, you have the basis for a negligence action. That action, if successful, could compensate you for your medical expenses, the money you lose because of the time you missed at work, the cost of rehabilitating your body and mind, the tuition fees for retraining your injured body for a new job, and your legal fees, and could earn you a sort of sad profit—compensation for the harm you suffered. Compensation for a major injury could run into six and seven figures, more for death.

Your starting point for a negligence action is to know what negligence is all about in the eyes of the law. *Did* the other person act negligently? It may look as plain as the cast on your arm, but the law could say no. And if the other person did act negligently, what are your rights in the case? The law of negligence has grown in the courts and on the statute books of England and the United States over the last thousand or so years into labyrinthine complexity. Tracing *your* rights could be a baffling experience—as witness the answers to the following questions concerning just the right to sue for negligence:

Do you have the right to sue a child for negligence? Yes and no.

Do you have the right to sue a member of your family for negligence? Yes and no.

Do you have the right to sue a branch of government for negligence? Yes and no.

Do you have the right to sue your landlord for negligence? Yes and no.

Do you have the right to sue your neighbor for negligence? Yes and no.

Actually, your only guide to this yes-and-no world of negligence rights is your lawyer. But with the information in this chapter you can become, in Judge Katz's term, a "good client"—

the kind of client who can assist his lawyer in personal injury cases, "thereby, providing greater income for each."

WHAT YOU SHOULD KNOW ABOUT NEGLIGENCE

· *What is negligence in a civil action?*

It's the commission of a civil wrong, a tort, that accidentally causes injury to somebody by reason of failure to perform an expected duty with the care that a reasonably prudent person would use with regard to the safety of others in a particular circumstance. (Negligence can also be a criminal offense.)

Let's see how these conditions work out in a hypothetical case. A motorist passes a red light as you're crossing the street. You leap backward, fall, and injure your leg.

The motorist had no intention of injuring you; the injury was accidental. It was a tort, not a crime.

By statute, it was the motorist's duty to stop at the red light. He failed to perform that duty.

As a reasonably prudent person in this circumstance, the motorist should have stopped at the red light, or, having passed the red light and seen you crossing, should have stepped on his brakes. He did neither; he was careless in regard to your safety.

The motorist's actions meet all the conditions for the legal definition of negligence. You have the grounds for a negligence action.

However, if the motorist passed the red light because he had a seizure and lost control of the car, or because a mechanical defect, such as a brake failure threw the car out of control, you do not have grounds for a negligence action. To prove negligence you have to show not only failure to perform a known duty, but also the defendant's ability to perform it (which he didn't have when he suffered the seizure), and his opportunity to perform it (which he didn't have because of his car's mechanical defect). However, the motorist would still be negligent if he knew he was subject to seizures or was aware that his brakes were defective.

· *Is "duty" as it's used in negligence cases limited to statutory responsibilities, like stopping at a red light?*

No. In regard to negligence, think of duty broadly as an obligation to protect the safety of others. That means doing something that a reasonably prudent person would do under the circumstances. Specific precedents for duty are found not only in statutory law, but in common law and court decisions. *Caution*: When you promise to do something—say, repair a neighbor's bike—you're assuming a duty. If you do the job negligently—and a wheel falls off and so does your neighbor, who is injured—you could be sued for negligence.

• *Does the law recognize that both parties in a negligence action could be negligent?*

Yes. If you're injured by the negligent action of another, but you contributed to the accident by your failure to exercise reasonably prudent care, you're guilty of contributory negligence. You may also be guilty of a form of contributory negligence if you voluntarily expose yourself to danger—by riding a roller coaster without using a seat restraint, or working with a neighbor's power saw or other dangerous tool if you're inexperienced or fail to use a safety guard. This is called *assumption of risk*.

• *Does my assumption of risk influence my right to negligence damages?*

Perhaps. If you knew, or should have known, about the built-in risk of the activity, assumption of risk may limit or negate your right to negligence damage.

• *Can I claim damages if I'm partially responsible for being injured as a result of somebody's negligence?*

It depends on the state in which the accident occurred.

In some states, the courts are guided by the rule of *contributory negligence*, which holds that you have no claim for negligence damages if any negligence on your part—no matter how small—contributed to your injury. The states are Delaware, Illinois, Indiana, Michigan, Missouri, and West Virginia. But laws are constantly changing, so check with your lawyer.

In the other states, the courts apply the rule of *comparative negligence*, which holds that even if you are guilty of contributory negligence, you may recover damages reduced in proportion to the amount of negligence for which you are responsible. However, in some of those states, if you're more than 50 percent responsible, you're not able to recover damages. The percentage of negligence is determined by the court and/or the jury.

• *In what states does the rule of contributory negligence apply?*

In all states except *Arkansas, Colorado*, Connecticut, *Hawaii, Idaho, Kansas, Maine*, Massachusetts, *Minnesota*, Mississippi, Montana, Nebraska, Nevada, New Hampshire, New Jersey, New York, *North Dakota, Oklahoma*, Oregon, Pennsylvania, Rhode Island, South Dakota, Texas, *Utah*, Vermont, Washington, and *Wyoming*. In the states italicized in the preceding list, the plaintiff can win only if he is less than 50 percent at fault. But state laws change constantly. Check with your lawyer.

• *Is there any exception to the rule of contributory negligence?*

Yes, one. If by the exercise of reasonable care, the defendant could have avoided injuring you despite your contributory negligence, you can recover damages. The legal doctrine involved here is called the *doctrine of the last clear chance*. Example:

You know that your car suffers from chronic stalling. You hear the hoot of an approaching train, but you drive onto the railroad track anyway. Your car stalls. You have committed a negligent act. But the railroad engineer has plenty of time to spot you and stop the train—giving you a last clear chance of avoiding injury. He doesn't give you that chance. You're hit. You could bring a claim of negligence against the railroad.

The doctrine of the last clear chance, though, has become obsolete in most states.

• *How is the amount of an award in a negligence case determined?*

From a consideration of the victim's dollar losses (from inability to work, medical costs, and so on) and the dollar value judged adequate to compensate for the victim's pain and suffering. The total is known as *actual damages*. If the defendant has shown flagrant disregard of the safety of the victim, due to negligence or malice, then punitive damages may be added.

In a recent suit, brought by the parents of a young woman who died when her 1974 Mustang was hit from behind and burst into flames, the jury found the Ford Motor Company negligent in failing to warn of the danger of fire from rear-end collisions of that model. The award for actual damages—based mainly on the pain and suffering of their daughter, who died from burns a week after the accident, and on the loss of their child—was $6,800,000. The punitive award was $106,800,000. Although reduced by a state district court judge to $26,800,000, it is still one of the largest punitive damage awards ever assessed.

· *What are lawyer's fees in negligence cases?*

Lawyers work on a contingency fee. For the pros and cons of this practice, see page 51.

WHEN YOU CAN SUE FOR NEGLIGENCE

· *Can I sue for negligence if I'm injured in a neighbor's house because of a defective condition, say a slippery staircase?*

If you're in your neighbor's house lawfully, yes, provided he knew of the hazardous condition and took no action to correct it, or warn you about it.

· *I slipped on a crack in the lobby floor of my apartment building and broke my hip. Can I sue my landlord?*

Yes, a landlord is liable for negligence for injuries caused by his failure to keep the common areas of the building—lobby floors, stairwells, elevators, and so on—in good repair, providing he knew or should have known of defective conditions.

• The wheel of my new motorcycle wobbled suddenly, and I lost control. The result was twenty stitches. Can I bring a suit against the manufacturer for negligence?

Yes, if you can show that the defective wheel resulted from lack of reasonable care in the manufacturing or design process.

• My beautician left me under the dryer too long, and I lost some of my hair because of it. Can I sue for negligence?

Yes. Since your beautician's work did not meet acceptable standards of performance for his trade, he was negligent. This test of negligence applies to all specialists and professionals, and is called, as readers of this book have learned in Chapter 2, malpractice. Remember, you must show that you suffered true damages.

• Can I sue a member of my family for negligence?

Generally, no if it's your spouse. Generally, yes if it's any other member of your family.

• Can I sue a child for negligence?

It depends on the state. In some states, the answer is no if the child is under ten, unless the parents could have prevented the injury caused by their offspring; and yes, when the child is over ten.

• Can I bring a negligence suit against a charitable organization?

It depends on the state. You have no right to sue a charitable organization for negligence in Georgia, Mississippi, and Montana. You can bring suit with certain restrictions in Arkansas, Colorado, Hawaii, Iowa, Maine, Maryland, Nevada, New Jersey, South Carolina, and Virginia. In New Mexico and South Dakota, there's no statutory regulation, and no clear-cut court decisions. In the remaining states you can sue, but in Massachusetts if you're a charity patient in a hospital, there's a $20,000 ceiling on your claim.

• Can I bring a negligence suit against the U.S. government?

Yes, when negligence results from the act of a government employee. That's a right guaranteed by the Federal Tort Claims Act, in which the U.S. government waives its sovereign immunity under that circumstance, to negligence claims. Cases are usually settled by administrative agency hearings, but can end up in court if you are dissatisfied with the decision.

• Can I bring a negligence suit against my state government?

You have no right to sue a state government for negligence, or your right to sue is limited, often severely, in the following states: Alabama, Arkansas, Connecticut, Delaware, Georgia, Iowa, Maryland, Massachusetts, Michigan, Minnesota, Mississippi, New Hampshire, Ohio, Pennsylvania, South Carolina, South Dakota, Tennessee, Texas, Virginia, and West Virginia. Generally, you have the right to sue all other state governments for negligence when you allege that the government itself or any of its employees committed a negligent act against you. But in Idaho and Oregon, the maximum collectible damages is $100,000; and it is only $50,000 in Oklahoma.

• Can I bring a negligence suit against my municipal government?

Yes, in Alabama, Alaska, Colorado, Delaware, Florida, Hawaii, Idaho, Illinois, Indiana, Kansas, Kentucky, Louisiana, Minnesota, Missouri, Montana, Nebraska, Nevada, New Hampshire, New Jersey, New Mexico, New York, North Dakota, Oklahoma, Oregon, Pennsylvania, Rhode Island, Tennessee, Texas, Utah, Vermont, Washington, West Virginia, and Wisconsin. But there's a plethora of ifs, ands, and buts whether you can bring suit against the municipality itself or any of its employees. Your lawyer can guide you through these generally complex statutes.

• How is negligence handled in the case of automobile accidents?

Two ways, depending on the state: by the fault system or the no-fault system. They're discussed separately in the following subsections.

HOW NEGLIGENCE IS HANDLED IN CAR ACCIDENT CASES: FAULT AND NO-FAULT SYSTEMS
The Fault System

· *What is the fault system?*

It's a system of determining liability based on showing that one party was at fault because of negligence which caused the accident. In other words, if the other driver is to blame for the accident, you can collect damages, and vice versa.

· *In what states does the fault system apply?*

Alabama, Alaska, Arizona, California, Idaho, Illinois, Indiana, Iowa, Louisiana, Maine, Mississippi, Missouri, Montana, Nebraska, New Hampshire, New Mexico, North Carolina, Ohio, Oklahoma, Tennessee, Vermont, Washington, West Virginia, Wisconsin, and Wyoming.

· *What do I do in case of an accident?*

Follow these Dos and Don'ts:

Do get medical attention at once in case of injuries. Since many serious injuries do not show up at the time of the accident, precautionary emergency-room treatment at a hospital is advisable.

Do exchange the following information with the driver of the other car: name, address, telephone number; license number and license plate number; year and make of car; name, address, and telephone number of insurance company and agent.

Do get the name, address, and telephone number of the owner of the other car, if the driver is not the owner.

Do get the names, addresses, and telephone numbers of witnesses.

Do get the names and badge numbers of police officers on the scene, as well as the police office where their report is filed.

Do make notes on all relevant details such as road and weather conditions. If possible, take photos of both cars at the scene of the accident from several angles. Aim at making the photos a graphic record of the collision, showing road and weather conditions, directions in which each car was traveling, the area of impact, traffic signs and traffic controls, and skid marks.

Do, whether the accident is serious or not, obtain a copy of the police report (it contains a detailed account of the accident); check it with your version; and, if the police version is in error, rectify it by means of a certified letter, return receipt requested. You can usually obtain the police report by paying a small fee at the police office at which the report is filed.

Do notify your insurance agent immediately. He may provide advice on how to proceed to press your claims and defend against claims against you.

Do, if you've been hurt, keep an injury diary. This should be a complete medical/financial record relating to the injuries suffered in the accident. Don't forget to enter the following:

- A daily record of your healing progress, indicating the length of time it takes for each injury to heal
- All stays at a hospital and the dates
- Your patient ID card number
- All outpatient visits, and the dates
- All visits by nurses and physical therapists, and the dates
- All other contacts with medical personnel, and the dates
- All medical treatments given
- All prescribed medicines
- All physician's names
- All medical bills (hospital, doctor, medication, nursing, others). Preserve each bill and record of payment.
- Lost work time because of your injury
- Lost earnings
- Car rental receipts

Don't discuss the issue of fault.

Don't reveal the amount of your insurance coverage.

Don't say whether or not you were wearing a seat belt.

Don't get into an argument.

Don't sign any statements or talk to anyone except your lawyer or your insurance representative.

In the following states, the accident report must be made not by you but by the police: Delaware, Idaho, Kansas, Michigan, and North Carolina.

· *How can I put a value on a personal injury claim?*

You can't. Too many factors are involved for a layperson to evaluate accurately the value of a personal injury. Rely on the knowledge and experience of your lawyer.

· *I'm injured. It was the fault of the other driver. What next?*

You may be contacted by an insurance adjuster representing the other party's insurance company. The adjuster will want a statement from you at once. Don't give it. He may want to tape the conversation with you. Don't do it. He may try to settle with the promise of quick money. Don't accept it. Instead, refer the adjuster to your lawyer. After that, the adjuster is prohibited from dealing with you directly.

· *What happens if my claim is disputed?*

Most claims *are* disputed. To expedite settlement, your attorney will normally institute suit against the wrongdoer. This procedure leads to negotiations, and settlement before trial in up to 97 percent of cases of this type. If *you* are being sued, your insurance company's legal division handles your case. Remember, negligence cases are won by meticulous preparation before trial. So be sure to keep accurate records and cooperate fully with your lawyers.

· *Must I submit an accident report if there are no injuries and the damages are small?*

In all states except Pennsylvania, you are required to submit an accident report to the state public safety or motor vehicle department within a few days if there are personal injuries, or if damages (usually, combined damages) exceed a certain minimum amount.

The minimum is $50 in Alabama; $100 in the District of Columbia, Florida, Maryland, New Mexico, and Oklahoma; $150 in Ohio; $200 in Indiana, Kentucky, Louisiana, Massachusetts, Michigan, New Jersey, North Carolina, Oregon, Rhode Island, South Carolina, Tennessee, and Vermont; $250 in Arkansas, Colorado, Delaware, Georgia, Idaho, Illinois, Iowa, Mississippi, Montana, Nebraska, Nevada, South Dakota, Texas, West Virginia, and Wyoming; $300 in Arizona, Hawaii, Kansas, Maine, Minnesota, New Hampshire, and Washington; $350 in Virginia; $400 in Connecticut, New York, North Dakota, Utah, and Wisconsin; and $500 in Alaska, California, and Missouri.

In Pennsylvania there is no damage minimum, but in case of injury or death, or in case any vehicle involved cannot proceed under its own power without further damage or becomes a hazard to other vehicles, an accident report must be made.

• *Suppose I settle a claim, and a few months later an injury appears that my doctor says is a result of the accident. Can I make an additional claim?*

Probably not if you signed the customary "Release of All Claims" form. It releases the party at fault and his insurance company from any future claims by you arising out of the accident.

If there's any chance at all of a hidden injury from the accident surfacing in the near future (let your doctor be your guide), you may not want to settle any claims until it surfaces and your doctor advises you of the full extent of your injury. You have from ninety days in some states to three years in others to file your claim. If you don't file before your state's deadline, you may not be able to file at all.

• *How can I be sure I'll collect personal injury damages from an uninsured motorist?*

Some states permit insurance companies to issue "uninsured motorist coverage." You take out the coverage, and if the uninsured motorist is at fault, your insurance company pays you. This type of coverage also applies if you're struck by a hit-and-run driver (provided you report the accident to the police within a specified period of time, usually twenty-four hours). Some companies provide up to $300,000 in benefits. Also available is "underinsured coverage," which provides additional benefits if the wrongdoer's own coverage is insufficient to compensate you for your injuries.

• *I'm worried about what happens if the accident is my fault. What coverage does my insurance give me?*

The coverage provided, known as "liability limits," is usually designated by three numerals separated by slash marks, for example: 100/300/25. Reading from left to right, the numerals, multiplied by 1,000, stand for the maximum the insurance company pays when you injure one person, when you injure more than one person, and when you damage property. With liability limits of 100/300/25, the insurance company pays a maximum of $100,000 for injury to one person, a total of $300,000 for injury to more than one person, and $25,000 for property damage. If you have to meet claims in excess of your liability limits, the money comes out of your own pocket. You can, though, insure yourself against that contingency by taking out an "umbrella policy" that boosts your total liability limits to $1,000,000 or more.

· *The person I injured in the accident is covered by catastrophic medical insurance. Am I responsible for his medical bills anyway?*

Yes, unless the injured person is insured in a no-fault state, in which case the policy usually covers his medical and hospital bills.

· *In what states does the no-fault system apply?*

Arkansas, Colorado, Connecticut, Delaware, Florida, Georgia, Hawaii, Kansas, Kentucky, Maryland, Massachusetts, Michigan, Minnesota, Nevada, New Jersey, New York, North Dakota, Oregon, Pennsylvania, Rhode Island, South Carolina, South Dakota, Texas, Utah, and Virginia. But the law in your state may have changed recently. Check with your lawyer.

· *Suppose I'm killed in a car accident. It's the other driver's fault. Who receives the damages?*

In most states, your spouse, children, parents, or your estate can sue to recover losses due to your "wrongful death." How much can be recovered depends on the laws of each state, and the available insurance and assets of the wrongdoer.

The No-Fault System

• *What is the "no-fault" system?*

Basically it's a system that separates your auto accident claim into two separate categories (claims).

- The first category provides you with reimbursement for all just and reasonable medical expenditures required to treat and rehabilitate your mind and body, as well as reimbursement for your loss of income during your disability (up to a specified amount allowed by statute, which varies from state to state). THIS PAYMENT IS MADE BY YOUR OWN INSURANCE COMPANY WITHOUT REGARD TO *YOUR FAULT*.
- The second category contains your right to seek recovery (make claim or sue) from the adverse party for pain and suffering, future loss of income (in excess of that covered by no fault), and recovery for the property damage caused to your automobile.

Note that while in the first category your fault has no bearing on your right to recover benefits, it may diminish or even preclude your recovery in the second category.

• *In no-fault states, am I required to purchase no-fault insurance and personal liability insurance?*

Both are optional in Arkansas, South Dakota, Texas, and Virginia. No-fault insurance is optional in Kentucky, but personal liability insurance is mandatory. In all other no-fault states, both types of insurance are mandatory. Personal liability insurance is required because, although the no-fault system is designed to reduce litigation, lawsuits are possible; and this insurance protects you as well as the plaintiff when an award is made against you.

• *When are lawsuits possible under the no-fault system?*

In some states when compensation demanded for the injury is greater than the maximum permitted under the state's no-fault system, or greater than the no-fault insurance; in other states when the injury results in dismemberment, cosmetic scarring, or death; and in still other states, when medical bills exceed a certain amount. But in other states there are no restrictions on suits.

· *I've been in an accident and suffered a minor injury. Under the no-fault system, what do I do?*

Report the accident to your insurance company, and request the no-fault claim forms. Fill them out and return them with the required backup documents to the insurance company as soon as possible. Basic information required: your doctor's report, amount of medical bills, and your employer's record of work time and income lost because of your injury. Sound advice: Don't do anything without guidance from your lawyer.

· *How soon after I submit the required forms do I get paid by the insurance company?*

Usually the law requires payment within thirty days. For delayed payment, the insurance company may be penalized 2 percent per month on the amount of your claim. The penalty is paid to you.

· *What happens if the insurance company disputes my claim?*

You won't be paid until the dispute is resolved.

· *To settle my disputed claim with the insurance company, does my lawyer go to court?*

He can, but usually he goes to arbitration. This is a proceeding in which both parties to a dispute agree to abide by the decision of an impartial third party, the arbitrator. (The arbitration machinery is made available through insurance companies in most states.) If your lawyer satisfies the arbitrator that your medical treatment was necessary because of the accident, and that the medical fees are reasonable, the arbitrator will direct the insurance company to pay your claim. But if the arbitrator is not satisfied that those two conditions have been met, he will rule that the insurance company is entitled to withhold payment. Your lawyer may then elect to go to court.

• In a claim dispute with the insurance company, who pays my lawyer?

If the arbitrator decides in your favor, the insurance company pays. The arbitrator fixes the fee, or arranges for your lawyer and the insurance company to negotiate the fee between them. If the arbitrator decides in favor of the insurance company, you pay the fee.

• Under the no-fault system, does the insurance company make up for my lost wages?

Yes, within limits. In New York, for example, you can get up to 80 percent of your wages up to $1,000 a month for three years. You can also get up to $25 a day for accident-related expenses other than medical (transportation is an example). Payments are reduced if you receive workmen's compensation or Social Security benefits. Ask your insurance agent for the forms to fill out.

• I'm self-employed. Does the no-fault system compensate me while I'm disabled?

Yes, if you hire somebody to take your place while you're unable to work. Then, in New York, you receive 80 percent of the money paid to your replacement up to $1,000 a month. You can also be compensated if you can prove your income for the previous year. Percentage of income as compensation is determined by state statute.

• Does the no-fault system compensate me for pain, suffering, and inconvenience?

No. You can't even sue for this type of claim unless your injuries pass a certain "threshold." In some states the threshold is monetary; damages must exceed X dollars before you can sue. In other states, the threshold is a "serious personal injury." As defined under some no-fault statutes, a "serious personal injury" involves one or more of the following: permanent loss or significant limitation of use of a body organ, member, system, or function; a medically determined injury or impairment of a nonpermanent nature which prevents you from substantial performance, for not less than 90 of the 180 days following the injury, of all the material acts which usually constitute your daily activities; fracture; significant disfigurement; death.

• *What are the maximum benefits my insurance company can pay me under the no-fault system?*

The maximum personal injury protection includes reimbursements for medical expenses, lost wages, death benefits to the survivors and funeral expenses (when permitted by the state), training in new job skills necessitated by the accident, and miscellaneous payments. The maximum is determined by statute or by the amount of no-fault insurance purchased, depending on the state.

The amount of insurance determines the maximum in Arkansas, Colorado, Kansas, Michigan, New Jersey, Oregon, Pennsylvania, South Dakota, Utah, and Virginia.

Statutory maximums in other states are as follows: Connecticut, $5,000; Delaware, $10,000 per injury or $20,000 a year, whichever is lower; Florida, $5,000; Georgia, $5,000; Hawaii, $15,000; Kentucky, $10,000; Maryland, $2,500; Massachusetts, $2,000; Minnesota, $30,000; New York, $50,000; North Dakota, $15,000; South Carolina, $1,000; and Texas, $2,500.

12

Crime: Your Rights When Under Arrest and on Trial

> • The rights of the accused—from the moment of arrest to the conclusion of the retrial

Statistics: During their lifetimes, one out of two American men and one out of eight American women will be arrested. Of all Americans, one out of 252 will be convicted of a crime and sent to a federal or state prison. As of June 30, 1984, according to the U.S. Justice Department's Bureau of Justice Statistics, 454,136 of us were behind bars.

But it's not likely that you could be one of those statistics. Or is it?

"One evening...I attended a party on the outskirts of Los Angeles," writes Tom Ballinger, an authority on arrest records. "It was a large group...drinking beer and cocktails, and enjoying the music and festive atmosphere. Then at the height of the evening, amid sudden bright lights and clamorous bullhorns, the police arrived.

"Eighty-six people—all who attended...were arrested, frisked and arraigned.... Two or three marijuana cigarettes and four or five illegally obtained pills were found by the police.... Six people were formally charged with minor drug possession. But eighty innocent citizens had been arrested."

You could have been one of those eighty innocents. Or one of the six accused.

What happens in either case?

Most of us don't know, and have nothing but the mythology of TV, movies, and best-sellers to guide us. Faced with the chilling reality of an arrest, most of us don't know how to get the ultimate protection the law affords us, because that means knowing our rights. Do *you* know them?

Do you know whether the cops can knock down your door without knocking?

Do you know whether the cops can search your place without a warrant?

Do you know whether the cops can take you out of your car, strip you, and search you?

Do you know whether the Miranda warnings must be given to you?

Do you know whether you have to answer the cops' questions?

Do you know whether you have the right to use the phone in the precinct house?

Do you know whether you have to stay in jail until the trial?

Do you know whether you can be released on bail if you don't have the money?

Some of the answers could shock you. And that's just for starters.

Do you know what your rights are as the case goes on—as it goes to a preliminary hearing, as it goes before the grand jury, as it goes to trial, as it goes to appeal?

Some of your rights as the accused have recently suffered significant setbacks in the opinion of some commentators on the legal scene. You can judge for yourself as this chapter unfolds. But today, guilty or innocent, you are protected through every step of our criminal procedure by a body of common law, Amendments to the United States Constitution, and supporting court decisions and state statutes that for fair and unbiased dispensation of justice are unmatched except for the British criminal law system. Our criminal law safeguards the rights of the accused and protects the innocent.

• *My daughter, who's an adult, is arrested for the illegal possession of narcotics. What happens at the time of her arrest?*

She's handcuffed and informed of her constitutional rights.

• *Why must she be informed of her constitutional rights?*

The mandate stems from the Miranda case. Ernesto Miranda, after two hours of police questioning, confessed to kidnapping and rape, and was convicted and sentenced to twenty to thirty years in the penitentiary. In a landmark decision in 1966, the Supreme Court in the case of *Miranda* v. *Arizona* held that Miranda's constitutional rights had been violated by the police. Miranda had not been aware of those rights. To prevent a miscarriage of justice of this type from ever occurring again, the Supreme Court decreed that the police must acquaint the suspect on arrest with his constitutional rights—a procedure known as "giving the Miranda warnings."

In 1984, the Supreme Court by a vote of five to four modified the rule in the Miranda case, citing "overriding considerations of public safety" as a justification of questioning a suspect in custody without giving the Miranda warnings. If, for example, your daughter's arrest took place in a supermarket and the police suspected her of concealing a gun somewhere on the premises, they could have asked her, "Where's the gun?" without first advising her of her constitutional rights. The majority opinion written by Associate Justice William H. Rehnquist stated:

"We believe that...concern for public safety must be paramount to adherence to the literal language of the prophylactic rules enunciated in Miranda. We do not believe that the doctrinal underpinnings of Miranda require that it be applied in all its rigor to a situation in which police officers ask questions reasonably prompted by a concern for the public safety."

This doctrine is now known as the "public safety exception" to the rule on the Miranda warnings.

In the same year, the Supreme Court also ruled that motorists could be pulled over and questioned by the police without being given the Miranda warnings, provided the motorist was not arrested first ("taken into custody"). The Supreme Court based its decision on the rule that the Miranda warnings apply only when the suspect is taken into custody. So if your daughter was in a car and the police stopped her, she could have been questioned, then arrested, then given the Miranda warnings.

· *Just how is my daughter informed of her constitutional rights?*

In the Miranda case, the Supreme Court further decreed that the way an arrested person is informed of his constitutional rights must appear on a card as follows:

"You are under arrest. Before we ask you any questions, you must understand what your rights are.

"1. You have a right to remain silent and refuse to answer any questions.

"2. Anything you do or say may be used against you in a court of law.

"3. As we discuss this matter, you have the right to stop answering my questions at any time that you desire.

"4. You have the right to a lawyer before speaking to me, to remain silent until you can talk to him, and to have him present during the time you are being questioned.

"5. If you desire a lawyer but cannot afford one, the Public Defender will be provided to you without cost.

"6. Do you understand each of these rights as I have explained them to you? Now that I have advised you of your rights, are you willing to answer my questions without an attorney?"

In practice, the arresting officer usually delivers the Miranda warnings from memory. But the officer may also read the warnings from a card and show the card to the person in custody. The Miranda warnings protect the suspect against self-incrimination—a privilege afforded by the Fifth Amendment.

· *Do the Miranda warnings mean my daughter doesn't have to say anything after she's arrested?*

Yes. Unless she voluntarily waives the rights that have been read to her.

· *Suppose the arresting officer doesn't give the Miranda warnings to my daughter, but just says he did?*

Some Miranda cards have a space for a signature. If your daughter signs such a card, that is evidence that the arresting officer complied with the law. But if there is no signed card, and your daughter claims the arresting officer did not comply with the law, then it's your daughter's word against the officer's. By and large, police departments nationwide instruct their officers to give the Miranda warnings immediately after an arrest.

Miranda warnings need only be given when the police take a statement from the suspect. If a statement is not taken, the Miranda warnings are not required.

• What happens after my daughter is arrested?

She's taken to the police station, booked, photographed, fingerprinted, and put into a cell. "Booked" means her name and the designation of the crime she's said to have committed are entered in a ledger.

• Does my daughter have any rights after she's jailed?

Generally, she can make a total of two phone calls to family, friends, or her lawyer. One call should be to her lawyer, or to you (or to some other member of her family or to a friend) to arrange for a lawyer if she doesn't have one. The lawyer, who should be a specialist in criminal law, will visit her at the station house.

• Does my daughter have to stay in jail until her trial?

No, unless the prosecutor can demonstrate that if released she will be a menace to society or likely to skip town. One of the ways she can be released is by posting bail. Bail is money or property pledged to assure her presence at subsequent legal proceedings. In the event she jumps bail—that is to say, doesn't appear for subsequent proceedings at the designated times and places—the bail is forfeit to the state, and a warrant is issued for her arrest.

• How soon can my daughter be released on bail?

If a state statute fixes the amount of bail for her offense, she can be released by a police officer immediately after booking on posting the amount of bail required. If the amount of bail is not fixed by statute, she must wait until her arraignment for a judge to fix bail. The judge at that time has the option of releasing her "on her own recognizances"—that is to say, without bail, but on her promise to show up at the subsequent legal procedures.

· What's an arraignment?

It's a legal procedure during which the judge details the charges against your daughter, acquaints her with her basic rights under arrest as prescribed by the Fifth, Sixth, and Eighth Amendments to the United States Constitution, and asks how she pleads— guilty, not guilty, or not guilty by reason of insanity. The arraignment may take place on the day of arrest or shortly thereafter.

· I want to post bail for my daughter. It's set by the judge at $50,000. I don't have the money. What can I do?

Provided you are credit-worthy, you can obtain a redeemable bond from a bailbondsman. All you have to put up is the bail-bondsman's fee, which can be as low as 10 percent of the bail— $5,000 instead of $50,000. The court will accept the bond in lieu of cash or property. The fee is not returnable to you after the case is settled. But if your daughter jumps bail—that is to say, if she doesn't appear at the specified times and places of subsequent legal procedures—the bailbondsman has to come up with the $50,000, and you're obligated to make good his loss. So you could be out $5,000 plus $50,000.

The police station at which your daughter was booked will supply you with the names of bailbondsmen, as will the clerk of the court. But the best way to put up bail is to have your lawyer arrange the details.

· What are my daughter's basic rights under arrest as prescribed by the Fifth, Sixth, and Eighth Amendments?

Here are excerpts from those Amendments. We've emphasized the rights most relevant to your daughter at this stage of the legal procedure.

FIFTH AMENDMENT. "No person shall be held to answer for a capital, or otherwise infamous crime, unless on a presentment or indictment of a Grand Jury, except in cases arising in the land or naval forces, or in the Militia, when in actual service in time of War or public danger; nor shall any person be subject for the same offense to be twice put in jeopardy of life or limb; *nor shall [any person] be compelled in any criminal case to be a witness against himself,* nor be deprived of life, liberty, or property, without due process of law; nor shall private property be taken for public use, without just compensation."

SIXTH AMENDMENT. "In all criminal prosecutions, *the accused shall enjoy the right to a speedy and public trial by an impartial jury* of the State and district wherein the crime shall have been committed, which district shall have been previously ascertained by law, and to be informed of the nature and cause of the accusation; to be confronted with the witnesses against him; to have compulsory process for obtaining witnesses in his favor, and *to have the Assistance of Counsel for his defense.*"

EIGHTH AMENDMENT. "*Excessive bail shall not be required,* nor excessive fines imposed, nor cruel and unusual punishments inflicted."

• *My daughter pleads not guilty, and she is out on bail. What next?*

She attends a preliminary hearing. (This is not mandatory in all states.) The hearing is held before a judge within a reasonable time after arrest. At the hearing the prosecutor is given the opportunity to demonstrate that a crime was committed and that there is *reasonable and probable cause* to hold your daughter as the one who did it. The prosecutor at this stage does not have to prove that she actually did commit the crime. The prosecutor at your daughter's hearing is probably an assistant district attorney. (In other cases, the prosecutor could be a district attorney or a state or federal attorney.)

• *My daughter claims that the police searched her apartment without a search warrant. Isn't that cause for having the case against her thrown out?*

Not necessarily. If the police make a lawful arrest, they can search the suspect and the immediate vicinity in which the arrest occurred. A lawful arrest can be based on a resonable cause for believing the person arrested had committed a crime. In your daughter's case, "the reasonable cause for believing" could be a tip from a reliable informant.

To curb possible police misconduct, the Supreme Court ruled in 1914 to *exclude* the use of evidence obtained illegally. This decree was called the "exclusionary rule." The rule held for seventy years. Then in 1984, the Supreme Court made a new ruling that in essence declared that some evidence obtained illegally can be used, provided it was obtained in good faith— for example, with an invalid warrant that the police didn't know was invalid. The new ruling is called the "good faith exception" to the exclusionary rule. Its effects on strengthening police power and weakening the Fourth Amendment guarantees against unlawful search and seizure remain to be seen.

· *My daughter claims the police broke down her door without warning. Isn't that reason for having the case dismissed?*

Not always. The police are required to knock, and give the person to be arrested a reasonable time to answer; but there are exceptions to this "knock rule." If the police have reasonable cause to believe valuable evidence is being destroyed, or their lives are in danger, or the person to be arrested is escaping, they have the right to break in without knocking. In your daughter's case, should the police officers testify that they had reasonable cause—based, say, on their informant's knowledge of your daughter's habits—to believe she would have flushed her half kilo of cocaine down the toilet had they knocked first, the case would not be dismissed because of a violation of the knock rule.

· *My daughter complains that on several previous occasions she's been stopped and frisked by the police. She claims harassment. Will that help her case or harm it?*

Your daughter lives in a state where it is legal for a police officer to stop and frisk anybody when the officer suspects the person has committed or is about to commit a crime. With your daughter's history of involvement in the drug scene, the police were probably acting within their rights and not harassing her. If the judge regards her previous experience with the police as at all relevant, the harassment claim is likely to harm her case, not help it.

The states where stop-and-frisk laws are in effect are Delaware, Massachusetts, New Hampshire, New York, and Rhode Island. In New Jersey, provided you're arrested for a motor vehicle violation or other petty offense, and the police have probable cause to believe you're concealing drugs, a weapon, or criminal evidence, you can not only be frisked but stripped and searched. In other states, police have the obligation to investigate suspicious circumstances—and that means that under those circumstances anybody can be stopped, asked for identification, and even arrested.

· *My daughter's lawyer asked her if she was entrapped. What does that mean?*

If a government agent persuades an unwilling person to commit a criminal act, that is entrapment. An entrapped person cannot be convicted of the crime. On the other hand, if the person is willing to commit the crime, "persuasion" by a government agent is not entrapment. Your daughter's lawyer was attempting to set up a defense.

· *According to my daughter, there was no entrapment. But she does claim that the police planted the cocaine in her apartment. Will her lawyer have the right at the preliminary hearing to question the police who made the arrest?*

Yes. But the arresting officers will deny it, even if it is true. The preliminary hearing is more or less a formality. The prosecutor calls in a minimum number of witnesses, usually just the arresting officers, to make out reasonable cause for advancing the case to the grand jury or directly to trial, depending on the state. He does not at this time want to preview the case, or give the defense attorney a chance to "discover" what the testimony of his other witnesses will be. That's why your daughter's ex-boyfriend who claims that he saw her receive and conceal the bags of cocaine shortly before the police arrived does not appear.

The defense lawyer is not required to call witnesses for the defense at this time, but in some states he's required to lay down lines of defense to be employed later at the trial. Your daughter's lawyer's defense is this: She's been framed.

• *At the preliminary hearing are there any grounds her lawyer can use to have her discharged?*

Yes. He can plead that there is no reasonable cause to believe a crime has been committed or that your daughter committed a crime. In your daughter's case, though, that would not be much of a plea. The judge would deny it, and hold your daughter for the grand jury. (In other states she may be held directly for trial.)

• *What is a grand jury?*

A group of citizens (the numbers vary from state to state; there are twenty-three in New York State) who determine whether the prosecution has made a valid case against the accused. The purpose of the grand jury is to prevent the government from bringing anybody to trial on insufficient evidence. The grand jury does not pass on the guilt or innocence of the accused. But if, after reviewing the evidence presented by the prosecution, the grand jury decides that a crime has been committed and that there's a reasonable assumption that the accused is responsible for that crime, the grand jury will return an indictment, called a true bill.

An indictment is a formal written accusation. It says, in essence: "We, the grand jury, accuse you of the following crime." After the foreman of the grand jury writes the words "a true bill" across the face of the indictment, it is presented to the court as the formal charge against the accused. The accusation is not evidence against the accused, and must be proved in court.

The grand jury hears only felony cases. A felony is a crime punishable by imprisonment in a state penal institution for at least a period of one year or by death. (A lesser kind of crime is a misdemeanor; punching a person in the nose is an example. A still lesser kind of antisocial behavior, called a violation — disorderly conduct, for example — may not be considered a crime, but it may be punishable by a fine or a short jail sentence.)

• *In my daughter's case, can she go before the grand jury to attempt to prevent an indictment?*

The accused has no basic right to appear before the grand jury, but she may be given permission provided she agrees she may be prosecuted on the basis of her testimony. (She then is said to "waive immunity from prosecution.") In your daughter's case, the defense attorney would see nothing to be gained by having her appear before the grand jury.

• *What happens after the grand jury presents the indictment against my daughter to the court?*

A date for trial is set. She may have to apply for bail again. Her attorney will attempt to gain access to all the evidence in the case held by the district attorney, a procedure called *discovery*.

• *Can my daughter avoid a trial by plea bargaining?*

It's possible. Her lawyer, the prosecutor, and the judge can agree on a lesser charge, provided your daughter changes her plea to guilty. But in this case, your daughter insists on her innocence and will not consent to a plea of guilty.

• *What are my daughter's basic rights at a trial?*

She has the right to a speedy public trial by a jury of her peers. She has the right to present witnesses on her behalf, and the right to cross-examine witnesses for the prosecution (both of these rights are normally exercised by her lawyer). She has the right to remain silent. Most important: She has the right to be considered innocent until she's proved guilty. That means the burden of proof is on the prosecution. If the prosecution fails to prove her guilt beyond a reasonable doubt, she is presumed to be innocent and the judge will so instruct the jury.

Formerly the jury had to be composed of twelve members, but in 1970 the Supreme Court of the United States ruled that the jury only need "be large enough to promote group deliberation and a fair possibility for obtaining a representative cross-section of the community." Six is the usual alternate to twelve. In general the procedure of a criminal trial follows that of a civil trial described in Chapter 1. The Supreme Court ruled in 1972 that a unanimous verdict is not necessary in a state court.

• *Can my daughter object to a specific juror sitting on her case?*

Acting for her, the defense lawyer has the right to question prospective jurors to determine if they can be fair and unbiased. If they can't, he has the right to challenge them for cause, in which case they are excused by the judge. This procedure for selecting jurors is known as *voir dire*. The defense lawyer also has the right to have jurors excused without cause by means of peremptory challenges. The number of peremptory challenges is limited, but he can make as many challenges for cause as necessary. The prosecuting attorney has the same rights and limitation as the defense attorney regarding the selection of jurors. When twelve jurors and one or two alternates survive the voir dire and the peremptory challenges from both sides, the jury is said to be satisfactory, and the trial begins.

· *Can my daughter object to the judge's rulings during the trial?*

Acting for her, the defense lawyer can. The procedure follows this pattern: The judge rules on the admissibility of evidence. The defense attorney objects. The judge overrules the objection. The defense attorney takes exception to the ruling. Objections are necessary as the basis for a motion to appeal the verdict in the event your daughter is convicted. The prosecutor has the same right to raise objections as the defense attorney.

· *My daughter is able to obtain photocopies of letters from the arresting officer to her ex-boyfriend proving that her arrest was a frame-up. During the trial can my daughter's lawyer use the letters to obtain an acquittal?*

The problem the defense lawyer faces is to have the judge permit the photocopies to be read and shown to the jury. Rules of evidence—based on the accumulation of judicial decisions over the years—determine what the judge will allow the jury to consider as evidence. The rules of evidence vary from state to state, but generally they hold that copies of documents cannot be admitted as evidence. In your daughter's case, the judge so rules. The jury is not informed about the contents of the letters.

· *The jury found my daughter guilty as charged. Can she get a new trial?*

Her lawyer can make a motion for a new trial based on any of the following reasons:

- The judge permitted the jury to listen to or view inadmissible evidence.
- The conduct of the prosecutor was prejudicial to your daughter.
- A juror fell asleep, or argued with the defense, or otherwise acted improperly.
- The jury's verdict clearly flew in the face of the evidence.
- The judge did not instruct the jury properly concerning the law governing the case.
- The jury's verdict disregarded the law.
- New evidence.

Because your lawyer realizes that none of these reasons apply to your daughter's case, he does not move for a new trial. A date is set for sentencing.

· How is my daughter sentenced?

According to the provisions of the criminal code in your state. In some states, the exact length of the prison term is set by statute (determinate sentencing). In other states, the prison term is set between a minimum and a maximum (indeterminate sentencing)—between two and five years, for example, for your daughter's crime. In those states, the judge determines the length of the sentence within the set limits. Presentencing investigation reports on the convict made by state probation departments and other sources help the judge come to a decision.

Your daughter is sentenced to five years in the state penitentiary. How long she'll actually serve is determined by the parole board.

· After sentencing, my daughter's ex-boyfriend gives her the originals of the letters proving her arrest was a frame-up. Can she get a new trial?

On that basis, her lawyer can make a motion for a new trial, producing an affidavit from your daughter asserting that she has discovered new evidence that would have produced a verdict of not guilty. The affidavit states that the new evidence was not accessible during the trial and was found only after the trial was over. (An affidavit is a sworn statement in writing.) The motion is then argued between the defense lawyer and the prosecutor before a judge. If the judge grants the motion, your daughter could go on trial again, and this time with a good chance of being acquitted. Or the prosecutor could drop the case, and your daughter would be free.

• *Suppose my daughter gets a new trial and is acquitted. Can the D.A. try her again, hoping another jury would find her guilty?*

No. To be charged or tried more than once for the same offense is double jeopardy, and that's forbidden by the Fifth Amendment.

• *Suppose my daughter were underage—say, fifteen—would she have been treated differently?*

Yes. Instead of being charged with a crime, she may have been charged with juvenile delinquency. A juvenile delinquent is someone below the age at which one is considered capable of committing a crime. That age—say, sixteen—is set by state statute. Should the juvenile court judge at a hearing decide that the child is in fact a juvenile delinquent, the punishment is less severe than for an adult who commits a similar crime. At the judge's discretion, the minor could be placed in the custody of his parents, or sent to a foster home, a state or county school, or a reform school. Your lawyer should represent your child's interest at the hearing. No conviction for a crime appears on a minor's record.

Nevertheless, treatment for juvenile offenders can be severe. The United States Supreme Court in 1984 upheld New York's pretrial detention law for juveniles, which permits confinement of alleged delinquents while awaiting trial, based on the presumption of a serious risk that the child would commit a crime if released. Associate Justice William Rehnquist, who wrote the decision, stated that pretrial detention provides "the youth with a controlled environment—separating him from improper influences pending the speedy disposition of his case." Moreover, since in New York there is no standard legal age for adults, a child of thirteen could be treated as an adult in a criminal case.

13

Caveat Venditor:
Your Rights as a Consumer

- The most common anti-consumer actions taken by sellers
- How consumer law strikes back
- How criminal law strikes back
- New trends in consumer law

Caveat emptor, which translates from the Latin as "Let the buyer beware," means that if the seller stings you, you have no recourse in law. And, though it may seem unbelievable to a generation of consumer rights advocates, that *was* the law in the U.S.A. not too long ago: The consumer had no rights.

But, as we've stressed in these pages, the law follows the economy—and in an economy largely dependent for its continued prosperity on the consumer, the consumer is always right. Pro-consumer legislation derives partially from a sense of social justice, but overwhelmingly from our business-oriented legislatures' abhorrence of killing the goose that lays the golden eggs. "We have reached the point," stated the 1966 court decision that gave birth to consumer law, "where 'let the buyer beware' is poor business philosophy." "The law," added another court decision in 1969, "is beginning to fight back." By 1984, state legislatures alone were enacting more than four-thousand pro-consumer laws a year.

It is no surprise, then, that consumer rights have been a major concern of this book. The book tells you what your rights are when you buy medical services (Chapters 2 and 3); when you buy credit and everything credit can buy (Chapters 4 and 5); when you contract for anything (Chapter 6); when you buy or rent a home (Chapter 7); when you buy a small business or stock in a corporation (Chapter 8); when you're hurt or your property is damaged by a product or service you've bought (Chapter 11); when you buy a lemon (Chapter 14); and when you buy beyond your means (Chapter 5).

The book introduces you to the landmark legislation from 1968 on that protects your rights as a consumer: the Consumer Credit Code, the Fair Credit Billing Act, the Fair Credit Opportunity Act, and the Truth in Lending Act (all in Chapter 4); the Magnuson-Moss Act, also known as the Warranty Act, and the groundbreaking New York Automobile Quality Products Act (both in Chapter 14); the Bankruptcy Reform Act of 1978 and its revision in 1984 (Chapter 5); and the Civil Rights Act of 1968 and the Rehabilitation Act of 1973 (both in Chapter 14), which shield the consumer against discrimination because of race, color, sex, religion, national origin, and handicap.

But as Stephen A. Newman, Associate Professor of Law at New York Law School and a leading authority on consumer law, wryly comments, "Even with favorable laws, too much consumer exploitation goes unpunished.... [While] printed contracts, legal representation, and middle-class appearances all confer an aura of respectability and legitimacy on sellers ... the most reputable [-appearing of these] sellers may stay in business for years, cutting corners on quality ... engaging in overbilling ... refusing to repair or replace shoddy goods ... and using false sales practices." On a certain level of business—Professor Newman characterizes it as business "dealing with poor persons," to which we add "and business dealing with unsophisticated persons"—it's a buyer-seller war.

But it's a war that the consumer can win. "Today," asserts Professor Newman, "any lawyer representing a consumer who has been treated unfairly can feel reasonably sure that a legal [basis] exists ... to support a claim for redress.... The chances for success are excellent." Consumer law, strong and getting stronger almost daily, is the weaponry of victory. A formidable new breed of lawyer—the consumer lawyer—is the striking force. "Let the seller beware, too!" exhorted the 1966 court decision with which consumer law began. In Latin, "Let the seller beware," is *Caveat venditor*—and that's the new battle cry of the consumer.

This chapter deals with some of the major ways the seller attacks the poor and/or unsophisticated consumer, and the potent legal ways that consumers can strike back. *Caveat venditor!*

THE MOST COMMON ANTI-CONSUMER ACTIONS TAKEN BY SELLERS

· *What are the top ten anti-consumer actions taken by sellers?*

Here they are, not necessarily in order of their frequency or dollar value:

1. BAIT-AND-SWITCH ADVERTISING. This is best described by an example. A seller of sewing machines advertises a model at an exceptionally low price. That is the bait. But the machine has been rigged to jam on demonstration, and the salesperson warns the consumer that when the machine jams, the needle could break, and people have lost eyes that way. "I recommend this other machine instead. It costs more, but it's safe." That is the switch.

2. FRAUDULENT SALES OF HEARING AIDS. While most hearing aid dealers are honest and reputable, some have tainted the reputation of the business with a pattern of fraudulent practices, misleading advertising, gross negligence, and price gouging— abuses so flagrant that in New York all hearing aid dealers must be registered with the secretary of state. Further, dealers may sell hearing aids only on a prescription from a doctor or an audiologist, and they must offer a thirty-day money-back guarantee. You have to be careful when you buy a hearing aid if similar regulations do not apply in your state.

3. UNCONSCIONABILITY. Unconscionability is a legal term defined in 1889 by the U.S. Supreme Court as a deal "such as no man in his senses and not under delusion would make...and no honest and fair man would accept." From the consumer's view-

point, that translates into modern language as a real raw deal. Today, consumer law recognizes two general types of unconscionability:

In *price unconscionability*, the price of goods or services is way out of line compared with normal retail prices, or even with the seller's own usual prices. The sale of *objets d'art* at twice or three times their value to unsophisticated consumers with no knowledge of the art market is unconscionable. So is the sale of a $300 food freezer to a non-English-speaking immigrant for $1,439.60.

In *nonprice unconscionability* the value you receive for your money is nil or almost so. It is unconscionable to take $1,200 for a data processing technician course from a young man who never got by the sixth grade, understands English imperfectly, and flunked the pre-course aptitude test. It is also unconscionable for a catering hall to refuse, on cancellation of a booking, to return a deposit of $350 on the grounds that there is no time to find a replacement booking—when the cancellation is made well in advance of booking date.

4. TRAVEL AGENCY MISCONDUCT. Some travel agencies have been known to misrepresent details of tours and personal travel arrangements (price and quality of hotels and meals, airport and bus transportation, guides, side trips, and so on), price-gouge on group-fare rates, leave tourists stranded by defaulting on payments to airlines, and fail to keep promises.

5. PYRAMID SCHEMES. This is how a pyramid scheme works. The promoter starts a pyramid at the apex with the sale of the right to sell distributorships for a product to at least four people. The buyer invests X dollars, and when he makes the four sales, reaps 4X dollars. That's a 400 percent return, sometimes in just a few days—and that's the almost irresistible attraction of the scheme.

The base of the pyramid has now broadened to four investors. They have to find sixteen buyers. Still easy. But the sixteen investors have to find sixty-four buyers. It's getting harder. The sixty-four investors have to find 256 buyers. Tougher yet. The 256 must find 1,024; the 1,024, 4,096; the 4,096, 16,784, and so on. As the base of the pyramid grows bigger and bigger, the probability of finding buyers becomes smaller and smaller. Only ten steps down from the apex, 67,696 investors would have to find 270,784 buyers. Are there 270,784 people in your community, let alone 270,784 buyers?

The point is: If you get in on a pyramid scheme early, while the base of the pyramid is small, you stand a chance of making a small killing. But if you get in late, when the base of the pyramid has become enormous, you have no chance at all. Moreover, when the offer comes to you—usually by mail—you have no idea of the size of the base. A pyramid scheme is not an investment; it's a pure gamble.

6. INFLATED JEWELRY OR ART APPRAISALS. Since the appraiser's fee is a percentage of the valuation, the appraiser may inflate the valuation, giving you a false appraisal and charging you too much in one fell swoop.

7. SENDING YOU MERCHANDISE YOU DIDN'T ORDER. Why would a seller send you something you didn't order? If it's food, you're tempted to taste it. If it's a gadget, you're likely to play with it. If it's anything at all, you may be too busy or too greedy to send it back. Then the bill comes.

8. UNASSEMBLED PRODUCTS. If you buy a packaged toy for your child and the seller does not inform you it needs assembly, that's a consumer ripoff. You're paying for an assembled product, but you wind up putting it together for hours on Christmas Eve, trying to decipher an instruction sheet that seems to be written in algebra.

9. THE CASH-OR-CREDIT SWITCH. The seller promises you a cash refund or credit if you're not fully satisfied. You're not, and you ask for the cash refund. Sorry, you're told, we promised a cash refund *or* credit, and the choice is ours: it's credit.

10. MAIL-ORDER FRAUD. Mail-order fraud works in several ways. Your order is never filled. Your order is filled, but not with the merchandise you ordered. You get the merchandise you ordered, but it doesn't match the advertising description. The merchandise that looked good in the catalog turns out to be shoddy or flimsy, or it doesn't work. The merchandise is everything the seller claims it to be, but it's outrageously overpriced. You send the merchandise back for a refund, but you never get it.

HOW CONSUMER LAW STRIKES BACK

· *Is there a uniform* caveat venditor *code?*

Unfortunately not. But remember, the concept of *caveat venditor* is new. It's only within the last two decades that the courts have begun to reject the centuries-old common law doctrine of *caveat emptor.* Federal, state, and local *caveat venditor* legislation and juridical decisions have proliferated in a disorganized way with no attempt at coordination. In the absence of a uniform code, your lawyer searches the multitude of laws and court cases governing fraud, unconscionability, and warranty, and the constantly expanding volume of specific consumer laws and court decisions elucidating them, to arrive at the strategy and tactics to win your *caveat venditor* action.

· What are the *caveat venditor* responses to the top ten anti-consumer actions taken by sellers?

Here, in essence, is how those various federal, state, and local *caveat venditor* laws strike back at the seller.

1. *Bait-and-switch advertising* is illegal, and subjects the seller to possible fines and criminal penalties. Merchandise purchased as a result of bait-and-switch advertising may be returned for a full refund.
2. Anti-consumer practices concerning *hearing aid sales* are effectively inhibited by mandatory registration of dealers with government agencies. Unregistered dealers are not permitted to engage in hearing aid sales; and misconduct may cause denial or loss of registration. Requirements of prescription-only sales and money-back guarantees further curtail the dealers' capacity for anti-consumer action. Violators are subject to fines and sometimes criminal penalties.
3. *Unconscionability* makes any agreement unenforceable. That means you don't have to pay for any unconscionable deal; and if you have paid, you can get your money back.
4. The penalties for *travel agency misconduct* include full

refunds, cancellation of contracts, fines, and, in some cases, payment of punitive damages. Some acts of misconduct are misdemeanors.

5. *Pyramid schemes* are banned in most states, and perpetrators are subject to criminal as well as civil penalties.

6. You can collect damages and reasonable attorneys' fees for fraudulent *appraisals of jewelry and art* (as well as watches and objects containing precious stones or metals).

7. *Unordered merchandise* is considered to be a gift. You can keep whatever is sent you, and you don't have to pay a cent or be obligated in any way. Should the sender harass you with continued bills and demands for payment, your attorney may sue to obtain an injunction to stop the harassment, and collect court costs and legal fees from the sender.

8. If a package contains more than a certain number of *unassembled parts* (usually six), a notice to that effect must be displayed prominently on the box, or on a sign very close to where the box is placed on sale; and the instructions for assembly must be clear and simple. In addition, advertisements must state in large type that the product is not assembled. Violation of any of these regulations entitles the consumer to cancel the sale and obtain a full refund.

9. When a seller promises a *refund or credit* if you're not fully satisfied, the choice is yours. The seller cannot switch you to credit when you demand a refund. If the seller insists on credit, a lawyer's letter usually gets you the refund fast.

10. *Caveat venditor* laws against *mail-order fraud* include these major ones: A mail-order business must deliver goods in thirty days or offer a refund. If goods ordered are not available, and a mail-order business sends substitute merchandise of similar or superior quality, the consumer need not accept it, and can return it for a full refund. A mail-order business must offer an if-not-fully-satisfied money-back guarantee of the full purchase price on return of merchandise. The legal name and street address of a mail-order business must appear in its advertising to facilitate complaints and legal action, if necessary.

• *Licensing of some sellers predates* caveat venditor *laws. Can I still take a* caveat venditor *action?*

Yes. If the seller of goods or services does not live up to the standards of conduct and performance set by the licensing agency, loss of license can result; and the seller cannot operate without a license. If a seller who should be licensed isn't, contracts with him may be rendered illegal and unenforceable— which is to say, you may not have to pay for goods ordered or services performed, and if you have paid, you may get a full refund.

Licensing is usually required of businesses or professionals associated with a high potential for incompetent or illegal activities. These include auctioneers, auto repair shops, banks, employment agencies, funeral directors, health spas and gyms, home improvement salespeople and contractors, insurance agents and brokers, insurance adjusters, loan companies, nursing homes, process servers, radio and TV service dealers, real estate salespeople and brokers, and private trade and correspondence schools.

• *Retail installment contracts have been known to contain provisions unfavorable to the consumer. Do* caveat venditor *laws help?*

Yes. Any of the following unfair provisions in a retail installment contract (page 81) are void, even though the contract as a whole remains valid:

- Any provision allowing the creditor to accelerate payment arbitrarily and without reasonable cause of all, or any part, of the amount due
- Any provision accelerating payments after a default and repossession, if the consumer then resumes making payments on time
- Any provision authorizing the creditor to enter the consumer's premises unlawfully, or commit a breach of the peace, in order to repossess the product
- Any provision relieving the seller from "liability for any legal remedy . . . the buyer may have had against the seller under the contract"
- Any provision creating a security interest of the seller's in

any property other than the property sold under the terms of the contract. (Example: if you're buying a TV set, you can't be required to put up your furniture as collateral)
- Any provision appointing the creditor as the consumer's agent to perform collection or repossession
- Any provision permitting assignment to the creditor of the consumer's wages in case of default
- Any provision that waives a trial by jury in case of dispute
- Any provision that waives the consumer's claims arising from illegal acts caused to be committed by the creditor in the course of collection or repossession

· *What misrepresentations are made by door-to-door salespeople, and what are the* caveat venditor *remedies?*

Typical misrepresentations include:

- Hiding the true purpose of the sales call. ("I'm making a survey. Would you mind answering a few questions?")
- Misquoting the total price as the cash price. ("This set of *Bible Stories* costs only $245," but no mention of credit costs of $187.12.)
- Accepting a very low down payment to draw attention away from the high cost of the merchandise. ("All your neighbors will be green with envy. And it's yours for only 99 cents!")
- Calling the contract just a receipt. ("You can cancel at any time. Nothing's binding.")
- Giving a "free" gift which has strings attached. ("Sure, this gift is yours—free—just as soon as I finish demonstrating this vacuum cleaner.")

Caveat venditor laws have declared such misrepresentations illegal. If you are victimized by such practices, you are entitled to a cancellation of the contract and a full refund, and you can possibly press for criminal charges.

The laws also provide that the consumer has the right to cancel any door-to-door contracts within three days; that the seller must inform the consumer of the right to cancel; that if the seller does not give the consumer notice of the right to cancel, the consumer's right to cancel can be extended indefinitely; that in the event of cancellation the seller must return all payments, and the consumer may retain possession of all goods until repayment has been made; and that, should repayment not be made in ten days, the seller is liable for a fine (usually about $100) and reasonable lawyer's fees.

· *Is a class action* caveat venditor *suit possible?*

Yes, and it has been since the early 1970s. A class action suit is brought not by an individual but by a group of people all of whom have allegedly been injured or had their property damaged in the same way by the same business or government agency. The group is called a class—hence, class action. When a consumer class action suit is won, the seller is likely to be required to pay damages far greater than the damages that would have been awarded to a single consumer—*caveat venditor* with a vengeance. Requirements for acceptance of a *caveat venditor* class action suit by a court are:

- The class has to be numerous.
- The basic questions concerning law and fact have to be common to all members of the class.
- The few consumers who actually take part in the litigation have to be typical of the class.
- Class action has to be judged by the court as better than any other type of action for adjudicating the claim.

Successful *caveat venditor* actions have been brought in state and federal courts against a wide variety of businesses, ranging from cab companies, travel agencies, and real estate sales organizations to banks, security investment firms, and pharmaceutical manufacturers.

· *What part do government consumer-protection agencies play in* caveat venditor *actions?*

On local levels, they can be effective in straightening out minor disputes between consumers and sellers in favor of consumers (but, often, consumer action departments of local newspapers and radio and TV stations are faster and more effective). On most state and federal levels, service to consumers can be frustratingly slow and tangled in red tape, but eventually satisfactory. At the very highest-level government consumer protection agency, the FTC (Federal Trade Commission), you can expect no action solely on your behalf. The FTC, which has the broadest consumer protection duties, is concerned not with resolving individual consumer problems, but with building cases against violators of FTC regulations. On all levels, no government agency will become involved with a consumer complaint if it is either in personal litigation or is best resolved by personal litigation.

You'll find local and state consumer complaint bureaus listed in your White Pages. Following is a list of major federal government agencies that act on consumer complaints, arranged alphabetically according to the type of complaint handled. Before seeking the help of any government consumer-protection agency, it is prudent to consult your lawyer.

Automotive Safety Complaints
National Transportation Safety Board
U.S. Department of Transportation
Washington, DC 20044

Communications (Radio, TV) Complaints
Federal Communications Commission
1919 M Street, N.W.
Washington, DC 20554

Credit Complaints
Bureau of Consumer Protection
Federal Trade Commission (FTC)
Washington, DC 20580
See also page 69.

Drug Complaints
Food and Drug Administration
5600 Fishers Lane
Rockville, MD 20852

Health Complaints
United States Public Health Service
5000 Fishers Lane
Rockville, MD 20852

Food Complaints
See *Drug Complaints*.

Mail-Order Complaints
Office of the Chief Postal Inspector
U.S. Postal Service
Washington, DC 20260

Product Safety Complaints
Consumer Products Safety Commission
Washington, DC 20207

Securities Complaints
Securities and Exchange Commission
500 North Capitol Street, N.W.
Washington, DC 20549

For an encyclopedic listing of government consumer protection agencies, including regional offices, consult the *Directory of Consumer Protection*, published by Academic Media, 32 Lincoln Avenue, Orange, NJ 07050.

HOW CRIMINAL LAW STRIKES BACK

· *Can I bring criminal charges against a seller for an anti-consumer action?*

Some *caveat venditor* statutes in some states carry criminal as well as civil penalties. In all states, some violations of the criminal code may be applied to anti-consumer actions. The more common criminal actions perpetrated by sellers include:

Fraudulently obtaining a signature. A salesperson makes false promises to obtain a signed contract.

Criminal impersonation. Pretending, with intent to defraud, to be a member of a business or a government agency. Example: A woman sells cosmetics door-to-door on the pretense that she's an employee of the Department of Welfare, and the proceeds will go to poor people.

Criminal usury. Interest rate above 25 percent per annum. Example: A retailer does a "favor" for a customer who can't obtain credit by selling him an appliance at 33⅓ percent interest.

False statement of credit terms. Example: A salesperson promises a special low rate of interest on purchase of children's clothes; actually, the interest rate is as high as permitted by state law.

Unlawful collection practices. Example: Sending a collection letter bearing what looks like the seal of the United States.

Fraudulent accosting. When you're deprived of money in a public place by a trick, swindle, or confidence game. Example: The $500 watch you buy from a street vendor in a "factory-sealed package" for $50 turns out to be a fake worth $5.

Scheme to defraud. When you're one of a group of people who are victimized by a scheme involving fraudulent pretenses, representations, or promises. Example: At a free dinner party for a hundred prospects given by a real estate development company, you and others are sold parcels of retirement land that turn out to be in a desert.

• *How do I bring a criminal complaint against a seller?*

Call the District Attorney's office or the State Attorney General's Office (see your White Pages). But before taking any action against a seller, civil or criminal, it's wise to consult your lawyer.

NEW TRENDS IN CONSUMER LAW

In the early 1980s, legislation strengthened consumer protection in traditional areas such as mail-order fraud and credit practices, and began to cover businesses which up to then were only flimsily covered by specific *caveat venditor* restraints. These businesses include funeral homes, fitness spas, home insulation companies, mobile homes sales companies, dealers in ophthalmic goods and services, vocational and home study schools, and used car dealers.

But in 1984, an innovative trend was initiated by the 98th Congress of the United States, which placed emphasis on consumer health legislation that not only permitted the consumer to strike back more effectively at manufacturers of health-harmful products but also encouraged health-service sources to meet previously unsatisfied consumer needs. Here is a capsule summary of the major 1984 federal consumer health legislation:

- New sterner and more explicit warnings against the dangers of smoking—called by the Surgeon General of the United States, Dr. C. Everett Koop, "the greatest public health threat in the country"—are required to appear on cigarette packages and advertising.
- Manufacturers of generic drugs—inexpensive but equally potent copies of brand-name drugs—are now permitted to market their products faster than before and with less red tape. (Generic drugs are less expensive than brand-name drugs.)
- Manufacturers of orphan drugs—medicines necessary to treat rare diseases, but seldom manufactured because of low demand and hence low profit—are now given incentives to go into production (longer patent time is one).
- About $31 million was appropriated for a computerized system designed to match organ donors with recipients at the time of implantation, which could avoid an estimated twenty-thousand deaths a year.
- The Consumer Products Safety Commission was authorized to recall dangerous toys (as well as cribs and other children's furniture) in days rather than weeks or months, with the object of drastically reducing injuries to children (123,000 in 1983 alone).

The same trend toward health-oriented consumer legislation was also evident on state levels. Statutes ranged from requiring the dating of hot dogs to mandatory checks on radiation leaks of microwave ovens to obligatory inspection of new homes for toxic substances. Numerous statutes are aimed at the prevention of injury, particularly of motorists and their passengers. Outstanding among 1984's automotive safety laws are these from New York State which help protect against the use of the necessary but dangerous product that the automobile has become (50,000 deaths and 500,000 injuries a year):

- The mandatory seat belt law requires that the driver of a car, all passengers in the front seat, and all children between the ages of four and nine wherever they sit be restrained by safety belts. Children under four must be restrained by a safety seat. The law covers private cars and school buses, but exempts other buses as well as taxis, trucks, and tractors. Violators are liable for fines of up to $500.

- The mandatory drunken driving license suspension law requires the suspension of the license of any drunken driver who is also charged with assault or homicide, or who has been convicted of drunken driving during the previous five years.
- The national precedent-setting "used car lemon law" aims not only to protect the consumer from a bad buy, but also to remove defective, and hence dangerous, used cars from the highways. The law (see page 271) requires the used-car dealer to provide a warranty, and to replace a defective car or provide a full refund if the car has a major defect or cannot be repaired.

If the trend that began in 1984 is to continue, then consumer legislation at all levels will be concerned less with traditional consumer matters such as retail ripoffs and scams—a plethora of legal coverage now exists—than with health, safety, and the safer use of dangerous products, such as cigarettes, motor vehicles, and some therapeutic drugs (including those that fight cancer), that cannot be recalled from the market. The stick of *caveat venditor* laws will be supplemented by the carrot of laws encouraging the seller to provide better products and services for the consumer's needs. The consumer, as he has since the 1960s, will enjoy increasing protection by the law; and, in a society largely based on consumption, that means he will enjoy life more. The law in America, as we said in the early pages of this book, is designed for *you*.

14

Restrictions on Your Everyday Rights: From Your Right to Love to Your Right to Nondiscrimination

The legal rights we explore together in this book are linked to the key moments and activities of your life from birth to death. But there's another complex of legal rights that is part of the day-in, day-out pattern of our lives. Some, such as the right to speak your mind and to attend a town meeting, stem explicitly from the Bill of Rights— the first ten Amendments to the Constitution of the United States. Others, such as the right to bring up your children and to eat and drink what you please, probably have their legal basis in the Ninth Amendment, which guarantees that the government cannot deny rights held by the people. And still other rights, such as freedom from slavery and women's right to vote, have come through combat and struggle culminating in emancipating Amendments to the Constitution.

Some of these everyday rights have been part of American life since the Bill of Rights became effective in 1791. But slavery wasn't abolished until the Thirteenth Amendment became law in 1865. The dictum that no state shall "deprive any person of life, liberty or property, without due process of law; nor deny to any person within its jurisdiction the equal protection of the laws" was not incorporated into the Constitution until the Fourteenth Amendment was ratified in 1868. The Fifteenth Amendment, which established that "the right of citizens of the United States to vote shall not be denied or abridged by the United States or by any State on account of race, color or previous condition of servitude," was enacted as late as 1870; and it took ninety-four more years before payment of a poll tax as a condition for voting was prohibited by the Twenty-fourth Amendment. Women didn't get the right to vote until 1920 (the Nineteenth Amendment). The flood of federal civil rights legislation which became the foundation for today's nondiscriminatory society didn't begin until the 1960s.

Born from a long, slow, and often painful gestation, our everyday rights are the crowning achievement of American democracy. But they're not pure rights; they're limited. They always have been, because unrestricted rights can lead to anarchy. Only when they operate within a framework of restrictions provided by law can our rights achieve their purpose: individual happiness and well-being within a stable and prosperous state.

Today new restrictions of another kind may be threatening to turn back the clock for women, blacks, the aged, the handicapped, and the believers that the state must not become entangled with religion. This chapter is a brief account of both kinds of restrictions—those rooted in tradition and those as fresh as the latest Supreme Court decision.

• Can the government restrict my right to make love?

Yes, under certain conditions. Intercourse with a minor with or without consent—"statutory rape"—is a criminal offense in most states. Many states have statutes against incest, adultery, bigamy, homosexuality, oral sex, sodomy, and intercourse with animals, but they are seldom enforced.

• Can the government restrict my right to have children?

Yes, in the following instances. Inmates of state penitentiaries in some states may be sterilized if they are the bearers of hereditary diseases causing insanity or imbecility. While the government cannot prevent you from having a child out of wedlock, it can deny your right to social services unless you name the father of the child and bring a paternity suit against him. (The purpose of a paternity suit is to place responsibility for the support of the child on the natural father.) In some states, you may not become a surrogate mother—that is to say, you are forbidden by law to carry a test-tube baby or another woman's embryo in your womb, or to be artifically inseminated for another women.

· Can the government restrict my right not to have children?

Only during the second and third trimesters of pregnancy (a trimester is a three-month period). During the second trimester many states will not permit an abortion unless it is necessary to protect your health. In the final trimester, pregnancy can be stopped only to preserve the life of the unborn child, which is the reverse of abortion.

But whether you're married or unmarried, you have the right to abort the fetus during the first three months of pregnancy if your doctor agrees with your decision.

· Can the government restrict my right to bring up my children?

Yes. Your state may limit, and possibly terminate, your right to bring up your children if you have been found guilty of abusing them, neglecting them, or placing them in foster care without attempting to secure their return. Compulsory education also limits your right to bring up your children. But you can send them to a private school of your choice, provided the school meets your state's standards.

· Can the government restrict my right to work?

Yes, directly by requiring licenses and permits for certain types of professional and business activities, and indirectly by granting unions the right to prohibit employment of nonunion members. Some states, though, have passed "right to work" laws which protect nonunion members against discrimination by unions. Federal legislation and many state statutes, though, protect your right to work by prohibiting discrimination in employment by reason of race, religion, national origins, sex, and advanced age. There is no federal protection against discrimination against homosexuals, but some states have enacted homosexual anti-discrimination statutes.

· *Can the government restrict my right* not *to work?*

Under certain circumstances, yes. You can be required by the government to work as a juror or as a member of the military establishment. A judge may dispose of a criminal case against you by making certain types of work obligatory. Work may be a condition of penal servitude. And in most states, you can't collect unemployment insurance or receive welfare benefits unless you certify your willingness to work.

· *Can the government restrict my right to select my customers?*

Yes. If you're serving the general public, the government denies you the right to reject customers because of race, color, creed, or sex. If you're not serving the *general* public—if, for instance, you're selling $2,500 custom-made suits or running a private club—it is questionable whether the antidiscrimination laws apply. However, whether you're serving the general public or not, affirmative action programs may require that you select certain types of customers. Many private clubs, for example, have been forced to accept women members and others against whom they had discriminated.

· *Can the government restrict my right to take care of my health and my family's?*

Yes. Vaccination, sanitation, and health laws limit that right. You may be denied the right to procure some therapeutic drugs which have been approved for use in other countries but have not been approved here. If you are a terminal case, kept alive by medical technology, your family may be denied the right to "pull the plug." You may be denied the right to treat yourself or other members of your family with nonstandard therapies, even though all standard therapies have failed.

· *Can the government restrict my right to eat, drink, and smoke whatever and wherever I like?*

Yes. Federal, state, and local laws prevent the sale of food and beverages which may be harmful to you.

State statutes set drinking ages—ages at which young adults are permitted to purchase alcoholic beverages—and control the times when alcoholic beverages can be purchased or consumed in a public place. In some states, hosts or barkeepers are held liable if drunken guests or customers are involved in auto accidents. A 1984 federal law will withhold some highway construction funds to those states that fail to enact a minimum drinking age of twenty-one by October 1, 1986.

Although smoking tobacco is, according to the U.S. Surgeon General, a potential health hazard linked to cancer, emphysema, and heart disease, it is not prohibited. However, since smoking can be a fire hazard, and the smoke itself can be harmful to others, local and state statutes prohibit smoking in many locations. The smoking of marijuana (except for medical purposes) is prohibited, but enforcement is loose.

· Can the government restrict my right to travel?

Yes, to an unfriendly nation. The restriction, which is based on the 1917 Trading with the Enemy Act, was sustained in 1984 by the United States Supreme Court in the case of curbs on travel to Cuba. Violation of the travel ban carries a possible penalty of up to $50,000 and up to ten years in jail.

· Can the government restrict my rights to life and liberty?

Yes, but only with due process of law. You can be detained for a short time before trial on suspicion of a crime, and for a long time if you fail to post bail. Should you be found guilty of a crime, you can go to jail or even be executed.

· Can the government restrict my right to my property?

Yes, if it's done with "due process of law." That is to say, the government can take over your home and land (say, to make room for a missile site), kill your animals (if they're dangerous, for example), destroy your harvest (should it be the carrier of a contagious disease), and so on. When the government takes over your property, you receive payment for it.

• *Can the government restrict my right to personal privacy?*

Yes. The I.R.S. and the Census Bureau invade your privacy, and so, in some instances, do other government agencies such as the FBI when they collect information about you. However, the Privacy Act of 1974 prohibits the federal government from using information collected about you for other than purposes prescribed by law. This act also gives you the right to obtain information about yourself held by an agency (say, the IRS), to control the transfer of that information to another agency (say, the FBI), and to request correction of misinformation and deletion of irrelevant information.

• *Can the government restrict my right to freedom of expression?*

Yes. You can't threaten to overthrow the government by force. You can't create a clear and present danger—by, for instance, crying "Fire!" in a crowded theater when there is no fire. Local laws prohibit numerous acts, such as doing an obscene monologue in a nightclub. You can't unjustly malign the reputation of another person; if you do, it's slander if spoken, libel if written. These restrictions apply to freedom of speech and of the press, which now includes motion pictures, graphics, and the electronic media.

• *Can the government restrict my right of freedom of assembly?*

Freedom of assembly permits you to come together in a public place to discuss issues affecting the general public; and yes, there are restrictions. The meeting must be peaceful, comply with local laws, and not infringe on the rights or affect the safety of other people. These restrictions govern picketing for labor and nonlabor purposes as well.

• *Can the government restrict my right to own a gun?*

Yes, even though the right to bear arms is guaranteed by the Second Amendment to the United States Constitution. The reason: The patriots who wrote the Constitution believed that the nation's survival depended on a citizen's militia. Hence, the right to bear arms was granted to every citizen. But the need for a citizens' militia has long passed, and now the possession of lethal weapons may constitute a threat to the peace. As a consequence, state laws control the sale, ownership, and possession of certain lethal weapons, and prohibit the sale of others. You can legally obtain handguns and hunting weapons, for example, but there are no legitimate consumer outlets for military armaments.

· *Can the government restrict my right not to be attacked physically?*

Yes. In 1983, the Supreme Court held, in effect, that the use of "choke holds" by the Los Angeles police is legal. A "choke hold" blocks a major artery in the neck and can cause unconsciousness and even death. Police may use force when necessary under the state's power to promote safety and welfare. But in all other cases, the government preserves your right against physical attack (an action known in law as "assault"). Charges of assault and battery can result in criminal and civil actions.

· *Can the government restrict my right to know what the government is doing?*

Yes, even though the Freedom of Information Act grants you the right to examine and copy all records on file with federal agencies. Critics of the Act contend that in practice, agency fees for search and duplication are unreasonably high; a substantial part of a fee must be paid in advance; and inordinately long times, often more than a year, are taken to fill requests. Moreover, each agency has the right to select certain categories of material as exempt from the act. However, if your request for information is denied because the material is in an exempt category, you have the right to challenge the agency's classification in a state or federal court.

To request information from a federal agency, write or appear in person. Addresses of all federal agencies appear in the *Federal Register*, which the government is required by law to publish. For information on how it can be obtained by mail, write the National Archives of the United States, Washington, DC.

· *Can the government restrict my rights not to buy a lemon?*

A background briefing before we answer that question.

A dictum of the common law was *caveat emptor*—let the buyer beware. But in the 1960s, the buying revolution (we introduced you to it in Chapter 13) focused the spotlight on a new phenomenon: The nation's economy depended in a large measure on the *consumer,* a term no one had even heard of before the 1960s when national prosperity and massive consumption became synonymous. The consumer had to be treated with respect, and a rush of 1960s legislation from federal to local levels saw to it that he was.

The basic thrust of the consumer protection laws was to put an honest product in the buyer's hand, so he'd come back for more. Deception, fraud, shoddy manufacturing, and sharp practices were sales deterrents destructive to the consumer confidence index, and, as far as law can change human nature, they were legislated out of existence.

The key legislation came in 1975 with the passage by the Congress of the Magnuson-Moss Act, also called the Warranty Act. A warranty is a truthful statement by the seller guaranteeing the performance of goods. There are two kinds of warranties: expressed and implied. "Expressed" means that the manufacturer states explicitly—that is, warrants—that, for example, the product is free of defects and a part which becomes defective within a certain period of time will be replaced. "Implied" means that with the sale of the goods the consumer understands implicitly that the goods are free from defect and will perform the way they should. The Magnuson-Moss Act linked the implicit warranty to all sales of consumer goods, tightened the regulations for explicit warranties, and provided for punitive action against vendors who don't abide by the provisions of the act.

In essence, the Magnuson-Moss Act granted you the right not to buy a lemon: The vendor has to stand behind his product. But there are loopholes; manufacturers in some cases can fob off a lemon on you with impunity. So the answer to your question—"Can the government restrict my rights not to buy a lemon?"—is yes, by an act of omission, by failing to plug the loopholes.

However, in some states the loopholes are being plugged,

particularly in the area of car sales, where up to just a few years ago the consumer had virtually no recourse when stuck with a lemon. In New York, for example, a "lemon law," the New York Automobile Quality Products Act, enacted in 1983, extends the warranty and requires that a new-car lemon be repaired or replaced by the manufacturer or agent, or a full refund (less a reasonable depreciation) be made to the buyer. In 1984, the law was extended to used cars—a national first.

· *Can the government restrict women's rights?*

The government did in the past by not specifically legislating rights to women. Let's start with a flagrant example: the right to vote.

The Fourteenth Amendment appeared to provide equal rights for all citizens of the United States. The Amendment states in part:

"All persons born or naturalized in the United States and subject to the jurisdiction thereof, are citizens of the United States and the State wherein they reside. No State shall make or enforce any law which shall abridge the privileges or immunities of citizens of the United States; nor shall any State deprive any person of life, liberty, or property without due process of law; nor deny to any person within its jurisdiction the equal protection of the laws."

That put a woman on an equal footing with a man, but it didn't specifically grant her the right to vote. It wasn't until 1920, fifty-two years after the passage of the Fourteenth Amendment, that she could cast her vote. The Nineteenth Amendment states in part:

"The right of citizens of the United States to vote shall not be denied or abridged by the United States or by any State on account of sex."

Still, there was no prohibition in the Constitution or its Amendments specifically granting women equal rights with men in all other respects. Because of this, women's liberationists proposed a Twenty-seventh Amendment—the Equal Rights Amendment (ERA)—which stated in part:

"Equality of rights under the law shall not be denied or abridged by the United States nor any State on account of sex."

Opponents of the proposed Amendment argued that it was not needed, since equal rights for women already had been guaranteed by the Fourteenth and the Nineteenth Amendments. The argument succeeded, and the proposal was defeated in a sufficient number of state legislatures to prevent it from becoming the law of the land.

However, the death of the Twenty-seventh Amendment, according to the American Civil Liberties Union (ACLU), "masked the larger victory of the women's movement." Some state legislatures have adapted the ERA Amendment to their state constitutions; and a wide spectrum of women's rights are now protected by specific laws.

However, the ACLU claims that there are "some serious problems of sex discrimination"—such as the confinement of women to low-status, low-paying jobs with no reasonable chance for advancement—which the ERA could remedy.

State laws as they relate to women's rights in case of domestic violence, employment, public accommodations, housing, and education are described in *Rights of Women*, published by the American Civil Liberties Union, 132 West 42nd Street, New York, NY 10036. This 406-page handbook also contains more than 115 sources of additional help and information concerning sex-discrimination problems.

Gay rights seem to be following the progress pattern of women's rights. With no specific federal legislation to protect their rights, gays have to wage a continuous fight in the legislature and in the courts to prevent discrimination and achieve equality. For an in-depth review of homosexual rights, see *The Rights of Gay People*, published by the American Civil Liberties Union, 132 West 43rd Street, New York, NY 10036.

• *Can the government restrict my rights to religious freedom?*

Maybe.

The First Amendment forbids the government to give preference to any religion or to adopt a state religion. Our founding fathers set up a wall between church and state. That means you can follow any faith you choose, believe in God or not, and the government cannot interfere in any way.

Yet, the Pledge of Allegiance, as revised by the Eisenhower administration, includes the phrase "one nation under God," implying that all loyal Americans are believers in a divine being.

Yet, in a 1971 decision, the Supreme Court said that "the line of separation far from being a 'wall,' is a blurred, indistinct and variable barrier depending on all the circumstances of a particular relationship." The decision said further that a statute satisfies the Constitutional requirement of separation of church and state when it has a secular purpose, does not advance or inhibit religion, and does not foster "*excessive* government entanglement with religion." (Emphasis ours.)

Yet, in spite of a 1961 Supreme Court decision barring prayer and Bible reading in public schools, in 1984 President Reagan signed into law a bill prohibiting public high schools from preventing voluntary meetings of students for religious purposes before or after regular school hours.

Yet, pending Congressional legislation would permit or require children to spend one minute of their public school day in silence, during which time prayer may be an option.

Yet, the Supreme Court in 1984 permitted the city of Pawtucket, Rhode Island, to include a Nativity scene as part of an official Christmas display. The creche, an explicit symbol of Christianity, did not appear alone in the display but was accompanied by a reindeer and other secular symbols of Christmas. The Supreme Court consequently viewed the display as symbolizing not a Christian holiday but a secularized American one. Whether the Pawtucket display would have been sanctioned if it did not contain the secular symbols is problematical. That problem may be settled in a case now before the U.S. Court of Appeals involving a display in a public park of only the Nativity figures.

It would seem, based on the Pawtucket case and other recent decisions including those upholding the constitutionality of tax deductions for parochial schools and of prayers by chaplains in state legislatures, that the Supreme Court is leaning toward some restriction of religious freedom as defined by the First Amendment. The explanation may be found in Chief Justice Warren E. Burger's statement in his Pawtucket decision that "the wall of separation" between church and state is "a useful figure of speech" but "not a wholly accurate description of the practical aspects of the relationship that in fact exists." What

Justice Burger appears to be saying is that there is a *de facto* government entanglement in religion, and the courts should recognize it.

• Can the government restrict my right to be protected from discrimination?

Never in human history has there been such an outpouring of legislation to protect your civil rights as there has been in this nation over the last several decades. You are protected against discrimination because of race, color, sex, religion, national origin, age, and handicap by specific federal laws, including the Civil Rights Act of 1968, the Rehabilitation Act of 1973, and counterpart state statutes. You cannot be discriminated against by the following:

- A bank, savings and loan association, credit union, store or any other source of credit
- A public or private school, college, or university
- An employer, labor union, or employment agency
- A real estate broker or a seller or renter of a house or apartment
- A hotel, restaurant, theater, sport arena, swimming facility, or park
- A voter registration office
- A courthouse or jail

Yet, in 1984, two Supreme Court decisions struck at civil rights legislation.

In the case of the Memphis firefighters, the Supreme Court ruled that white firefighters could not be laid off to protect the job rights of black firefighters with less seniority. This was, in essence, a repudiation of affirmative action programs as provided for in the Civil Rights Act of 1964. Affirmative action requires employers who, in the judgment of a court, have practiced job discrimination against blacks or women to give favorable treatment to them in the workforce by means of hiring quotas or otherwise.

In the case of the Grove City College, the Supreme Court ruled that a federal law prohibiting sexual discrimination by schools and colleges receiving federal funds applied only to offending departments and not the school or college as a whole. This has been interpreted as a weakening not only of laws protecting against sexual discrimination involving government funding, but of similar laws protecting against discrimination because of race, age, and handicap.

Congressional legislation is pending to remedy the decisions of the Supreme Court with a civil rights act that reaffirms the civil rights laws that stood prior to the Supreme Court's decisions.

The following U.S. government nondiscrimination guides are free.

A Compilation of Federal Laws and Executive Orders for Nondiscrimination and Equal Opportunity Programs may be obtained from: U.S. General Accounting Office, Distribution Section, Room 1518, 441 G St., N.W., Washington, DC 20548. Include the order number (HRD-78-138) and date of publication (August 2, 1978).

A Guide to Federal Laws and Regulations Prohibiting Sex Discrimination is available from: Publications Management Division, U.S. Commission on Civil Rights, Washington, DC 20425.

You and Your Lawyer:
The Client's Bill of Rights

Not too long ago, we sent a special, and we think a milestone, memo to all the attorneys on our staff. In this book, we're making that memo public. It contains the first Bill of Rights ever put together by a law firm for the benefit of its clients. This is the memo:

"A Client-Oriented Practice" by J. Harris Morgan, which appeared in a recent issue of *The National Law Journal*, reports some extraordinary findings concerning what clients look for in an attorney.

Summing up the results of numerous surveys of client opinion conducted by prestigious legal groups, the author concludes that:

1. Most lawyers are not client-oriented, and what they think is good for the client is, in the opinion of the client, wrong eight times out of ten.
2. What the client wants most—even more than results (although the client wants results)—is a clear demonstration of effort and concern. The client wants to know that you have his interest at heart, and that you're at work *for* him.

That's always been our credo at Jacoby and Meyers, but with the *American Law Journal* article in mind, let's firm it down. As of this day, let us declare—

A BILL OF RIGHTS FOR CLIENTS

- All clients have the right to receive copies of all paperwork and/or periodic status reports.
- All clients have the right to talk to you over a clean and uncluttered desk. The client must feel, and rightfully so, that you've cleared the desk for action—for *him*.
- All clients have the right during discussions to your full

and exclusive attention, without interruptions, especially telephone interruptions.

- All clients have the right to have their calls returned by the end of the business day, or at longest within twenty-four hours.
- All clients have the right to tell you what they want from you, and suggest how you can get it for them, and to have you proffer advice based on that right.
- All clients have the right to be treated in a businesslike manner, including full explanation of fees in the first consultation, and regular billings.
- All clients have the right to know how you intend to reach their goals: the options open, and the efforts you intend to make.
- All clients have the right to be treated with respect and dignity—and that starts with a friendly smile from the receptionist and up-to-date periodicals in the waiting area.
- All clients have the right to expect you to be a good and sympathetic listener—even though you've heard the story three hundred times before from three hundred different clients.
- All clients have the right to good, sound legal work.

People have always said to us, "Let's face it. The only way we can find an attorney is by recommendations or by reading ads. How do we know the attorney is right for us?" Our answer now is: A lawyer is right for you when he lives up to *A Bill of Rights for Clients*. You can get a good idea whether he does on your first consultation.

There's one proviso: The lawyer should be familiar with the field of your problem. You don't want a negligence lawyer handling a real estate case, any more than you'd want a pediatrician operating on you. That's another advantage of our type of law firm. We have attorneys with specific experience in most fields. And all our attorneys adhere to *A Bill of Rights for Clients*.

When you come to the right attorney as the kind of informed client this book has made you, you and he can work toward your goals cooperatively, efficiently, and with the least cost to you. We think that's the winning formula.

Gail Koff, for the partners of
Jacoby & Meyers, Summer 1984

GLOSSARY

Abstract of title is a short summary of the legal history of the title (ownership) of a house or other real property.

Adjective law deals with the forms and procedures for carrying out substantive law, which deals with principles.

Administrative agencies are arms of the government that have the statutory right to make their own regulations and enforce them.

Affidavit is a sworn statement in writing.

Affirmative action requires employers who in the judgment of the court have practiced job discrimination against blacks and women to give them favorable treatment in the workforce.

Annulment is a decision of the court that voids a marriage on the basis that there never was a legal marriage.

APR, annual percentage rate, is the true interest rate, arrived at by taking into consideration all finance charges.

Arbitration is a method of settling some civil disputes by a person or persons (arbitrators) chosen or approved by both parties.

Arraignment is a procedure by which a criminal suspect is acquainted with the charges against him, his Amendment rights, and asked how he pleads— guilty, not guilty, or guilty by reason of insanity.

Assault means threatening substantial bodily harm while demonstrating the ability to carry out the threat.

Baby Doe cases involve the right to a life-support system for irreversibly malformed newborns with short projected life expectancy.

Bail is money or property pledged to assure that a criminal suspect will appear for subsequent legal procedures.

A battered wife is one who is the victim of assault or battery by her husband.

Battery is the act of inflicting substantial bodily harm on another person.

A binder may be a deposit on the purchase of a house or other real property, or a purchase agreement for a house or other real property.

Chapter 7 is a section of the Federal Bankruptcy Act which grants a debtor the right to clear himself of debt by paying a percentage or nothing of what he owes.

Chapter 13 is a section of the Federal Bankruptcy Act which grants a debtor the right to pay off all or part of his debts on an easy payment plan under the protection of the court.

Circuits are the eleven geographical divisions of the federal court system; twelve, when the District of Columbia is included.

Civil law determines the rights of individuals to protect their persons and property against the wrongful, but not criminal, acts of others.

Closing is a legal ceremony to consummate the purchase of a home.

Codicil to a will is a legal amendment to a will.

Common law is a body of law derived from custom, usage, and court decisions.

Common-law marriage is a form of marriage entered into by a couple who live together and announce they're married but do not obtain a marriage license or participate in a marriage ceremony.

Community property is property, including earnings, acquired after marriage by the work and efforts of both spouses, which is shared equally according to the law of the state.

Community property states are states which mandate community property distribution for married couples.

Comparative negligence is a legal doctrine holding that a party who has contributed in part to injuries caused by another's negligence can recover damages only in proportion to the amount of negligence for which the injured party was responsible.

A condominium or condo is a multiunit dwelling project in which each unit consists of a dwelling plus interest in the areas and facilities designed for common use.

Constitutionality refers to whether a law conforms with the letter and spirit of the Constitution of the United States.

A contract is an agreement upon sufficient consideration to do or not to do a particular thing.

Contributory negligence is a legal doctrine holding that a party injured by another's negligence has no claim for damages if the injured party contributed in any way to the injury by his own negligence.

A cooperative or co-op is a multidwelling project in which the person who leases an apartment at the same time purchases shares in the corporation that owns the project.

A corporation is a form of business regarded by law as a person, different from the persons who own it, who are therefore not responsible for the debts of the corporation.

A credit profile is a report issued by a credit reporting agency on the credit payment performance of a debtor.

A credit reporting agency is an organization that records your credit payment performance and issues reports on it.

Crime is the violation of criminal law.

Criminal law provides governmental protection against acts harmful to the peace and order of society.

Death is now defined in many states as the irreversible cessation of the spontaneous action of the heart, lungs, and the whole brain.

A **deed** is a document that transfers title of real property from the seller to the buyer.

The **defendant** is the person against whom a legal action is brought.

Direct evidence immediately establishes the facts to support a claim.

Divorce is the legal dissolution of a marriage.

Earnest money is a deposit on the purchase of a house.

Emancipated describes a person who has not yet reached statutory adult age but whom the law regards as an adult because he has met certain statutory conditions.

An **encroachment** is an illegal intrusion on your property.

Entrapment occurs when a government agent induces a willing person to commit an illegal act.

Equity is a branch of law involving violations of civil law which cannot be redressed by money or by money alone.

Evidence is facts introduced to support a claim.

Exceptions are objections by lawyers on both sides to the decisions of a judge, and can form the basis of an appeal.

The **exclusionary rule** excludes the use of illegally obtained evidence in a criminal trial.

A **fault divorce** is granted on the premise that one party is at fault.

The **fault system** is a method of determining liability in an auto accident based on showing that one party was at fault.

Fraud is intentional deception.

A **garnishment** is an official notice to an employer to pay part of a debtor's wages directly to the creditor. The wages are said to be *garnished.*

General partnership is a partnership in which each partner is responsible for the acts of the other partners and for all partnership debts.

The **good faith exception to the exclusionary rule** permits the use of illegally obtained evidence in a criminal trial when the evidence was obtained without knowledge that the action by which it was obtained was illegal— that is to say, the person who obtained the evidence illegally was acting in good faith.

HP actions are taken to obtain a court order mandating that a landlord make repairs within a specific time.

Indirect evidence establishes a fact from which the fact to be proved can be inferred.

Informed consent is a legal doctrine stating that a doctor is required to inform his patient about everything concerning his illness and the proposed treatment and, on the basis of that information, obtain the consent of the patient before proceding.

An **inter vivos trust** or living trust names the beneficiaries who will inherit the trust after the death of the person who set up the trust. It can be employed as a tax-saving and probate-avoiding device.

Intestate means without a will.

Joint tenancy is a legal term for two or more people holding any kind of property together.

Joint tenancy with the right of survivorship grants one party the right to dispose of his share of the property without the consent of the other party.

Judgment is a formal entry of the court's decision in a civil action that the defendant is legally required to pay the plaintiff the sum awarded by the court.

Jurisdiction is the limits or area within which a court is empowered to make decisions.

Lemon laws provide recourse to the consumer stuck with a defective product, particularly in the purchase of new and used cars.

Liability limits are the maximum amounts your auto liability insurance pays in three categories: when you injure one person, when you injure more than one person, and when you damage property.

A lien is a legal claim against property, usually as a result of a debt.

A limited partnership is a partnership in which the liability of some of the partners, the limited partners, is limited to the amount of their investments.

Litigation means carrying on a legal contest by judicial process (rules).

Living together is an alternative to marriage based on an implied or expressed contract between the partners.

Living trust. See *inter vivos trust.*

A living will is a directive to disconnect a life-support system in the event of terminal illness or existence in a vegetative state.

Malpractice is a form of negligence committed by a professional whose departure from standard practice in the performance of his duties results in harm to others.

Medical malpractice is malpractice committed by medical professionals.

Miranda warnings, which advise a suspect of his constitutional rights, must be given immediately after arrest, except when the *public safety exception* is applied.

Misrepresentation is a false statement which may or may not be intentional.

A mortgage is a method of financing a house by putting up the property as security.

Negligence occurs when a person or persons are injured accidentally because another person or other persons act without reasonable care in the circumstances.

A no-fault divorce does not require either of the parties to be at fault.

The no-fault system is a means of collecting directly from one's own insurance company for damages resulting from injuries sustained in a car accident, regardless of whose fault the accident was.

A noncupative will is an oral will.

Palimony, for a couple who had a living-together arrangement, is the equivalent of alimony.

Partnership is an agreement of two or more persons to conduct an unincorporated business.

A plaintiff is a person bringing a civil action.

A postnuptial or postmarital contract is a contract executed after marriage, defining the nonstatutory rights and obligations of the partners in a marriage.

A prenuptial or premarital contract is in principle the same as a *postnuptial contract* except that it is executed prior to marriage.

A prima facie case is made when the presentation of the claim seems on first view by the court to be supported by sufficient evidence.

The public safety exception to the Miranda rule permits the police to omit or defer the Miranda warnings when the public safety is at stake.

Quid pro quo means "something in return for something," usually a condition for a valid contract.

Real property refers to items which are part of the land or affixed to it. It is synonymous with *real estate.*

Reciprocal wills are drawn up by a man and wife designating each other as sole beneficiaries.

Remedy at law involves violations of the civil law which can be remedied by the payment of money.

Rent control is a method of setting a ceiling on rents.

Rent stabilization is a method of setting a ceiling on periodic rent rises.

A rent strike is a method of obtaining tenants' rights by legally withholding rents.

Res ipsa loquitur means "the fact speaks for itself." Used in open-and-shut cases, particularly in malpractice suits in which, for example, a surgeon leaves an instrument inside the patient.

Right to die is the controversial right to reject a life-support system in the event of terminal illness or of continued existence in an irreversible vegetative state.

Right to live is the controversial right to a life-support system in the event of terminal existence, continued existence in an irreversible vegetative state, or being born with expectancy of a short, abnormal, and painful life.

Rules of evidence determine what means of proof of a claim the jury is permitted to consider.

Separation is a state of marriage in which the partners live apart.

7A proceedings provide the legal means for at least one-third of the tenants in an apartment house to request the court to appoint an administrator to run the building until all violations have been cleared up.

Sole proprietorship describes an unincorporated business with a single owner.

Spousal support, formerly called alimony and now also known as maintenance, is money paid by one spouse to the other under the terms of a separation or divorce agreement.

Statute. A statutory law.

Statutes of descent prescribe the disposition by state law of a person who dies intestate.

Statutory law is a body of law enacted by legislators.

Substantive law defines the rights and duties of the individual.

Summation is a closing speech to a jury.

A summons is a device to bring you to court.

Tenancy by the entirety is a form of joint tenancy in which none of the parties can dispose of an interest in the property without the consent of the others. It applies only to real property.

Tenancy in common is a form of joint tenancy that, in the absence of a will, passes the share of the property owned by the deceased to his heirs-at-law according to state laws.

Testimony is a form of evidence given orally.

Title as it refers to real property is usually a legal document which contains all the necessary facts to prove the right to possession and ownership of a property.

Tort. A wrongful act, damage, or injury, often willfully or negligently performed, for which a civil suit can be brought.

A Totten trust, or bank account trust, is a bank account that names the beneficiary who will inherit the trust.

A trust is a device for transferring assets to another person to hold in trust for you or any other person or persons you designate.

Unconscionability means "a real bad deal," and includes price gouging and obtaining money for services and merchandise of little or no value.

Voir dire is a procedure for questioning prospective jurors by opposing lawyers to sift out those who, in the opinion of the lawyers or their clients, cannot be fair and impartial.

A will is a legal declaration of the deposition of a person's property after death.

SOURCES AND RECOMMENDED READING

A good deal of recommended reading, intended to give you access to additional specific information in concentrated areas of the law, appears throughout this book. The works listed here will expand your general basic grip on the subject, chapter head by chapter head. The material in the recommended publications is accurate, well organized, and reasonably translated from legalese to plain English. Actually, they are so good we have used some of them as sources for this book.

Since this is a book for laypersons, references to legal citations, which would go on and on and on and mean nothing to you, have not been included. But if you'd like to track down the law yourself—it's a marvelous kind of treasure hunt—there's a magnificent guide that can get you started. It's *Finding the Law: A Workbook on Legal Research for Laypersons* by Al Coco, Professor of Law/Librarianship and Law Librarian at the University of Denver. You can get a copy from the Superintendent of Documents, U.S. Government Printing Office, Washington, DC 20402. Write first and ask for the current price.

There are some other institutional publications in this list. Those that are asterisked (*) are available from Consumer Information Center, Pueblo, CO 81009; and those that are daggered (†) from American Bar Association, 1155 East 60 Street, Chicago, IL 60637. Some may be free, but write first for catalogs, order blanks, and current prices.

CHAPTER 1. **The Law in Action**

The Legal Guide for the Family, Donald L. Very, Doubleday and Company, Inc., 1982.
Your Introduction to Law, George Gordon Coughlin, Barnes and Noble Books, 1979.
Do I Really Need a Lawyer? Stuart Kahan and Robert M. Cavallo, Chilton Book Company, 1979.
Handbook of Everyday Law, Martin J. Ross and Jeffrey Stevens Ross, Harper & Row Publishers, New York.

CHAPTER 2. **Medical Malpractice: Your Right to Standard Medical Care**

Medical Overkill, Ralph C. Greene, George F. Stickley Company, 1983.
Live or Die, Thomas H. Ainsworth, Macmillan Publishing Company, 1983.
Your Personal Vitamin Profile, Michael Colgan, William Morrow and Company, 1982.
Health Facts, Maryann Napoli, Overlook Press, 1982.
Malpractice, Donald J. Flaster, Charles Scribner's Sons, 1983.
Making Health Care Decisions, President's Council for the Study of Ethical Problems in Medicine and Biomedical and Behavioral Research, U.S. Government Printing Office, Washington, DC 20402.

CHAPTER 3. **Medical Life-Support Systems: Your Right to Have Them, and to Reject Them**

Defining Death: Medical, Legal and Ethical Issues on the Determination of Death, President's Council for the Study of Ethical Problems in Medicine and Biomedical and Behavioral Research, U.S. Government Printing Office, Washington, DC 20402.

CHAPTER 4. **Credit: Your Right to It, and to Its Fair Use**

Credit Cardsmanship, Martin J. Meyer, Farnsworth Publishing Company, 1971.
How to Turn Your Plastics into Gold, Martin J. Meyer and Mark Hunter, Farnsworth Publishing Company, 1974.
Don't Bank on It, Martin J. Meyer and Joseph M. McDaniel, Jr., Farnsworth Publishing Company, 1972.
How Women Can Get Credit, National Organization for Women, 2000 P Street, N.W., Washington, DC, 1982.
*Consumer Credit Handbook, 578M, 1981.
*Fair Credit Billing, 407M, 1978.
*Fair Credit Reporting Act, 408M, 1980.
*The Arithmetic of Interest Rates, 406M, 1983.

CHAPTER 5. **Debt: Your Right to Get Out of It**

Get Out and Stay Out of Debt, Anne David, Cornerstone Library/Simon & Schuster, 1981.
How to Get Your Creditors off Your Back, Melvin J. Kaplan, Contemporary Books, 1979.
*Alice in Debitland, 579M, 1980.
*Budgeting for the Family.
*Fair Debt Collection, 409M, 1981.
*Avoiding Mortgage Default, 575M.
†*Your Guide to Consumer Credit and Bankruptcy*, 1983.

CHAPTER 6. **Contracts: Your Rights of Agreement**

Sylvia Porter's New Money Book for the 80's, Avon Books, 1979.
  See also under Chapter 1.

CHAPTER 7. **Your Home: Your Rights When You Buy or Rent**

Bernard Meltzer Solves Your Money Problems, Bernard Meltzer, Simon &
  Schuster, 1982.
Lawyers Title Home Buying Guide, Lawyer's Title Insurance Corporation,
  Ventura Associates, 1980.
The Complete Real Estate Adviser, Daniel J. de Benedictis, Cornerstone
  Library/Simon & Schuster, 1971.
The Condominium: A Guide for the Alert Buyer, Dorothy Tymon, Avon Books,
  1976.
Tenants' Rights and How to Protect Them, City of New York Commission on
  Human Rights, 1983.
*The Mortgage Money Guide, 418M, 1982.
*Selecting and Financing a Home, 174M, 1980.
*Settlement Costs, 175M, 1983.

CHAPTER 8. **Small Business: Your Rights as an Entrepreneur**

*Checklist for Going into Business, 513M, 1983.
*Starting and Managing a Small Business of Your Own, 136M, 1982.
*Starting and Managing a Small Service Business, 137M, 1981.
**Women's Handbook: How the Small Business Administration Can Help a
  Woman Establish a Business,* 514M, 1983.

CHAPTER 9. **Wills: Your Right to Determine the Distribution of Your Property
  After Your Death**

The Essential Guide to Wills, Estates, Trusts and Death Taxes, Alex J. Soled,
  an AARP Book, Scott Foresman and Company, 1984.
†*Planning for Life and Death.*
†*Wills: Why You Should Have One, and the Lawyer's Role in its Preparation.*

CHAPTER 10. *Man and Woman: Your Rights in Marriage and when You Live
  Together.*

†*Law and Marriage, Your Legal Guide,* 1983.
*Plain Talk About Wife Abuse, 571M, 1983.
Living Together, Marvin Mitchelson, Simon & Schuster, 1980

CHAPTER 11. **Negligence: Your Rights When Somebody Injures You Accidentally**

Damages and Recovery: Personal Injury and Death Actions, Jacob A. Stein and Roland F. Chase, Bancroft-Whitney Company, 1972.
Winning Your Personal Injury Suit, John Guinther, Anchor Press/Doubleday, 1980.

CHAPTER 12.   **Crime: Your Rights When Under Arrest and on Trial**

Clean Slate, Tom Ballinger, Harmony Books/Crown Publishers, 1979. See also under Chapter 1.

CHAPTER 13.   *Caveat Venditor:* **Your Rights as a Consumer**

Caveat Venditor, Stephen A. Newman, Consumer Law Training Center, 1984.

CHAPTER 14.   **Restrictions on Your Everyday Rights: From Your Right to Love to Your Right to Nondiscrimination.**

*Consumer's Resource Handbook, 601M.
Getting Uncle Sam to Enforce Your Civil Rights, United States Commission on Civil Rights, Clearinghouse Publication 59, Superintendent of Documents, United States Government Printing Office, Washington, DC 20402.